The Sociology of Architecture

PAUL JONES

The Sociology of Architecture
Constructing Identities

LIVERPOOL UNIVERSITY PRESS

First published 2011 by
Liverpool University Press
4 Cambridge Street
Liverpool
L69 7ZU

British Library Cataloguing-in-Publication data
A British Library CIP record is available

ISBN 978-1-84631-076-8 cased
978-1-84631-077-5 limp

Typeset by XL Publishing Services, Tiverton
Printed and bound by CPI Group (UK) Ltd, Croydon, CR0 4YY

Contents

Acknowledgements

This is my first single-authored book and, looking back over the long process that has led to its publication, thanks are due to a group of people who have been supportive and encouraging in different ways during the writing of this book.

A number of colleagues past and present at the University of Liverpool have taken an interest in the ideas as they have developed from my PhD on architecture and national identity. Of this group I would like in particular to thank Roy Coleman, Matthew David, Phil Davis, Gerard Delanty, Matt Donaghy, Barry Goldson, Kevin Jones, Andrew Kirton, Marion Leonard, Chris MacIntosh, Michael Mair, Ruth Melville, Steve Miles, Gabe Mythen, Paul Rafferty, Roger Sibeon, Nicole Vittelone, Sandra Walklate, Dave Whyte and Stuart Wilks-Heeg. Students on the MA *Cities, Culture and Regeneration* programme have also stimulated my thinking in this area. I would also like to say a big thanks to Robin Bloxsidge and Anthony Cond from Liverpool University Press for their support for me and the project.

Conversations at conferences, in pubs or by email with colleagues from the wider academic community have given me much food for thought. From this growing group, particular thanks are due to Ana Beatriz da Rocha, Ash Amin, Paul Blokker, Heike Delitz, Chris Grant, Engin Isin, Kjetil Fallan, Simon Guy, Heather Hopfl, Bob Jessop, Paul Kennedy, Michał Krzyżanowski, Natalia Krzyżanowska, Graeme Owen, John Pløger, Ngai-Ling Sum, Ruth Wodak and Sharon Zukin. Extra special thanks for extended inputs go to Rob Imrie, Liz Kingdom (who is very sadly missed), Suzanne MacLeod, Maurice Roche, Leslie Sklair, Trevor Skempton and the late Paul Stringer. While the book is all the richer for the contributions of the above, the usual disclaimers apply.

I would also like to thank my mum and dad and brother Graham, who have all been very supportive throughout the duration of the book and the studies whence it came. And last but not least a very big thank you to Leah M. Chidgey.

Illustrations

Introduction

> The question is not whether architecture constructs identities and
> stabilizes meanings, but how and in whose interests.
>
> Kim Dovey, *Becoming Places: Urbanism/Architecture/*
> *Identity/Power* (2009), 45.

The architect-sociologist Garry Stevens suggests it would take one day
to read sociology's contribution to our understanding of architecture
(1998: 12), and while this is an exaggeration it is only a slight one. With
the exception of some of the notable contributions assessed throughout
this book, the relationship between architects, their work, and social
order has not been subject to sustained scrutiny by academic sociologists.
In the light of this book's title it is perhaps unsurprising that I feel this
represents something of a missed opportunity, and what follows here is
my attempt to contribute to this underdeveloped field of inquiry. A
central contention of *The Sociology of Architecture* is that the application of a critical 'sociological imagination' (Wright-Mills 1959) to
architects and their work is one way in which the tensions associated
with the political mobilization of culture can be revealed.

By using 'sociology' in the title of the book, and elsewhere, I am
ascribing some significance to the term. Sociology, by now a heavily
contested and increasingly fragmented disciplinary label, is used here as
a proxy for a critical approach to the connections between the architectural field, political power, and the construction, maintenance and
mobilization of collective identities. Using the label 'sociology' represents
one way to foreground the social production of architectural practice and
form from the perspective of a research tradition that can make a distinctive contribution to such questions. Here I suggest that a central task of
a sociology of architecture should include situating architectural practice, and the objectified results of that practice, within the
political-economic conditions that give rise to it.

A major concern of sociology, in its critical manifestations at least,
involves revealing the ways in which power is socialized in the cultural
sphere, with such an approach seeking to question how structures of
power come to be taken for granted as legitimate and 'natural'. From this

1

perspective, addressing the role that architecture has in codifying and reproducing social identities requires analysis; architecture is one cultural space in which political projects attempt to become socially meaningful, and where particular visions of publics are forged. Getting to grips with this fascinating context requires a theoretical approach sensitized to the specificity of architecture as a form of cultural production, which involves revealing the contingencies (Till 2009), complicities (Dovey 2000) and contested processes that characterize the incorporation of elements of the built environment into frames of social and political meaning. This in turn means taking seriously questions of architectural form, meaning and discourse – concerns that define certain rarefied parts of architectural practice and production – while not neglecting the broader political and economic conditions of action within which build- ings are commissioned and become meaningful.

Accordingly, a critical sociological perspective would seek to disrupt any taken for granted assumptions about architecture as an unproblem- atic signifier of national identities. Categories such as collective identities are constructed and maintained through social action, with the cultural forms and discourses – such as those emerging from/centring on archi- tecture – crucial to sustaining, and giving meaning to, these relations. As states continue to mobilize architecture as part of a repertoire of cultural symbols that serve to present the category of the nation as a natural and inevitable social category, then traditionally understood 'sociological' concerns addressed to the relationships between culture, politics and ideology become highly relevant.

To this end I have sought to approach architecture with a sense of the ways in which it is drawn into state projects at the forefront. Architecture has historically been an important way that states have sought to codify collective identities such as the nation (see, for example, Lasswell 1979; Vale 1992; Crinson 1996; Heynen 1999a; Jones 2002; 2006; McNeil and Tewdwr-Jones 2003), with the commission of major architects revealing the intent of regimes from ancient Rome to the European Union to express something of their self-understanding in the cultural sphere.[1] From the point of view of states, the promise of architecture is in its poten- tial to connect citizens meaningfully into political projects through material forms of buildings, which can resonate sufficiently with a range of lived social experience. Untangling this relationship requires engage- ment with the ways in which architects and architectural projects are mobilized by political regimes. Despite the symbiotic relationship between high-profile architects – dependent on commissions for material and symbolic capital – and those states eager to materialize power and otherwise abstract values, any satisfactory sociological account of architecture must move beyond a tautology that would simply observe that those who commission architecture are powerful because they commission architecture. A key challenge is to interrogate both (1) how particular political regimes have used architecture to materialize their power and simultaneously to help legitimate it and (2) how architects respond to the constraints and opportunities associated with major commissions in their designs and their wider discourse.

Until now I have been using the term 'architecture' in a slightly portmanteau fashion. The first three chapters of the book flesh out this definition, but initially it is worth observing that architecture is used both as a collective designation for a profession, and also to describe those parts of the built environment that are designed by this profession. This basic definition is complicated by a number of factors, not least of which is that the types of buildings that can 'properly' be considered architecture are in themselves sites of significant controversy and struggle, as is the right of designers to be recognized as an architect (a legally protected title in many countries). However, given that only a fraction of the world's built environment is designed by professional architects, it is also necessary at this stage to explain that the focus of the present book is by and large on an elite group of internationally famous architects' discourses, practices and buildings. Such an emphasis runs the risk of sustaining an elitist and problematic conception of architecture, in which the stand-alone buildings designed by critically acclaimed architects are considered primarily as objects of autonomous practice, and canonized in teaching (Stevens 1998), the architectural press (Dovey 2009), the wider media (Larson 1994) and politics (Sudjic 2005). Such a partial focus is most often at the expense of the typically unheralded, 'everyday' buildings – such as houses and flats, factories, shops, offices, bus stations, hospitals, universities, prisons, schools, pubs etc. – that provide the background to the vast majority of social life. Although such buildings do have a crucial role in giving spatial form to broader social relations, and reflect the hierarchies and assumptions of social order – a perspective explored in the essays in Anthony King's excellent collection *Buildings and Society* (1990) – they are seldom legitimated in 'sociological' terms by architects and politicians relative to collective identities or major political-economic shifts . In other words, while many buildings outside the formal canon definitely *do* come to have a 'landmark quality' for a given public, city, nation etc., the architects responsible for such buildings are not compelled by the nature of the commission to situate their work relative either to an 'imagined community' (Anderson 1983), such as the nation, or to a major social or political change.

As collective identities are in part produced and sustained through artefacts such as architecture, pertinent questions centre on to whom are buildings being addressed, and how architects and others seek to connect social values and identities to the material forms of architecture. In *The Signature of Power* (1979), an often overlooked but very useful contribution to research on architectural production, the political scientist Harold Lasswell addresses 'landmark' buildings, which he defines as those parts of the built environment that come to have a strong *symbolic* association to a political project or to a place. Through analysis of state-led buildings that have recognizable forms and silhouettes – and that are widely disseminated in the media and famous outside the architectural field – Lasswell observes that architecture need not physically dominate the landscape to be a significant landmark for a political project. Crucially, Lasswell draws our attention to the material political struggles that exist around the ways in which given regimes represent themselves in the built environment, hinting at the centrality of architecture for the social construction of political imaginaries. Similarly, the focus of *Architecture, Power and National Identity* (1992), Lawrence J. Vale's excellent account of architecture in post-colonial contexts, is the attempts made by architects to signify national identity and state power in those buildings that house parliaments and other parts of a state's administration ('capitols'). In this work Vale is particularly interested in those state contexts in which architecture is consciously mobilized as part of a broader attempt to reposition a state relative to internal and external publics, with crucial questions centring on representations of social pasts and futures and the role of the nation in the world.

I mention Lasswell's and Vale's accounts in particular as my focus in *The Sociology of Architecture* is comparable to theirs inasmuch as I address buildings that are 'famous' outside of the architectural field and that, because of the social and political contexts in which they are commissioned, delivered and used, are inextricably bound up with a wide range of social struggles centring on questions of politics and collective identity. While the buildings assessed in *The Sociology of Architecture* are not all 'political' buildings in terms of their explicit function – as they are in Vale's account of parliament buildings – they *are* all situated within highly politicized contexts in which identity has become a central concern of states. While the architecture assessed in this book has been put to a wide range of different uses, the buildings are all 'landmark' in the sense that they have been positioned relative to major social claims vis-à-vis an 'imagined community' (Anderson 1983). Indeed, in most cases fully or partially funded by states, the high-profile architecture addressed here has been bound up with political claims that go far beyond the design and delivery of elements of the built environment; the highly politicized contexts that surround the commission and delivery of the building projects assessed here have necessitated that the architects responsible for their design fully engage with the relationship between architectural form and social meaning, between politics and publics.

As my focus is overwhelmingly on individual buildings, this leaves me open to the valid criticism – often levelled at architectural theory and criticism – of considering architecture as a series of 'isolated and monumental objects' (Borden et al. 2002: 3). Such an object-centric approach runs the risk of overlooking the crucial connections *between* elements of the built environment in the broader urban fabric and discounting the crucial social externalities that often go unremarked in accounts narrowly focused on a building's form. In common with much of the work cited in this book I agree that the focus on stand-alone, monumental buildings can risk mystifying both the social relations that are constitutive 'outsides' of architectural production (including both the material interests that benefit from their construction) and the broader political projects they help make meaningful.

However, in seeking to illuminate the broader social production of architecture, it is important not to discount analysis of the architectural object altogether. It is in part the promise of architecture to reflect social values in a tangible, material form that leads political agencies to commission architecture, and architects' attempts to position their building relative to an identity project or public requires engagement with the slippery relationship between social values and architectural form; drawing attention to political mobilization of such projects requires analysis of the connections and disjunctures between the two. Furthermore, situating the emergence of particular cultural forms relative to broader political and economic transformations can open up research questions centring on, for instance, attempts to embed a particular political project in a socially meaningful, resonant form and aesthetic (Jessop 2004; Jones 2009).

While drawing on a range of scholarship from a variety of disciplines and intellectual traditions, my own perspective is shaped primarily by a concern to reveal the underlying power relations inherent in the cultural strategies employed by states and other political regimes. Focusing on high-profile landmark buildings allows for analysis of the written, spoken and built work of the small group of architects responsible for their conception. This group of architects that are the focus here are by definition successful in gaining the major commissions for the type of building defined above, and represent a very small fraction of those working in the profession at any one time (see Gutman 1988; Stevens 1998). Such a focus overlooks what the majority of architects do most of the time, but my focus in this respect is guided by a desire to 'study up' (see Becker 1967) to question, first, the ways in which political projects are served by associating architecture with a particular social discourse, and, second, the role of architects' public discourse in such contested processes.

A significant component of high-profile architects' work, from the competition stage through to the subsequent dissemination of the meaning of completed buildings in the media, centres on the 'discursive construction' (Wodak et al. 1999) of an appropriate social meaning relative to their material architecture. High-profile architects, owing to the rarefied structural positions within which they operate, are conditioned to connect their work to social values and identities. Precisely because so-called 'starchitects' – a somewhat contentious designation assessed in more detail elsewhere (Sklair 2005; 2006; Faulconbridge 2009; McNeill 2009) – are inherently bound up with place marketing activities beyond designing buildings, the distinction between what is said and what is done becomes increasingly blurred. Celebrity beyond the architectural press may suggest a reinvigorated public role for architects (Wigley 2005), with the capacity to intervene in social and political debate beyond the formal limits of architecture and what is actually built, but such wider public engagement means treading an uneasy and uncertain terrain relative to the competing social claims that often centre on major built projects. Furthermore, given the symbiosis between high-profile architects and political projects, the basis and legitimacy of any such interventions into political debates are objects for critical analysis rather than unproblematic contributions to the public sphere. From this perspective questions about the role of high-profile architects must include an assessment of whose interests their work serves, the parameters within which they intervene into public discourse, and the ways in which broader political-economic conditions of action shape the social meaning of their work. The architects assessed in this book have all been very active in the public sphere, disseminating interpretations of their respective buildings and so becoming inextricably bound up with the highly politicized nature of state-led identity projects. In focusing on attempts to position buildings relative to social categories such as the nation, I hope not to have fetishized the work and words of powerful architects, but rather to have drawn out the political mobilization of architecture in various social contexts, revealing something both of the exploitation of architecture by states and the necessity to analyse the contingent forms and practices within which this wider pattern is manifest.

All seven chapters seek to open up a set of related questions about architectural projects from a social scientific standpoint. Chapters 1 and 2 are primarily conceptual, and set up some of the general theoretical perspectives that inform the rest of the book. Chapter 1 draws on the influential work of Pierre Bourdieu to position architecture as a field of cultural production characterized by a range of symbolic and material conflicts. Assessing the relationship between culture and social power relations from what Bourdieu referred to as a 'structuralist constructivist' or 'constructivist structuralist' position (2003), this chapter is designed to draw attention both to the constitutive and socially conditioned nature of architectural production and to some of the internal field logics that characterize architectural production in capitalist society. Chapter 2 develops some of the initial questions concerning the relationship between the architectural field and the socially dominant, foregrounding the constitutive role of discourse in the social construction of architectural meaning, suggesting that what is said by architects about their buildings is one way in which architecture is positioned relative to political projects and collective identities; the case of the extension to the Jewish Museum in Berlin by Daniel Libeskind is assessed against this backdrop.

The case studies of particular architectural projects contained in Chapters 3–7 are not intended to 'prove' any kind of argument, but rather to illuminate some of the central theoretical claims concerning the tensions that emerge when landmark architecture is positioned relative to collective identities. Chapter 3 gives an overview of the role of states' architecture in the context of nineteenth-century nation-building. This chapter positions architecture within the literature on national identities. Focusing on Victorian architects' quest for an 'appropriate' historical style to codify the British nation provides an entry point into the wider symbolic and material struggles that underpin the connection of social meaning to architectural form. Chapter 4 is also focused on the relationship between states and their landmark architecture, with attention here turning to the spectacular buildings that house the large-scale 'mega[-]events' (Roche 2000) designed to showcase national technological and economic achievements. As materializations of wider state visions, such events – and their architecture – have often been mired in controversy. The Millennium Dome project reveals much of the uneasy balancing act inherent in state-led codifications of national identities in contemporary social contexts; this case is understood against the backdrop of the New Labour government's attempts to present a 'new' convergence of cultural and economic production in Britain at the millennium.

Chapter 5 interrogates the positioning of landmark architecture within memorial frames of reference. While a cursory glance at the names of some major buildings in capitals attests to architecture's long-established commemorative function, what is significant today is the highly reflexive approach that characterizes such commemoration; the decline of the conventional forms of memorialization has seen significant losses of life in wars and other socially significant events increasingly transposed onto major architectural projects. It is against this backdrop that Daniel Libeskind's master plan for the Ground Zero site in New York City is understood. Chapter 6 assesses the role of spectacular 'iconic' architecture in place marketing strategies characteristic of regeneration processes in 'post-industrial' cities. The last decade has seen high-profile architects incorporated into entrepreneurial regeneration strategies that attempt to rebrand cities in such a way as to attract tourists and inward investment from the private sector. This rejuvenated role for celebrity architects and their spectacular architecture in this context raises a number of interesting tensions around community participation, cultural democracy and mobilization of urban identities; the aborted Fourth Grace project in Liverpool is situated relative to this highly contested backdrop. Finally, Chapter 7 is concerned with the role of architecture in the contemporary European context. There are two substantive cases assessed here: first, attempts by the European Union to mobilize 'European' architects and architecture to develop socially significant forms, and, second, the role of state-led architecture in a 'New Europe', with the rebuilding of the Reichstag by British architect Sir Norman Foster interrogated as an example of a building that was positioned in a 'post-national' cultural and political frame.

Although the scope of this book is broad, the fundamental aim is to position architecture as a cultural form and practice inherently bound up with the politicized construction of collective identities. The aim is to suggest a set of research questions emerging from the mobilization of architects and their buildings by political regimes, with a general contention that architecture is a field in which competing identity claims are played out in a wide variety of ways, and which, when interrogated against wider political–economic contexts, can reveal much about the tensions and conflicts inherent in state-led collective identity discourses.

Note

1 Vitruvius' *Ten Books on Architecture*, written in 27 BC and widely considered the foundation of architectural scholarship, bears a chapter of dedication to Augustus Caesar (Haladane 1999: 9).

1

Architecture, Power and Identities:
Surveying the Field

Every power to exert symbolic violence, i.e. every power which
manages to impose meanings and to impose them as legitimate by
concealing the power relations which are the basis of its force, adds
its own specifically symbolic force to these power relations.
                    P. Bourdieu and J.-C. Passeron, *Reproduction in
                    Education, Society and Culture* (1977), 4.

Introduction

In his discussion of military architecture, the British sociologist Paul Hirst
(2005) positions those buildings emerging from the architectural profession as being both configured by social power relations and a resource
for their consolidation and legitimation. Framing architecture in this way
is a useful starting point, as it expresses a sense of, first, the durable, structural relationship between architects and the powerful actors and
institutions that commission buildings, and, second, the ways in which
this relationship is normalized through practices within the architectural
field. Pierre Bourdieu's work, broadly within the 'sociology of culture'
research tradition, allows for development of this initial observation by
providing a framework that facilitates analyses of architecture's relationship to commissioning elites while avoiding the reductionisms
associated with economistic explanation on the one hand and overly
culturalized approaches on the other.

Bourdieu researched widely on the links between culture and social
values, which for him were never neutral or unproblematic but rather
ways in which social reproduction and the legitimation of existing power
relations were practised (1989a; 1989b; 1993; 1996; 2000). A major
concern of Bourdieu's widely influential research is to reveal the ways in
which culture maps onto social inequalities, all the time legitimating them
as natural, fair and taken for granted. Within his broader project, and
crucially for this context, Bourdieu attempts to clarify the role that state

11

institutions have in constituting and reproducing the existing social order (see, for example, Bourdieu and Passeron 1977; Bourdieu 1989a; 1993; 2003; Bourdieu and Wacquant 2000). As such, Bourdieu's work has become a crucial reference point for those concerned with the ways in which cultural discourses and hierarchies are mobilized by socially dominant institutions and individuals.

Thanks to its application into a number of empirical studies by scholars working in the tradition, Bourdieu's work has also contributed greatly to our understanding of how power functions in the architectural field itself and also of how architectural production is implicated in wider social relations. Many have sought to develop his framework to support engagement with elements of architectural practice (Stevens 1998; Dovey 1999; 2009; Dovey and Dickson 2002; Lipstadt 2003; Fowler and Wilson 2004; Jones 2009), with these approaches all situating the architectural field as a social space characterized by many different symbolic and material struggles. When thinking with Bourdieu about architecture (a topic he never addressed directly in his wide-ranging accounts of cultural and intellectual production),[1] any assumption that architects are involved in a social process characterized by artistic freedom, autonomy and neutrality must be banished.

Drawing on some of Bourdieu's master concepts – such as 'field', 'capital', and 'habitus' – this chapter also positions architectural production as a space of cultural contestation in which architects struggle over symbolic and material capitals. The general suggestion is that Bourdieu's approach to the study of culture can not only help in contributing to our understanding of how power operates *within* architecture but – and in keeping with the focus of this book – also in positioning the architectural field relative to those actors and institutions responsible for its commission. From this standpoint, crucial questions centre on the contribution of architecture to the legitimation of state power and on the extent to which the reliance on commissions from the socially dominant conditions the practices and self-understanding of those within the architectural field.

Thinking with Bourdieu about the Architectural Field

As a critically engaged researcher, Bourdieu's studies were characterized by a desire to puncture those legitimating and normalized representations emerging from the discourses of the powerful. With this in mind, Bourdieu suggested that the category of 'profession' is one such representation, bound up with a number of valorizing and partial self-characterizations that social scientists should seek to defamiliarize in their research. Those utilizing Bourdieu's framework to reveal the social contexts in which architecture is commissioned, produced and understood have heeded this call, identifying the gains associated with framing their studies with the concept of 'field' and jettisoning that of 'profession' (see Stevens 1998; Dovey 1999; 2000; 2009; Lipstadt 2003; Fowler and Wilson 2004; Jones 2009). As Bourdieu pointed out, the value-laden nature of the category of profession has been 'uncritically smuggled' into social science thinking via 'representation fostered by professional groups themselves' (Lipstadt 2003: 390). The 'field' concept is one way to problematize the assumptions associated with those self-characterizations developed by professionals themselves.

A 'heuristic tool' (Bourdieu 1993: 182) that provides a number of analytical gains over the term profession, a field is a 'veritable social universe where, in accordance with particular laws, there accumulates a particular form of capital and where relations of force of a particular type are exerted' (Bourdieu 1993: 27). The field concept functions as an *aide mémoire* to remind researchers of, first, the *relational* nature of any social space, and, second, the fundamentally conflictual nature of social relations relative to various types of socially contingent capitals (Bourdieu 1989a; 1996). Any field is a social space constituted by the practices of individual agents who are engaged in competition for a range of capitals (more on which later) and the institutions of which they are a constitutive part. As Garry Stevens points out in his excellent book *The Favored Circle: The Social Foundations of Architectural Distinction* (1998: 435), the concept of field in Bourdieu's work has two distinct but related meanings: first, that of a *battlefield*, a site of symbolic and material struggle, and, second, that of a *field of force*, whose influence shapes and conditions the values and practices of those individuals and institutions operating within it.

Within any field the element of struggle and competition is key, and 'the most general thing that can be said about a field is that it is a contest for authority over the field itself; without this struggle, there can be no field' (Lipstadt 2003: 398). As a social site of competition the concept of the field has features akin to a sports field, inasmuch as those on a football pitch, for example, are defined in relation both to each other (how closely someone is being marked, or if they can time their forward run to avoid being offside) and to the parameters of the pitch itself (how close they are to the goal, whether they (individually and collectively) are making the most of the width of the pitch etc.). Of course, these positions on the pitch are not absolute or fixed, and, as with the concept of field, analysis must be sensitized to their shifting and dynamic nature.

So, a promise made by the concept of field is the transcendence of undifferentiated, flat accounts of practice that are implied by the obfuscating catch-all 'profession', which in this particular case suggests a coherence *within* the category of 'architects' that is not evident in practice. Drawing attention to the internal hierarchies and struggles that characterize architectural production sensitizes us to the relationship between symbolic and material struggles in specific social contexts and provides a frame for researching the processes by which value is attributed, or denied, to certain objects and practices within the field at a given time. While all architects gain something of the status of being a member of the field in general terms, internal field distinctions are such that the practice of those in some parts of the field can be far removed from the work of those in others. To draw another analogy, although we may both operate in the same academic field, the differences between my working week and that of an internationally renowned sociologist are perhaps more notable than the similarities.

The mass part of the architectural field is occupied by the vast majority of architects whose work is overwhelmingly concerned with those functional buildings and domestic commissions that fail to capture the attention and plaudits of their colleagues, critics and wider publics; these designers are by and large 'anonymous' (and sometimes are denied the label 'architect' altogether; see Chapter 3).[2] To extend a sporting analogy (not for the first time), the field should not be considered a 'level' one; for Bourdieu, an indication of power within a given field involves having the capacity to determine the stakes over which 'the game' is being played. Stevens' refers to this conception of the field as congruent to a *battlefield* in the sense that it is a social space that provides the terrain on which *and* over which struggle and competition over capitals take place. In other words, fields are sites of contestation not only over positionality within the field but also about what the rules of the game are and what the goals are.

Ascendancy in the field confers an increased capacity to condition what aesthetics are prized (and ultimately even over who can gain access into the field to compete for its cultural capital). Indeed, one of the distinctive characteristics of the powerful in any field is their capacity to shape the field as well as being shaped by it. Commenting on the relative capacities to do this, Stevens makes a crucial distinction between the practices and orientations of those in the 'mass' and 'restricted' architectural subfields (1998: 74–91).

The group of architects operating in the restricted part of the architectural field have greater capacity to define the capitals worth competing for – to define what is valuable and what is not (whether in terms of aesthetics, practices and so on). Such architects are the taste makers, those who can ascribe and remove capital to others; the rarefied group of architects competing for symbolic capital to a greater extent than are the vast majority of practising architects, who are more concerned with economic reward and professional recognition. In short, famous architects are in a 'dominant position within a field configured by the changing outcome of competitive struggles for symbolic capital' (Larson 2004: 324). However, even given their *relative* power to shape the field, the consecrated elite of architects still 'find themselves under the sway of the entire range of the (conscious and unconscious) interpellative codings at work in architecture' (Rakatansky 1995: 14). From this perspective architects are recipients of the rules of the field who respond to the contexts in which they find themselves in ways that seem to make sense from those positions; in other words, and with apologies for the clumsy paraphrasing of Marx, architects design buildings but not within conditions of their own making.

The ability to present arbitrary values about worth as seemingly natural, neutral and unproblematic constitutes a 'symbolic violence' (Bourdieu 1977), a 'gentle, invisible violence, unrecognized as such, chosen as much as undergone' (Bourdieu 1990: 127). Symbolic violence is effectively the process through which the constitutive 'force-field' effect of the field comes to seem normal, fair and taken for granted.[3] The values and capitals of any field come to represent 'an absolute index of intrinsic worth' (Jenkins 1992: 13), and from Bourdieu's perspective it is the very mystification of this index and its subsequent acceptance that are of concern. Symbolic violence involves the attachment of legitimacy and value to a particular aesthetic or practice within the field, and the more that this process is hidden from sight and left unchallenged the more powerful it is in reproducing dominance; Bourdieu argues that it is the very *latency* of such symbolic violence that imbues it with legitimacy. Indeed, from Bourdieu's perspective, one of the crucial social functions of architecture is to produce 'instruments of taste' to divide populations rather than consolidate or unite them (Stevens, 1998). In this regard, those in the restricted subfield are 'producers not only of classifiable acts but also of acts of classification which are themselves classified'

(Bourdieu 1989a: 222). This function of architects as taste-makers means they are 'inextricably enmeshed in practices of symbolic domination' (Dovey and Dickson 2002: 290), both within the field and external to it.

Challenging the notion of the architectural field as a coherent, undifferentiated space means that the struggles *within* the field, between groups of individuals who perceive a common interest, become significant questions for research. Drawing attention to the ways in which some individuals within the field have greater or lesser potential to define aesthetic beauty, or a 'good' or 'appropriate' building (Bonta, 1979), reveals the distinct nature of practice in the restricted and mass parts of the field. Struggles within the field over material and symbolic capitals produce field-specific hierarchies. Perhaps betraying a residual materialism, Bourdieu observes that most fields divide quite neatly into subordinate and dominant positions: those in subordinate positions can find solidarity with those in subordinate positions in other fields, while those in powerful positions in one field can identify commonalities – and indeed often common interests – with those in dominant positions in other fields (this is a central reason why cultural capital serves the function of integrating actors dominant in different fields) (Stevens 1998: 103).

While the dichotomy between mass and restricted subfields may seem a little flat, it does remind us of the inherently relational nature of the architectural field. As Stevens observes, the 'mass' subfield is also by and large responsible for the design of buildings – albeit very important ones – *for* mass consumption, such as factories, schools, bus stations, shops and so on (1998: 85). Stevens' discussion of the ambivalent relationship between the restricted and mass parts of the field is worth quoting at length:

> Not only are they [architects] not a unified social entity, their linkages are weak. The mass subfield has a vested interest in the restricted field as the producer of legitimate architectural form, but it [the mass field] takes its images at second hand, and must forever be ridiculed by the [restricted field] for imitating form without understanding meaning. In the other direction, the restricted subfield sometimes looks to its subordinate sibling, but only to aestheticize what it takes. (Stevens 1998: 88)

The obfuscation of these conditions of action is characteristic of accounts that focus solely on architectural aesthetics and internally constituted practice at the expense of a broader account of architecture's relation to society, and in particular to dominant political–economic structures.

So, in sum, the concept of field allows us to frame architecture as a form of materially conditioned cultural production that operates within an internally differentiated social space.[4] The objective positions within the field of architecture would be what Bourdieu calls 'the space of possibles', which includes the generalized and accepted ways of being an architect; this includes a knowledge of the things that have gone before in the field, the things that have been dominant, and what the general areas of internal struggle and power are. In teaching I often compare this concept to those pathways that have been treaded down in an overgrown garden: there are other paths through it that could be pursued, but the routes of least resistance – that seem the 'sensible', 'natural' ones to pursue – are those that are most travelled by those who had the best tools to make the paths.[5] This process of transmitted values and practices that are internalized in the context of the field and, despite their arbitrary basis (the 'paths' *could* be elsewhere), come to be considered as natural, universal and fair is described by Bourdieu as habitus. A descriptor of how 'chains' of practices and meaning that come to be valued or devalued within the parameters of particular fields (Jenkins 1992) thanks to implicit rules that Bourdieu refers to as a 'feel for the game' – habitus, captures how unthinking responses are learned and actually come to characterize different positions within the field.

Engaging Bourdieu's framework to situate his study of architects, Stevens has contended that the 'central function of the discipline of architecture is to produce instruments of taste', with his conclusion that architects' success 'owes *at least* as much to their social background and to the social structures within which they are embedded as it does to their native talent' (1998: 2–3). It is through mobilizing Bourdieu's concept of habitus to ask awkward questions of architectural production and 'creativity' that Stevens manages to draw out some of architecture's central assumptions with regard to the value assigned to taste. Larson's recent work has also engaged with this theme, drawing attention to the distinctly symbolic manifestation of many of the wider struggles in architecture, with the architect's habitus contingent on caring 'about symbolic capital; they must care in one way or the other about participating in the discourse of architecture, about playing in the field where struggle determines the standards of architectural beauty and worth' (Larson 2004: 324). Although tending towards the structural, habitus directs us to a non-determinist account of creativity, reminding us how definitions of aesthetic beauty – or other forms of architectural capital for that matter

– can only be understood as those things consecrated by those in the field with sufficient capacity to make such definitions 'stick' and become widely agreed, consecrated goals worth pursuing. This approach is particularly useful for present purposes, as it helps us to move away from the idea of the architect as an asocial, romantic, creative genius (Lipstadt 2003: 400; Hill 2003) and towards an understanding of the collective relationship between the architectural field and, for example, the political field. The 'space of possibles' also explains one of the reasons it is necessary to step outside of architecture to understand it: as we will see an important part of the logic of architecture and architectural education is about refuting the social production of architecture.

Another category that is crucial to making sense of architecture as a field is capital, essentially Bourdieu's way of explaining how power operates in highly differentiated ways in different subsets of society, with individuals mobilizing a range of resources in struggles over widely varying objects of power and status. In drawing attention to the field-specific nature of much competition within given sectors of society, Bourdieu's framework departs with those reductionist strands of Marxism that see all forms of power relationship reverting ultimately to economic relations (Schwartz 1997). However, some capitals also resonate across fields; for instance, economic capital – although taking different forms in different fields – will almost always confer some advantage on the bearer, but in Bourdieu's schema – by definition – every field necessarily contains capitals specific to itself (in large part this is precisely what distinguishes it as a field apart from others). Field-specific capitals are those distinctive goals and statuses that cannot readily be translated into those from outwith the field; architecture has specialized capitals and currencies that are not reducible to relationships with external economic or political agencies, no matter how fundamental these connections are to architectural practice and production (Gutman 1988; Dovey 1999). It is important to note that symbolic capital is a crucial site of struggle in the architectural field, and takes place with reference to aesthetics; I will come back to this point in subsequent chapters.

An Architectural Paradox: Autonomy from Constraint

In one of the classic sociological studies on architecture, the American scholar Robert Gutman suggests that states and the economically powerful represent the 'natural market' for architecture:

> Rare is the building not designed by an architect that represents the

supreme values of a civilization. This has been true for temples, palaces, libraries, and city halls in Greece, Rome, and Europe during the Renaissance, and for museums, university buildings, and corporate headquarters more recently. The design of great seminal monumental buildings is the unique province of architecture, its 'natural market'. (Gutman 1992: 40)

From Bourdieu's perspective a number of fundamental questions emerge from this initial observation. First, architects require clients if they are to be architects. Those architects wanting to practise within the restricted part of the architectural field – its 'natural market' – are fundamentally reliant on their clients' patronage (Stevens 1998; Dovey 1999; Lipstadt 2003). Magali Safuri Larson (2004) notes that while other cultural producers can still operate in the face of being overlooked by their target market – an artist without a market can still paint or draw, a writer without a publisher can write, a songwriter without a deal from a record label can sing – architects are reliant on their clients' patronage in a way that by and large other cultural producers are not. Larson has framed her seminal analyses on architectural production with the observation (2004: 324) that 'architecture is never, and cannot be, an autonomous field, for buildings cannot be mere drawings ... buildings must be *realized* ... architects must design for *someone*'. Comments on this client dependence have also come from prominent architects, with Edward Luytens reputed to have remarked that 'without great patrons there would be no great architecture', and Frank Lloyd Wright noting three things every architect should learn: one, how to get a commission; two, how to get a commission; and three, how to get a commission.

Certainly, and as is explored throughout the book, architecture's professional identity is bound up with wealthy and powerful clients who feel themselves to require monumental statements in the built environment. This represents a highly restricted and specialized 'natural' market, essentially comprised of the state, the corporate market and extremely wealthy private individuals. This reliance on elite patrons means a highly niche market for architects seeking major commissions, with struggles over what architecture is and should be recast through this fundamental relation. Gutman (1988) is concerned to show that the struggles for such commissions – always limited in number and so creating competition between architects and a subsequent hierarchy of professionals – exists in the context of architects' attempts to retain distinction from other related design professionals, which is crucial to architecture's continued monopoly over this sphere of activity.[6] Garry Stevens convincingly demonstrates how the demography of architects is inextricably linked to the 'natural market' for architecture, found among those political-economic elites who want to symbolize major civilizational achievements and social transformations in 'great, monumental' buildings (Stevens 1998). There is a scarcity within this market and no way to increase the stock of commissions that are available at any one time, which means that the vast majority of architects have to operate outside of this context.

The symbiotic relationship between those architects who aspire to design such works and the powerful elites who commission them, from Bourdieu's standpoint, should not a priori position architecture as a compliant field, as an adjunct or handmaiden to capitalist or state projects; no field has total autonomy or is hermetically sealed off from other fields, and the fact that they all exist in society means contingency is a characteristic factor of any such production (Till 2009). Perhaps counter-intuitively, in Bourdieu's conception this reliance on clients for commissions does not in itself deny the architectural field autonomy. One crucial aspect of Bourdieu's definition of a social field concerns the degree of autonomy one field has from others, in other words the capacity of actors within one field to translate the logic and the 'rules of the game' from other fields into their own distinct logic. Thus, autonomy does not require complete rejection, but can mean the field's ability to define capitals from outwith into its own capitals; in *The Field of Cultural Production* (1993: 163–64) Bourdieu suggests that this is comparable to the way in which a prism refracts light. For example, we can think about the relationship between the 'rules' of one field – such as the economic – relative to another, such as the higher education field: people would seldom observe that the more money a student's parents earn the better degree the student stands to get or that a lecturer's burning ambition to be a professor as soon as possible is because they want to earn more money. While there are perhaps elements of truth about both these claims, the higher education field has sufficient autonomy from economic capitals to be able to frame these correlations in its own logic (the student with wealthy parents has sufficient education-specific capital to achieve a first class degree 'fairly' or the professor is remunerated commensurate with their experience and reputation etc.; in fact reducing the status associated with being a professor to money shows a lack of understanding of the status and capitals at stake within the higher education field itself).[7]

Crucially, the relative autonomy of a field is derived from a field being able to recast the values of other fields – such as the economy – in a way that translates into something meaningful, outside of economic reward, to architects. In this respect at least, the restricted part of the architectural field paradoxically enjoys a greater degree of autonomy from economy than does the mass subfield, as those in the restricted field are arbiters of taste and typically have the field-specific power to recast their major works in terms of aesthetic development, symbolic value and so on. In other words, they can refract economic reward into their own terms to a greater extent than can those in the mass part of the field (this claim is developed more fully in subsequent chapters).

The highly aestheticized discussions that characterize much of the symbolic capital at stake in architectural theory and practice can lead to an apolitical vision of architecture in which a disconnect exists between architectural form and wider social questions ('the politics of architecture' or architect's social responsibilities framed as issues from 'other fields'). Margaret Crawford concludes that a number of manifest contradictions in the constitution of the architectural field sees representations of practice absorb as much energy as the practices themselves, due in large part to more fundamental and unresolved contradictions at the heart of the field. She suggests that despite the fact that, as individuals, many architects

> sincerely assert that they are deeply concerned about issues of social and economic justice ... as a profession they have steadily moved away from engagement with any social issues, even those that fall within their realm of professional competence, such as homelessness, the growing crisis in affordable and appropriate housing, the loss of environment quality, and the challenge posed by traffic-choked, unmanageable urban areas. (Crawford 1994: 27)

Fundamental to the unresolved tensions on which the profession is built is the relation between 'actual practices and ideological representations' (Crawford 1994: 31); such struggles are over the parameters of the field itself, over what architecture is and what it should be. This element of the field effect is in evidence in many of the major architectural studies (such as Nikolaus Pevsner's books on national and stylistic traditions within architecture; see, for example, Pevsner 1968) that seek to position buildings within a hierarchy and as entirely aesthetic objects and as expressions of particular visions of beauty, seldom considering the politics and struggles that characterize such judgements. Such discourse is significant, as it acts to reinforce the 'rules of the game' and to consolidate the parameters and capitals of the field – for example, with regard to aesthetic preferences (Bonta 1979), gendered practice and values (Fowler and Wilson 2004), or relationships with unscrupulous, powerful clients (Sudjic 2005). Architecture – like many other fields of cultural production – is a highly reflexive field, that has its own habitus (Stevens 1998), including dispositional and linguistic (see Wolfe 1999 [1981] for a parody; Saint 1983 for a more considered engagement).

Kim Dovey and Scott Dickson have also pointed out (2002: 283) that the very definition of what architecture is, and who can claim to be an architect, represent crucial struggles within the architectural field. It is indeed the case that questions concerning the types of buildings that can 'properly' be considered architecture, and the types of people that can legitimately claim to be architects, have historically constituted signifi-cant sites of struggle (Rudofsky 1981 [1964]), with attempts to define the parameters of the architectural field, as distinct from other building professions, key to the maintenance of the field's boundary (Stevens 1998; Hill 2003). In dominant Anglo-American definitions, the archi-tectural profession is framed simultaneously in terms of its functional component – as a design solution to material issues such as shelter – and also with reference to aesthetics/questions of beauty and semiosis/questions of social meaning. Recasting these contradictory foundations of the field – those of artistic creativity and technical rationality – Margaret Crawford (1994: 29–31) suggests that that this dual heritage creates scope for sufficient specialization within the field to make possible a disengagement from technique and building, effectively removing a certain group of architects, critics and theorists from the material building basis of the profession (1994: 29).

The avant-garde tries to disrupt the capital at stake in a particular cultural field by challenging the fixity and seeming legitimacy of mean-ings and values (punk's version could be a 'do it yourself' ethic; modern art challenges realism; architecture's disrupts the relationship between form and function or challenges conventions of beauty, or what is possible with scale or materials etc.). Within this subfield sometimes the symbolic is all that is at stake, with challenges to the taken for granted values of the field; ostensible challenges or disruption can actually be a way of retaining autonomy. For example, and as noted by Thomas Dutton and Lian Mann (2000: 120–22), and more recently Dovey (2009: 47), Diane Ghirardo's (1994) critique of the deconstructive work of Peter Eisenman – the 'self-proclaimed theorist of strategies of resistance' in architectural theory and practice whose 'adventures in appearance substi-tute for challenges in substance' (Ghirardo, cited in Dutton and Mann

2000: 121) – goes to the heart of this separation. Ghirardo's critique concerned the emergence – and celebration within the architectural field – of the 'aesthetic formalism' emerging from the postmodern deconstruction of 'bourgeois humanist values' and its personification in Eisenman (Dutton and Mann 2000: 121). While acknowledging the cleverness of the symbolism of Eisenman's architecture, Ghirardo was highly sceptical of his claims to criticality, which she viewed as being aestheticized rather than political; she suggests Eisenman's project was one in which 'dissent is inscribed in such a narrow circle of formal choices that it loses any capacity to challenge all but the most banal of issues' (1994: 73).[8]

Rare is the architect who, due to *his or her* transferable capitals, can dictate terms and conditions to a client (Stevens 1998: 95); the autonomy of the field is thus a paradoxical one, which is not about freedom from political or economic constraint but rather the capacity to recast structural contingencies and reliances into an aestheticized architectural language. Certainly, the tendency to aestheticize the architectural field – including the focus on individual architects' practices and discourses and readings of aesthetics – is again significant here, as it can serve to romanticize a creative authorship for architects at the expense of an acknowledgement of ideological production of architectural values in the context of the durable and continuous mobilization of architecture by the politically powerful. It is the tension inherent in this form of the field that has led Thomas Dutton and Lian Mann to identify three ideal-typical ways in which this conflation occurs: when the distinction between form-making and meaning-making is collapsed; when a critique of architecture replaces a critique of society; and when radical academic theory replaces radical social action and engagement with projects of social change, including through new social movements (Dutton and Mann 2000: 118–19). Wanting to recover the critical potential of architectural practice, Dutton and Mann seek to challenge any 'co-opted' versions of 'critical' architecture not committed to transformatory politics.

Conclusion

The architectural theorist Kenneth Frampton points out that, relative to other forms of cultural production, architecture is 'the least autonomous … conditioned not only by its own technical methods but also by productive forces lying outside itself' (1990: 9–17). Positioning architecture relative to the social forces 'lying outside' of the field can seem to leave architects a compromised, constrained and compliant profession, dependent on the vicissitudes of the market and the whims of states and other commissioners. But, crucially, architects *do* enjoy a kind of an autonomy within these constraints (indeed, it is precisely the capacity to claim autonomy from political regimes that makes architecture such a politically useful cultural field). Architecture's own principles – including a highly aestheticized self-conception – can serve to obfuscate the durable relationship between architecture and dominant interests. The separation of architecture's form and wider programme is part of the way in which complicities with power are kept 'silent' (Dovey 2000; 2009). Paraphrasing his wider resistance to attempts to position architecture as a neutral, art-centred endeavour, Kim Dovey has noted that any 'critical architecture will not separate meaning from action' (2009: 46); the separation of the two leads to a focus on the aesthetic and the art, not on the way architecture is used, the way it is understood in 'everyday' contexts.

Getting to grips with this complex relation between constraint and autonomy requires a theoretical framework sensitized to the interplay between political economy and culture. This chapter has followed, among others, Dovey (1999), Stevens (1998) and Lipstadt (2003) in suggesting that a number of Bourdieu's major conceptual tools can be utilized to help reveal the tensions that characterize the architectural field. The individual architect operates in a complex field, which is characterized by a range of technical qualifications regarding entry to the field (not anyone can 'play the game'), their relationship with clients (Sudjic 2005), building-regulations regimes (Imrie and Street 2009) and – just as crucially – by their own objective position within the architectural field (Stevens 1998). In this context, and against the backdrop of the reliance of high-profile architects on states and capitalist organizations for funding, claims to either value neutrality or disinterested social intervention must be approached critically.

A sociological approach to architecture must also avoid focusing solely on these political-economic externalities to the exclusion of analysis of the complex specificities of the architectural field. A criticism that can be levelled at architectural theory is that, in common with other forms of disciplinary-bounded knowledge, it tends towards an internal schema and classification and criticism from 'within' that takes for granted a number of assumptions relative to architecture's and architects' relationship with society more broadly (Dovey 2009). In the restricted part of the architectural field this autonomy can be seen in the tendency for architects to frame what they do relative to aesthetic values, to social identities or to anything other than those responsible for their commission. However, critical social scientific engagements that emphasize the political mobilization of architecture can be in danger of developing ahistorical, overgeneralized accounts that overlook the specificities of the actual social and political conditions in which architecture is conceived, commissioned and made meaningful.

The field category helps us in understanding how the distinctive, internal logic at work within architectural practice translates and mediates the logics of symbolic domination into field-specific capitals. In sensitizing us to the self-validating nature of fields of cultural production, which includes the rejection of certain capitals and practices and the valorization of others, Bourdieu's work helps us situate these practices and knowledges of the architectural field against a broader political and economic backdrop. Revealing the ways in which institutions and agents constitute, and are in turn shaped by, the architectural field thus becomes a primary concern for critical academic work in this tradition, and leads us to confront a

> deep complicity of architecture with social order ... as the practice of imagining and building a new world, architecture will always be political. A primary imperative is that architecture be stripped of the illusion of autonomy; there is no zone of neutrality in [architectural] practice. Architects must enter into and understand some necessary complicities. (Dovey and Dickson 2002: 90)

Interrogating the complicities identified by Dovey and Dickson necessitates acknowledging that durable social power relationships not only condition the relationships within the architectural field but that beyond this they also shape the practice and remit of architecture vis-à-vis the politics of identity.

Notes

1 As Hélène Lipstadt points out (2003), Bourdieu does engage with architects *en passant* in his discussion of family dwellings both in his early ethnographic work in Algeria (*La reproduction* (1970)) and thirty years later in *The Social Structure of the Economy* (2005 [2000]). Interestingly, Bourdieu was also the original translator of Panofsky's *Gothic Architecture and Scholasticism* (1951), a seminal work on the social meaning of Gothic architecture.

2 Larson (1993: 5) also comments on the architectural field's heteronymous nature, observing the architect's fundamental dependence not only on clients but also on other building and design professionals (see also Imrie and Street 2009).

3 There is a great deal of evidence to point to the persistent functioning of a range

of inequalities in the architectural field (Cuff 1991; Stevens 1998; Fowler and Wilson 2004).

4 What follows here is no more than a working definition (what Bourdieu referred to as a 'temporary construct') of the concept of field, designed to facilitate subsequent enquiry. For more detailed discussion, see Bourdieu 1989a; 1993; 1996; Fowler and Wilson 2004; Jenkins 1992; King 2000; Lipstadt 2003; and Stevens 1996; 1998.

5 Parsons' (1968 [1937]) concept of the unit act, which he used to explain the relationship between socialization and the reproduction of social structures, also has a voluntaristic conception of action at its heart, although he loses sight of practice fairly early on in his structural analysis.

6 Larson has also noted (2004: 324) that 'elite architects may have as much trouble finding clients as anyone else, and sometime more, because they are expensive, and reputed to let budgets run out of control. This means they are as dependent on anyone else on the "client class", and the latter is dominant in the larger field of class relations within which architecture as expert service is subsumed'.

7 Cultural capital involves knowing when and how to use one's existing capital to its maximum advantage (which can, of course, involve 'switching off' certain aspects at some points).

8 Eisenman's response (1995), along with comments from seventeen of his supporters (published in a special edition of *Progressive Architecture* a year after Ghirardo 1994), suggested that an aesthetic radicalism could be a foreshadowing of a political radicalism. While radical political institutions frequently use radical architectural forms to signal a desire for a shift in policy, or to mark a shift from a previous regime, this does not mean a 'radical' aesthetic leads to social change or political engagement; 'the agreement that form and political content are not opposed does not mean they are the same' (Dutton and Mann 2000: 122).

2

The Public Discourse of Architecture:
Socializing Identities

The architect is a thoughtful person, a person who is able to think
in situations in which other people cannot think, and a person who
is able to allow other people to think differently. This is why the
architect talks so much ... The architect is a certain kind of commu-
nicator, a certain kind of *public intellectual* ... the role of the
architect is not to make buildings, but to *make discourse about buildings*, and to make buildings as a form of discourse, and this is the
most fascinating form of *social commitment*.

Mark Wigley, *Architecture Australia* (2005)
<www.architectureaustralia.com> (emphases added).

Introduction

As well as a material construction, architecture also represents a distinctly
social production, whose cast of characters is far more extensive than
those professionals who formally inhabit the architectural field. Works
of architecture are used and conceptualized by a wide range of citizens,
who not only organize their spatial practices in response to them (Hillier
1996) but who also come to understand buildings as symbols of wider
social order (Scruton 1977). Accordingly, architects' attempts to make
their work resonate with publics outside of the architectural field go far
beyond what is actually built, with the work of high-profile architects in
part concerned with discursive strategies to make their architecture
socially meaningful to non experts. However, owing to the ambiguous
nature of the architectural object relative to the construction and stabi-
lization of social meaning, those operating in the part of the architectural
field that demands engagement with questions of social identity tread on
uncertain political terrain.

This chapter focuses on but one aspect of the process through which
buildings become socially meaningful (or not), namely the role of architects' public utterances in positioning their buildings relative to identity

projects and social values. Those architects competing in architecture's 'natural market' (Gutman 1992) are compelled by the rules of this part of the field to engage with competing value and identity claims, not only in the actual forms and styles of their buildings (discussion of which is a traditionally understood concern of architectural theory) but also through the identity discourses within which they situate their work. The constitution of the restricted part of the architectural field not only shapes architects' aesthetic preferences, it also necessitates those within its *'field of force'* (Stevens 1998) to articulate the relationship between the architectural object and social meaning. The competition is discussed as one component of architectural practice in the restricted subfield through which architects compete for the award of commissions and seek to situate their work relative to social discourses. By interrogating the work of Hélène Lipstadt, who has drawn on Bourdieu to assess the competition stage (2003), this chapter contends that the process represents a struggle to define the social parameters of the architectural object itself, and is thus a crucial space in which the dialectic relationship between form and meaning is manifest.

The general argument of this chapter, concerning the tensions between discourse and form, is illustrated via discussion of the Jewish Museum in Berlin, a building situated in a highly politicized and contested political position. Daniel Libeskind, the architect who designed the extension to the state-funded museum, has been incredibly active in connecting/disseminating narratives and social meanings to the spaces within this project, in the process illustrating a number of the claims of this chapter relative to the centrality of discourse for architectural practice in the 'restricted' part of the field.

Architecture as Discourse: The Struggle for Meaning

A crucial challenge for sociological research in this area is to take seriously what could be called the 'soft' elements of architectural production (including the range of discourses attached to buildings by various social actors) while also maintaining a sense of the durable ways in which architects and their work are mobilized by states as part of political projects (Jones 2009). A contention here is that pluralist accounts of architectural meaning, stressing the status of architecture as an 'open' signifier, can leave us ill-equipped to understand the operation of power in the cultural sphere by flattening out the differential capacity of actors in different positions in the field to construct what become definitive claims about the world (see Jessop 2004 for a developed critique of this tendency). Avoiding the relativist position that sees interpretation of architectural meaning as 'equal but different', Bourdieu's concept of the field – discussed in Chapter 1 – sensitizes us to the differing capacities of actors and institutions within architecture to construct arbitrary values as natural, taken for granted and fair. The suggestion is that the ascription of social values to architectural form is complex, contingent and always contested, and reveals something about both the operation of power within the architectural field and the mobilization of architects and their work in the context of political programmes.

All but the most functionalist of definitions of architecture would position the built environment as a carrier of social meaning, as one way in which actors and institutions within society seek to objectify, represent and reconstruct themselves. Architecture is thus a 'discourse', inasmuch as it is a form and a set of practices through which social meanings are communicated and visions of the social world are sustained. The promise of cultural self-understanding through architecture hinges on the capacity of buildings to provide a 'concrete' reflection of abstract social values and identities, to give otherwise abstract histories and perspectives a tangible reality. However, overstating the correspondence between form and meaning 'essentializes', inasmuch as architecture is positioned as an unproblematic quarry of meanings that (with assiduous reading after the correct training) can be revealed to correspond to stable sets of authentic social values. John Gloag encapsulates something of this perspective when suggesting that '[b]uildings cannot lie; they tell the truth directly or by implication about those who made and used them and *provide veracious records* of the character and quality of past and present civilisations' (Gloag 1975: 1, emphasis added). The perspective of Gloag, and the others who seek to position architecture as a direct and unproblematic reflection of social values, can gloss over the heavily negotiated processes inherent in the cultural and political construction of architectural meanings.

Presupposing an independent basis to professional practice, such positions attribute an 'authentic' social reality that can be captured in material form. The formalistic assumption that particular styles or buildings have an 'authentic' essence has an affinity with this perspective. Commenting on this essentialist tendency in architectural theory, the critic Deyan Sudjic questions:

> Is there, in fact, such a thing as a totalitarian, or a democratic, or a nationalistic building? ... Can classical columns be described as the

signs of fascist or democratic buildings, as some have claimed? Are
these fixed and permanent meanings, or can they be changed over
time? (Sudjic 2005: 6)

As Sudjic himself concludes, the short answer to these questions is: no,
there is no such thing as an inherently 'democratic' building, and yes,
socially constructed meanings are by definition contingent on practices
existing in the context of wider social forces. This is both the basis of
much struggle within the architectural field and also the reason that the
social meanings associated with particular buildings are in themselves
highly dynamic.[1] Paraphrasing Bourdieu, Stevens has noted that 'the
essential arbitrariness of [architectural] symbols is what allows them to
be the object of struggles, in which groups try to convince others to value
their capital more than that of their rivals' (1998: 69). From a sociological perspective, an interesting line of inquiry concerns the ways in which
the practices of architects – and others within the field – seek to attach
social values to built form. As suggested previously, architects operating
in the restricted part of the field are required by the very 'rules' of the
subfield within which they operate to position their buildings relative to
a set of social values. The increasingly crucial *discursive* interventions of
high-profile architects into public debate is a key way in which social
meanings are attached to particular buildings, be they 'democratic',
'fascist', 'beautiful', 'progressive' or whatever.

Bourdieu and Loïc Wacquant's definition of a field as a 'space within
which the effect of the field is exercised' in which 'what happens to an
object ... cannot be explained solely by the intrinsic properties of the
object in question' (1992: 100, cited in Lipstadt 2003: 395) serves us as
a reminder of the fact that architecture is characterized by struggles over
meaning, and also serves as an ideal introduction to the work of the architectural theorist Juan Pablo Bonta. Bonta has demonstrated how
orthodoxies on architectural meaning occur through a process of 'collective plagiarism' (1979) within the field, in this process revealing how the
relatively coherent meanings that coalesce around buildings, their
aesthetics and their meanings are socially constructed, and thus are wont
to change across time and space. Bonta positions powerful architectural
critics as a crucial group within the field, as – in Bourdieu's sense although
not necessarily in Bonta's language – they have the capacity to define the
aesthetic capitals over which actors within the field struggle (architecture
as a *battlefield*).

Furthermore, and in a foreshadowing of Bourdieu's notion of the field
as a *field of force* shaping the behaviours and values of those within it,

Bonta observes a process whereby critics' aesthetic judgements are shaped by the architectural field and in turn shape subsequent judgements. Arguing persuasively against essentialisms, Bonta suggests that 'the meaning of architecture can be removed – and sometimes even dissociated – from what architecture actually *is*' (1979: 14, emphasis in original); for instance an influential critic's judgements on a particular building represent not only the personalized taste of the asocial individual critic but the mediated position of the field itself. In this way what is arbitrary is presented as 'an absolute index of intrinsic worth' (Jenkins 1992: 13). It is the very mystification of the judgements informing this index – and the agents within the field responsible for them – that are the general concern of Bourdieu's writings on symbolic violence.

Bonta's study of Ludwig Mies van der Rohe's German Pavilion at the Barcelona Expo in 1929 (Fig. 1) illustrates the wider point about the relative power of voices within the architectural field. Focusing on the published views of critics, Bonta traces reviews of the building from when it was first built – as a temporary structure – until the time he was writing in the late 1970s. The changing interpretations of the building and the motifs it employs are illuminating, with the field's 'discovery' of the building as a masterpiece of modernist design principles occurring many years after the 1929 exhibition. Bonta shows how influential critics' retrospective judgements contributed to this initially unremarked struc-

Fig. 1. Ludwig Mies van der Rohe's German Pavilion at the Barcelona Expo in 1929

ture becoming central to the modernist canon. Bonta's 'architectural orthodoxy' and 'collective plagiarism' effectively entail a shift in the collective judgement of significant figures in the architectural field. Ultimately, Bonta argues that Mies' architecture cannot, as some critics claim, 'speak for itself', but rather that 'value judgements originate and disappear with time' (1979: 138); styles come to be attributed with meanings over and above the actual built form, with understandings developing from historical and symbolic associations that architects – and others in the field – attach to buildings.[2]

Bonta's work also resonates with the contribution of Magali Safuri Larson, whose recent classic *Behind the Postmodern Façade: Architectural Change in Late-Twentieth Century America* (1993) draws attention to the discursive element of architectural practice and the power relations within the architectural field. Larson analysed the speeches of the judges of the prestigious annual American Progressive Architecture Award between 1965 and 1985, in the process revealing how different conceptions of the architect's social role were reflected and constructed through the judges' terms of reference. Reflecting on the contribution of her influential book, Larson has suggested that this study gives a 'micro-history of [an aesthetic] shift, seen from inside the profession by individuals constituted as gatekeepers, [identifying] the "anointing" function that elites have' (2004: 327). Both Larson's and Bonta's studies show the construction of architectural meaning as contested, but, while ostensibly open to challenge, also reflecting power relations within the field. These arguments can be situated as a clear example of Stevens' contention regarding the architectural field both as a *field of force* and as a *battlefield* (1998). Both Bonta and Larson also remind us of the arbitrary nature of the social meanings attached to architecture, and in so doing reveal the ways in which what Bourdieu would call 'symbolic violence' (1977; 1989a; 1989b) operates in the field. In presenting certain aesthetic or social meanings as definitive, individuals and institutions reveal both their competition on the architectural *battlefield* (struggles over relative capacity to frame the conditions in which they operate are also evident here) and also the simultaneous power of the architectural *field of force* over them (again, see Stevens 1998).

The observation that there is an arbitrary foundation to the architectural field leads us to ask far-reaching questions of the claims made by architects and others in the field. Of course, opinion about the beauty or otherwise of specific buildings or broader styles is always contested, with a variety of judgements within and without the field struggling for primacy; the impossibility of consensus is because ultimately these differing tastes reflect different field positions within which people learn values and taste (the *battlefield* component of Bourdieu's field concept identified by Stevens).

The Architectural Competition: Capital in the Field

While it can be noted that architectural meanings and values are constructed in the context of the field, it is necessary further to interrogate the processes that underpin the construction and maintenance thereof. One of the 'internal' sites of struggle within the restricted part of the architectural field is the competition. A crucial way in which the social meaning of the built environment is constructed and disseminated, the architectural competition is a cornerstone of elite architects' practice, and one that gives the field some of its distinctiveness from others. Although not the way in which the majority of architects get their work, competitions form the institutionalized route to commissions for major public and private buildings that are, as Gutman (1992) has shown, the 'natural market' for architects in the restricted part of the field.

Lipstadt has made significant contributions to our understanding of the architectural competition, and her definition of the event is well worth quoting at length here:

> Competitions are those events in which entire buildings are designed in a general manner, stopping short of construction drawings, by 'two or more architects for the same project, on the same site, at the same time', at a great cost of labour, presentation materials and opportunity costs, for clients who select – at relatively little cost to themselves – the best design for their purpose, most often through the intermediary of designated independent experts constituted as a jury. (Lipstadt 2003: 395)

Recalling the field as a *battlefield*, it should be noted that the competition process involves competition *between* architects for material and symbolic capital. A mainstay of elite architects' practice, competitions are to some extent unrestricted by 'real-world' constraints, the competition stage allowing the architect to embrace fully the aforementioned aesthetic and artistic dimensions of their role.[3] The basis of the competition is drawings, models and other renderings, which give the participating architects something of a distance from the prosaic considerations that characterize the realization of designs. As Lipstadt points out (2003: 396), the competition is thus a paradoxical space in which the constraints that impinge on architecture – including the client's wishes – are revealed, but within which architects can also enjoy a degree of autonomy otherwise not associated with the practice. In other words, competitions allow architects to embrace the 'artistic' component of practice. The fact that competitions prize drawings and other aestheticized constructions of the building is crucial in this regard.

In her research on the romantic origins of the profession, Larson (1994) shows how architecture was originally 'owned' by the patron: early renaissance architects were usually unknown designers (and builders) with their designs most closely associated with the commissioner. The question of architects' capacity for self-definition of the field is significant here, with the emergence of the profession bound up with the capacity of renaissance architects to frame their work as a design practice separate from that of construction (Hill 2003). The professional project of architects was contingent on two distinct but related aims: definition and maintenance of the parameters of the market for a particular set of skills relating to the built environment (Crawford 1994). Membership of the profession, which is protected by the professional bodies' accreditation of particular schools, confers economic and social status.[4]

Still, competitions are also a clear expression of the close relationship between social elites and the architectural field, and reveal the nature of the political-economic constraints that impinge on the architectural field. In this regard the competition process is a component of 'the technical and symbolic services [architects] *render to the dominants* (notably in the reproduction of the established symbolic order)' (Bourdieu 1996: 222, my emphasis). Stating the case forcefully, Garry Stevens argues that the competition:

> allows the elites to remind the [architectural] field that, in the end, it serves *them* ... [at the same time allowing architects] to make a ritual demonstration of allegiance to the elites, by showing architects to be the loyal and dutiful servants of the powerful. If the competition obliges the economically and politically dominant to aver in the most public manner their symbolic dependence on architects, the architects always reavow the covenant by affirming their material dependence on the wealthy and powerful. (Stevens 1998: 97)

Architects' willingness to embrace competitions is in some sense surprising, insofar as entry costs time and other material resources, and

– although the benefits of winning a commission can potentially be high – the odds are also typically quite long. Paradoxically, given the client-led nature of the process though, the competition is one of the most autonomous spaces in the architectural field (Lipstadt 2003); the capital at stake in such competitions is also consecrated by the field in aesthetic terms and certainly cannot be reduced solely to an economically motivated action. Architects submit to this element of practice willingly, as the capitals it yields are consecrated by the field, with the material and symbolic capital generated by success in a competition bringing celebration within the profession (and the money from without).

The competition is also an important part of the way in which a building is constructed relative to different publics. When entering a design competition for a major building, high profile architects are engaged in a normative debate about why the world is the way it is and what should be done to change it, thus 'express[ing] the will to build and rebuild, that is to engage and represent the world as a continuous opportunity for reconstruction' (Grezner 2000: 219). The competition is a key stage of the process through which buildings are 'discursively constructed' (Wodak et al. 1999) relative to publics, and a point at which architects are required by the rules of the field to position their vision socially, beyond a functional solution to a design problem. Accordingly, architectural competitions are an interface between architects and their publics. In the European and North American contexts, at least, the architectural competition is usually held only to decide on architects for high-profile buildings of social significance that constitute Gutman's 'natural market' (1988). In short, the architectural competition is an important part of the elite subfield, in which symbolic conflicts over power and identity – as well as economic capital – are played out.

Architects are faced with a very complex cultural terrain to negotiate at this stage, with the dangers of symbolically privileging one identity discourse over another, or overstretching the social claims of what a building will do, an ever-present threat. Charles Jencks refers to the competition stage as a 'litmus test is to see how the architect negotiates the very difficult terrain between the explicit sign and the implicit symbol: a false step on this thin ice and he or she falls into one of the twin dangers that come with the territory, either vacuity or bombast' (2004: 21).

Deconstructive postmodernist claims drawing attention to the 'death of the author' (Barthes 1968) are a significant backdrop to the contemporary relationship between architects, citizens and the social values attached to the built environment. Simplifying to the extreme, postmodern currents within architectural theory and practice attempted to release the democratic potential inherent in architecture by emphasizing multiple readings of buildings' styles and meanings. In general, these perspectives claimed that architecture should become a more 'opened' discourse that supported a plurality of 'voices' and meanings, in the process challenging the elitist conceptions of architecture that had been dominant in modernism (Venturi, Brown and Izenour's *Learning from Las Vegas* (1997) is a notable statement of this project). Crucially, notions of multiple truths associated with postmodernism rendered the architect's reading of the symbolism in their building as just one among many, which opened the way for playful architecture that challenged the relationship between signifier and signified and between architect and user.[5]

In general terms, postmodern perspectives were underpinned by a commitment that architecture should become a more 'opened' discourse and practice, with the spaces created by architecture reflecting a plurality of social standpoints and supporting a range of different ways of being in the city, generally emphasizing democratic rights to public space. Accordingly, postmodernism sought to challenge some of the elitist conceptions of architecture – as profession and social practice – that had been dominant in modernism, including the capacity of the architect to offer definitive 'truths' about the correct use and interpretation of urban spaces. Critical scholars engaged with the postmodern debate sought to demonstrate the superficial nature of much of postmodern architecture's promise for new 'open' spaces by drawing attention to the synergies between postmodern discourse – albeit as one that unquestionably did disrupt previously deeply held values and practices within architecture – and the recasting of long-standing compliances with the economically powerful. However, to consider the built environment as an 'open field', characterized by multiple interpretations, is to disconnect architecture from social relations and thus to overlook the inherently conscribed nature of architectural production (Albrecht 2002).

Without offering a strong interpretation of their own buildings, architects are in danger of leaving the interpretation of their work 'open'. Instead of actually etching text on to buildings or loading them with ostentatious ornamentation to signify national victories, as was often the case in an earlier modernity, contemporary designers tend to use more narrative associations when attempting to insert their buildings into political discourses such as, for example, democracy, transparency or openness. Given the aforementioned tensions surrounding architecture as communicative medium, the capacity of the architect to manage the interpretation of their buildings both inside and outside the field says much about the operation of power within the field. Crucially, for prominent architects, the competition stage is a site not just of narrowly defined architectural realization but of the wider social production of their project and practice.

The Discursive Construction of the Extension to the Jewish Museum in Berlin

The case of Daniel Libeskind's extension to the Jewish Museum in Berlin illustrates the centrality of the constitutive 'discursive construction' of social meaning within the restricted part of the architectural field. Libeskind, one of the most active architects in terms of his written and spoken reflections on his own work, is perhaps disingenuous when suggesting that '[w]hatever an architect says about his work may only seem a redundant commentary on what is obviously built' (cited in Langer and Steglich 1995: 24). Originally an architectural theorist rather than a practitioner, Libeskind was an influential presence in global architectural debates before his first building was completed. In his writings and built work, Libeskind embraces the political component of architecture and this reflexivity can be explained at least in part by the politically charged contexts in which he has worked, which has necessitated a reflexive approach to the relation between architecture, loss and collective identities. Accordingly, his writings and interviews provide clear examples of how architects working in the restricted subfield develop and disseminate the symbolic discourses within which their buildings are understood. Libeskind's general position (see, for example, Libeskind 2001) is that major events in world history demand more than a functional architectural response, and one that engages directly with the complex social questions of memory and loss. Over the last decade, Libeskind's radical aesthetic design has become associated with major global commissions, such as that for the Imperial War Museum in Salford; a number of buildings and spaces on the Ground Zero site in New York (see Chapter 5); the Contemporary Jewish Museum in San Francisco; and numerous other shopping centres, museums and residential spaces the world over. Libeskind is sufficiently famous to have become familiar to all inside the architectural field and many outside of it.[6]

With the extension to the Jewish Museum in Berlin, sociologically pertinent questions about how best to represent a traumatic loss of life come to the fore.[7] Previously, Libeskind has argued that any kind of Jewish memorial in Berlin must reflect a paradoxical 'permanent presence of absence … [a] presence in the city even though you don't see it in an obvious way but it is there, it's part of the void which the city also carries in its own absence' (quoted in Langer and Steglich 1995). James E. Young discusses the memorials of Horst Hoheisel, whose 1995 entry to a Holocaust memorial competition called for the destruction of the Brandenburg Gate. Young suggests that

> [a]t least part of its polemic is directed against actually building any winning design, against ever finishing the monument at all … Hoheisel seems to suggest that [the] surest engagement with Holocaust memory in Germany may actually lie in its perpetual irresolution, that only an unfinished memorial process can guarantee the life of memory. Better a thousand years of Holocaust memorial competitions in Germany than any single 'final solution' to Germany's memorial problem. (Young 2010)

Hoheisel engages what Young calls 'negative form', which entails the subversion and inversion of the perpetual, universalizing monument.

As a materialized engagement with the Holocaust, Libeskind's extension to the museum – on a former site of the Berlin Wall at Lindenstrasse (Fig. 2) – posed many problems in terms of a material representation of trauma and loss. Libeskind sought to create a sense of 'disrupted tradition' with the building's spatial organization, and with that in mind it is significant that the original competition stated that the entrance to the museum should be through the Kollegienhaus, a symbol of Berlin's baroque history. Libeskind met this criterion by connecting the two buildings not by a ramp (as did all other competition entrants) but via an underground passage: a 'conscious tear' (James-Chakraborty 2000: 119) in the urban fabric to represent the void left in the city by the absence of its Jewish population. By juxtaposing the two cultures in the new extension to the old building, Libeskind suggests a 'reconnecting [of] two cultures to the present time, saying something new about the Berlin of today and tomorrow … There is something deliberately ambiguous about the building: as wrenching as the history of this city' (interview with Daniel Libeskind).

The five-storey building is organized around empty spaces, what Libeskind calls 'voids' that cut through the corridors. But rather than offering access they deny it: 'as visitors follow the zigzag pattern through

Fig. 2. The Kollegienhaus, Berlin and Daniel Libeskind's extension to the Jewish Museum

the museum as dictated by the layout ... they are repeatedly confronted by these voids, which are accessible from nowhere and which seem to be senseless' (Heynen 1999a: 202). The voids are closed-off spaces into which visitors can see, but to which they have no access. Inside the museum there are numerous information points that tell of the representative voids around which the building is organized. One such text tells the visitor that 'the building is cut through by a tall space that has little in it. His [Libeskind's] building invites us to ask what this means'. Empty space is often used in memorials designed to represent trauma and loss (see Chapter 5). James E. Young (2000) also identifies an affinity between Holocaust memorialization and radical art and architecture, not just because the scale of the tragedy seems to demand a radical reflection in form but also because those seeking to represent genocides often want to reflect a deep mistrust and rejection of an existing social order that could allow such a tragedy. Libeskind's radical aesthetic is certainly one of the ways in which he attempts to reveal Berlin's 'disrupted tradition'.

The design for the windows further illustrates the centrality of narrative in the connection of form to meaning. In the competition entry, in interviews and in published texts, Libeskind has described how the design for the scar-like windows (Fig. 3) is based on linkages of sites of signifi-cance for Jewish cultural figures – such as Walter Benjamin and Mies van der Rohe – drawn across a pre-war map of Berlin. Provided with such explanation, we understand the social significance of the form of the windows, but without this narrative it is improbable that the viewer

Fig. 3. Libeskind's scar-like windows in the Jewish Museum in Berlin

would make this highly symbolic association. Without prior knowledge of Libeskind's own interpretation the windows do not locate the building into the history of the Jewish population of Berlin, but by offering a 'strong' interpretation the architect is able to locate it within this history. According to the museum's official pamphlet, other crosses on the zinc facade of the building (Fig. 4) make one 'feel compelled to think about

Fig. 4. Zinc facade of the Jewish Museum in Berlin

the links between the cross and destruction. You wonder about the connections between the church and the Holocaust'; one certainly does when prompted to do so.[8] Commenting on the symbolism of the Jewish Museum, Filler also suggests that '[n]one of Libeskind's allegorical references is readily apparent to the average viewer without prior knowledge of the architect's intentions', and while the 'hyper-cleverness' (2001) and referential nature of Libeskind's references further ground his work to place, meaning and context, this underlines the point being developed here: architecture is discursive and relates to any given identity only to the extent that links can be constructed and maintained in a way that connects form and meaning convincingly. Celebrating the architect's highly interpretive approach, Kathleen James-Chakraborty has suggested that 'Libeskind is virtually alone among architects building today in Berlin in the trust he puts in architectural form and the spaces it shapes to create an emotional rather than a rationally ordered environment' (2000: 120).

In discussing his own building, Libeskind has actually dismissed form as a 'superficial issue', suggesting that '[w]hat is important is the experience you get' from the building (*Guardian* 2002a). This is a highly ambiguous claim given the amount of symbolism he has worked into the

Fig. 5. The Garden of Exile, Berlin

architecture's form, and the sustained effort to connect narrative values to aspects of the building. However, in denying the centrality of architectural theoretical readings of the building's form, Libeskind is attempting to draw attention to the experience of being in and around the spaces he designed. Certainly a number of the spaces within the museum are affective, encouraging contemplation and reflection. The ways in which the building elicits an emotional response is by linking such spaces to historical experiences via a range of slight misalignment of walls, sloping floors, plays of dark and light, and angular, slashes of windows. This powerful combination of form, spaces and experience is

Fig. 6. The Holocaust Void in the Jewish Museum in Berlin

clearly evidenced in the Holocaust Void, a ninety-foot-high concrete
bunker that is lit only through a small opening at the very top, which
also allows some muffled street noises to filter in (Fig. 6). Entrance and
exit only through a heavy black door that slams shut behind the visitor,
and the experience of sensory deprivation in the space, are designed to
add to contemplation. The only thing on any of the concrete walls is a
ladder, which starts about fifteen feet up – too high to reach. It is by
confronting the visitor with such radical spatial experiences that
Libeskind attempts to force reflection of the Jewish experience in Berlin.

Filler has gone so far as to suggest that this space is 'the definitive statement on the Holocaust in architectural form' (2001: 5), and regardless
of such claims Libeskind has certainly created an experience that utilizes
space in a very direct, emotive way, reflecting that 'the museum will be
a permanently disorientating and reorienting experience to make the
historical experience more intensely concentrated. It is the exposing of
things which are irreconcilable' (cited in Langer and Steglich 1995). His
building, he has claimed, emphasizes the 'necessity to integrate physically
and spiritually the meaning of the Holocaust into the consciousness and
memory of the city' (Libeskind 2001: 23). James E. Young declares a
deep suspicion of the suggestion that materialization of memory through
art or culture approximates any kind of resolution; Libeskind's architecture in Berlin – while not a Holocaust memorial per se – engages with
this context in a way that on the one hand seems to claim a kind of essen-
tialized relationship between form and memory, but on the other – thanks
to the highly affective connection between social practice and meaning
that the building engenders for many visitors – is a dynamic and highly
socialized 'memorial'.

Jacques Derrida raises the question of whether or not a realized design
can ever avoid being a memorial (Heynen 1999a: 207–08). The bold
claims Libeskind makes about the representative capacity of architecture
certainly place a huge burden on the architecture's capacity to capture
such memories across a range of lifeworlds, the success of which places
a tension on the interface between what is built, what is said and how
the space is incorporated in people's practices. The Jewish Museum relies
on the combination of narratives attached to the building interior and
exterior spaces and spatial disruptions and sensory challenges, which
have the cumulative effect of disorientating the visitor, to this end. While
the numerous design tricks – such as the stairs that lead to a wall, the
dead ends, sloping floors, and clever plays of light and shade – *may* make
us reflect on the experience of alienation, it is by framing his work rela-

tive to otherwise abstract social values and identity discourses that the architect ensures we do. Far from leaving the viewer to weave meaning into the space – as per one critic's review (*Guardian* 2002a) – the very opposite is quite often true, with Libeskind actively offering 'strong' readings of what the museum architecture and the spaces within it mean.

James E. Young's work (1993; 2000) has revealed how Holocaust memorialization has been inflected by national agendas and politics. Libeskind sums up this ambiguity relating to the Jewish Museum extension by calling for the 'non-identity' of Germany, adding that he does not think the concept of the nation, and more specifically national architecture, is 'relevant' any more (Libeskind, cited in Leach 1999: 135). The 'particularistic' architectural devices of the nation code are not suitable for this building, and accordingly the flags and overt symbols synonymous with national architecture are absent, with empty spaces in their place; Libeskind's notion of a German 'non-identity' could be recoded as a desire to move away from the particularistic forms of national identity and towards a more universal, post-national identity, however – and as is illustrated by the way in which Libeskind framed his work at the Ground Zero site within a highly nationalized discourse (see Chapter 5). While the architect has suggested that the Jewish Museum 'speaks a visible language' (quoted in Spens 1999: 42), this complex architectural 'language' of form – and experience – is in need of the architect's own translations, which are often necessary to situate this building in relation to a particular social discourse of memory, loss and trauma. As a result this building illustrates much of the centrality of discourse in the work of those architects operating in the restricted parts of the architectural field.

Conclusion

Commenting in typically succinct fashion on the coupling of social meaning to architecture, Kim Dovey surmises that 'architecture is a multiple "framing" wherein representations are framed by spatial structures that are in turn infused with narrative interpretations' (2009: 46). Foregrounding the discursive element of architectural production – characteristic of the restricted part of the field – directs our attention to the myriad social struggles that centre on the political positioning of major architectural projects. The processes through which buildings come to represent collective identities or social values are always and everywhere highly contentious, involving the coupling of material form to abstract belongings and, relatedly, to a narrative order imposed on diverse experiences, meanings and events, processes explored in more detail in subsequent chapters.

Arguing against essentialist approaches to architectural meaning, in this chapter I have suggested that one prominent practice through which architecture comes to be socially meaningful is via the public pronouncements of architects, which also serve to connect major buildings to wider social or political values, social groups and memories. Precisely because architecture provides a focus for public discussion of identities and memories in a way that other symbols more abstract and distant from 'everyday' concerns do not, the potential of such buildings to act as a touchstone for wider public discourse reminds us of architecture's status as 'the most social of the arts and the most aesthetic of the professions. As an art it carries the obligation to imagine a future world; as a profession it carries the obligation to practice in the public interest' (Dovey and Dickson 2002: 294). Accordingly, when competing for a landmark state-led architectural project, architects are essentially engaged in a 'sociological' debate about social meanings (including collective futures and pasts). The extent to which architects manage to situate their buildings within a given identity discourse is a key part of a wider social production whose 'broader frames' include the political contexts in which architecture becomes meaningful. The practice of high-profile architects, increasingly adept at negotiating contentious symbolic ground when positioning their work (Delanty and Jones 2002; Baydar 2004), extends to the authoring of appropriate social and political meanings relative to particular publics.

The case of the Jewish Museum in Berlin illustrates this case, with Daniel Libeskind's nuanced discourses crucial to the positioning of elements of the building both as 'post-national' and as balancing form with memory and experience, which reminds us that the connections between buildings and meanings only exist insofar as they are forged and realized in the practices of architects and users. Libeskind expresses much of how successful architects move between framing their commissions both in an 'architectural' way – essentially for capital *within* the field – and in more understandable fashion for those outside of it. While architecture has its own 'specialized vocabulary, enabling critics [and others in the field] to talk seriously, technically, and precisely about the architectural object as distinct from other kinds of objects' (Hays 1984: 17), switching these field-specific codes (concerned with symbolic capitals such as aesthetics) into more publicly resonant frames is crucial to

Libeskind's particular strategy here. Foregrounding the *experience* of being in the building, and stressing the disjunctive and isolating character of some of the spaces – albeit carefully framed and guided by the architect's narratives – reminds us that the increasingly central element of the work of architects acting in the restricted part of the field is to make different types of discourses about buildings.

Notes

1 Debates about essentialism find an expression in the discussions around the work of Albert Speer, Hitler's architect. Leon Krier, a staunch defender of Speer's work, has suggested 'there is neither authoritarian nor democratic architecture ... it is just as childish to read a particular colour or the immanence of a political system into a row of Doric columns as it is to accept kidney shaped tables ... as the authentic expression of a libertarian and democratic regime. Architecture is not political; it is only an instrument of politics' (Krier, cited in Dovey 1999: 67). Speer himself, in some of his interviews and writings, sought to forward a similar argument about his work. Although highly effective at controlling the symbolism associated with the Nazi projects he sought to socialize and aestheticize, Speer has observed that '[c]olumns do not stand for dictatorship, nor glass for democracy' (cited in Wise 1998: 37–38). This position reveals the problematic nature of architectural 'autonomy' when configured as a retreat into analysis of form separate from the politics that gives rise to it.

2 From a philosophy of science perspective, Thomas Kuhn's work on paradigms is an important supplement to Bonta's initial framework. In *The Structure of Scientific Revolutions* (1962) Kuhn argued that the interpretation of the results of scientific enquiry differs according to which particular paradigm ('normal' or 'revolutionary') the wider scientific community is operating within, therefore drawing attention to the context within which experiments are carried out and interpreted. Linking this notion explicitly to architectural meaning, we can see how significant the architectural community is for the development of orthodox 'canonical' interpretations: from Bonta, we can see how significant the architectural field is for the development of 'canonical' interpretations, with 'the interpretation of a single work ... affected by interpretations of other works taking place within the same social or historical context' (Bonta 1979: 65). In other words, 'though political symbols may impress us as having "always" had the same connotative signification and societal meaning – because their representational form (as signifiers) stays the same – it is nevertheless far from uncommon for the same symbolic material to change its functions and connotations over time, and even at the same temporal intersection to imply different meanings to different groups' (Hedetoft 1995: 122). When commenting on critics' attempts to arrive at a definitive reading of his painting *Guernica*, Pablo Picasso foreshadowed these debates when suggesting: 'this bull is a bull and this horse is a horse ... If you give a meaning to certain things in my paintings it may be very true, but it is not my idea to give this meaning. What ideas and conclusions you have got I obtained too, but instinctively, unconsciously. I make the painting for the painting. I paint the objects for what they are'. Public Broadcasting Service (n.d.).

3 For a more detailed ethnographic exploration of the architectural competition, see Cuff 1991 and Blau 1984.

4 The role of drawing is a significant part of this story, as it allowed a form other than the finished building that could be understood as the intellectual property of architects (ongoing conceptions of the 'architect as artist' must also be understood

against this backdrop). On this point Stevens has observed that, compared to other forms of cultural productions such as poetry, music or art, architecture has only limited capacity to expand the stock of symbolic capital within the field, as there are only ever a small number of major commissions and competitions to enter; the centrality of drawing (Hill 2003) to the professionalization of architecture and its emergence as an intellectual property reveals this struggle for symbolic capital, with 'the fact that drawings of buildings are at least as important as the objects they depict' (Stevens 1998: 97), an interesting development in this regard.

5 Jonathan Hill's work on 'passive/reactive' and 'creative/proactive' users (2003) is also a useful conceptualization of this division in the reception and perception of social meaning in the built environment. Both Bourdieu (1989a) and, following him, Stevens (1998) would perhaps foreground class in their analysis of these cultural capitals/capacities to a greater extent than does Hill.

6 See, for example, his early writings on theory (Libeskind 2001). Libeskind did not actually build anything until 1998, when his Felix Osabaum Museum in Dessau was completed.

7 From the time of winning the competition to design the extension to Berlin's Jewish Museum in 1987 to delivering the building in 2001, with Germany's political climate witnessing 'seven changes of government, six name changes to the museum, five senators of culture, four museum directors, three window companies, two sides of a wall, one unification' (*Guardian* 2002a). The extension to the Jewish Museum, costing about 77 million Deutschmarks (about US $43 million at 1999 rates), was delivered slightly over budget.

8 A further discursive link between the building and identity is evident alongside the building at 'The Garden of Exile' (Fig. 5), which is accompanied by the following text, written not in Hebrew but in both German and English: 'Here architect Daniel Libeskind asks us to think about the disorientation that exile brings.'

3

Architecture and the Nation:
Building an 'Us'

Look and see the constant flaggings of nationhood ... Their unob-
trusiveness arises, in part, from their very familiarity.

Michael Billig, *Banal Nationalism* (1995), 174.

Introduction

The historian Bo Stråth has argued that a central concern of European
nation states in the nineteenth century 'was to mobilise and monumen-
talise national and universal pasts in order to give legitimacy and meaning
to the present and to outline the future culturally, politically, socially'
(2008: 26). Certainly states in this period were incredibly active in
commissioning culture so as to embed their political projects and values
into socially meaningful forms designed to help create/mobilize national
publics. Illustrating something of the general argument of this book,
architecture was central to the cultural self-understanding of nation states
in this period, as it provided an opportunity for emerging states to give
material form to their political power, while at the same representing one
way in which the national community was presented as a continuous and
'natural' entity. In other words, architecture was a part of a broader
historicist repertoire (that included flags, currency, anthems and art),
which was mobilized to 'invent' national traditions (Hobsbawm and
Ranger 1983) in order to forge feelings of belonging.

   The attempt to use culture to sustain the nation as 'natural' and
'continuous' raises interesting sociological questions about the political
construction and mobilization of culture; approaching this question from
a constructivist perspective – and drawing particularly on the work of
Benedict Anderson and Michael Billig – architecture can be framed as
part of a broader repertoire of cultural symbols that states have long
mobilized to construct and maintain national identities. Not only were
major national buildings objects used to this end, they also housed many
of the institutional rituals crucial to such invented traditions (Vale 1992:

54). The politicized search for national architectural styles best to reflect a state's aims and aspirations opened up a lucrative market for those newly professionalizing architects able to materialize 'appropriate' values in the built environment. Which architectural styles architects and states aligned themselves with was in many circumstances a highly contested question, with the social meanings attached to particular historicist styles and buildings taking on a 'moral' dimension.

Discussion of Anderson and Billig serves as backdrop to this chapter's focus on the 'Battle of the Styles' in Victorian Britain, a highly politicized struggle centring on the quest for an 'appropriate' architectural style in which to design major public buildings (including the Palace of Westminster, better known as the Houses of Parliament). The Battle of the Styles was fought out between the two great hostile camps, each advocating a different historicist style in which to build: this tussle between the Gothic Revivalists and neo-Classicists drew in actors far outside the formally understood parameters of the architectural field, in large part due to the fact that styles were imbued with questions of the cultural representation of the civilizational aspirations of the British nation state. As such, the Battle of the Styles is an interesting way into some of the major concerns of the book, with respect to how and why architects and their work get drawn into state projects at particular junctures.

States Constructing Nations: Politics and Collective Identities

Clifford Geertz observed that national cultural symbols are 'devices designed to render one or another aspect of the broad process of collective self redefinition explicit, to cast essentialist pride or epochalist hope into specific symbolic forms ... [that] can be described, developed, celebrated and used' (1973: 252). Geertz's anthropology tends towards a 'thick description' of these cultural symbols, but for the present discussion the broader significance of his observation is that a collective identity is always and everywhere a social co-construction, which does not exist outside of practices and social actions that attribute shared meanings to things.[1] Such an approach emphasizes that collective subjects, such as the nation, are constructed through a whole range of practices and discourses about internal and external populations – in crude terms about 'us' and 'them' – that help to represent such boundaries as natural and self-evident. Such an impression is bolstered by the development of cultural forms imbued with symbolic significance for respective communities.

Benedict Anderson coined the now-famous term 'imagined community' (1983) to capture a number of arguments associated with the construction of such belongings in the cultural sphere. Situating the emergence of the nationalism in the latter part of the eighteenth century, Anderson's study has been so influential because it addresses one of the paradoxes of the modern nation state, namely the fact that although many feel the nation to be their 'natural' community, we do not know the vast majority of the other people with whom we constitute this group. For Anderson, this raises the issue of how we come to 'know' the nation – an abstraction distinct from everyday life and conceptualization – through our cultural practices (1983: 3–6). Anderson thus defines the nation as *imagined* 'because the members of even the smallest nation will never know most of their fellow-members, meet them, or even hear of them, yet in the minds of each lives the image of their communion' (1983: 6) and a *community* because 'regardless of the actual inequality and exploitation that may prevail in each, the nation is always conceived as a deep, horizontal comradeship' (1983: 7). It is crucial to note that 'imagined' in this context does not mean false, but instead points to the socio-cognitive element in the construction of the nation, suggesting that nations and associated national identities are constructed through a range of social practices and emergent cultural productions.

Anderson emphasizes the roles of culture and the chance yet highly dynamic coincidence of the emergence of print culture and the development of industrial capitalism in the eighteenth and nineteenth centuries. This period saw advances in printing technology, accompanied by increased literacy, which allowed the concept of the nation to be (relatively) widely disseminated through media including literature. This technological affordance also facilitated communication increasingly taking place within national linguistic boundaries – and markets – allowing the emergent bourgeoisie to 'imagine' themselves as part of a group with shared interests, dispositions and lifestyles and to form 'imagined' solidarities not based on family structures, religion or other traditional social bonds. The extent to which these literary and other representations in turn shaped practices is an interesting related question. For Anderson, then, the promise of the nation as an 'imagined community' is as both a mechanism for social integration among strangers – a key concern for modern states – and as a coherent narrative of progress based upon a constructed remembering (and just as importantly a forgetting); the impression is of a united, coherent group moving together through history towards a common future (facing – and usually defeating – common enemies in the process).

Anderson's framework raises significant lines of inquiry when assessing architectural projects from a sociological standpoint. Pre-empting something of the subsequent discussion on architecture in Victorian Britain, an important point that emerges from Anderson's work is that (aside from the claims that can be made for the lineage and historical associations of a particular architectural projects or style) national continuities cannot be taken for granted as self-evident, but nor should they be dismissed as mere fictions. The extent to which the social meanings that political regimes (and cultural producers working under their auspices) seek to attach to architecture resonate with particular populations at particular junctures is a question of sociological interest and an object for empirical inquiry.

The social psychologist Michael Billig also makes a very useful contribution to our understanding of the relationship between states, culture and national identities with his central argument in *Banal Nationalism* that 'in the established nations, there is a continual "flagging" or reminding of nationhood ... a continual background for political discourses, for cultural products ... daily, its [the nation's] symbols and assumptions are flagged' (Billig 1995: 8–9). For Billig, it is impossible to define the nation in terms of 'objective' geographical, political or cultural principles, such is the huge degree of variation between existing nations (1995: 19); we are left then with the more abstract idea of the nation as a 'specifically modern form of collective identity' (Arnason 1990: 208) based around a cultural community.

The work of Billig and Anderson reminds us that the continued expansion of the nation state in the modern period has been accompanied by a consolidation of cultural boundaries, in part through the wide dissemination of nationalized cultural discourses/objects/images. The myriad architectural outcomes of this active process of cultural construction, expansion and consolidation are still to be witnessed in capitals and major cities that have been – and often continue to be – sites of state expression in the built environment (Therbon 2002). Indeed, architecture has been an important and effective way not only of 'inventing' (Hobsbawm and Ranger 1983: 4) but also of 'flagging' the nation in this way, as states have long used landmark buildings to supplement a historical narrative of collective memory when seeking to construct such 'bonds of loyalty' (Hobsbawm and Ranger 1983: 263) among citizens. When informed by the work of Billig and Anderson, such architecture reminds us that national identity is itself a cultural and political construction, and as such any architecture that is designed to sustain this category is inherently contested. Recast into Anderson's famous phrase: to what extent do architects and their designs contribute to the construction and maintenance of imagined national communities? And, from Billig, what is the role of architecture in 'flagging' – and thus in part constituting – national publics?

The Victorian State and 'National' Architecture: Constructing Continuities

Harold Lasswell notes that large-scale architectural expansion tends to be associated with the emergence or expansion of a new political regime, a period when 'the elite of a nation state ... tries to create symbols capable of setting it apart from older symbols of authority ... and to emphasize the existence of a brave new identity that enjoys excellent prospects for its values and institutions' (1979: 11–14). Britain's Victorian Age (1837–1901) saw the construction of a massive number of buildings designed by architects who were self-consciously attempting to reflect the state's sentiments and aspirations in an 'appropriate' way.[2] Many British public buildings of the period 1850–1901 give testimony to the self-confidence of the Victorian nation state as an imperial power; architecture – alongside other important codifications such as art, flags, national anthems and a nationalized discourse of history – was drawn closely into the state's cultural project and mobilized to give tangible form to abstract 'national' values (Jones 2002) and to codify a national public.

The Victorian period in Britain was one in which a self-conscious national construction was taking place in architectural production and explicit attempts were being made to use architecture to develop and reflect appropriate national identities. As such, it is a good place to illustrate broader theoretical debates about the relationship between the built environment, the state and social meaning. This backdrop saw struggles over social and political values become manifest in the architectural field, refracted into embattled discussions of styles and meshing with contemporaneous architectural-specific shifts and developments: during the early part of the Victorian period, British architects were engaged in an ongoing, and deeply entrenched, debate about what constituted a 'suitable' style for landmark British public buildings.[3] In this context, architectural styles such as Roman, Gothic, Greek and baroque (which, ironically, had all originated elsewhere as vernacular constructions with highly localized meanings) had taken on stylized qualities and had come to be read as cultural codes loaded with a wide range of social meanings.

A desire for representation, with attempts to construct and express idio-syncratic national cultural codes against the more universalizing tendencies inherent in modernity, was key to this cultural project. Although many of these civilizational styles reflected a particularized 'national' culture (with, for instance, French and British versions of Gothic – see below), the universality of architecture as an expression of *civilization* was always also evident, as states sought to connect their particular interpretations of styles to wider civilizations. As we shall see, the role of architects in designing such monumental, national buildings in imposing national styles through such particularistic cultural refer-ences was beset with tensions, and while the period was one of explicit and creative 'flagging', innovation and experimentation proliferated.

This struggle over 'correct' interpretations of styles vis-à-vis previous civilizations conspired to give the British 'Battle of the Styles' a moral dimension, with both Gothic and neoclassicism coming to connote sets of social values. Explicit debates took place about what styles would be suitable to express the colonial and ethnocentric meanings that European states often wanted to align themselves with and revealed much of the 'logic of "monumentalisation", intended to commemorate, or to radiate power ... [that] belongs to the nineteenth century grand narrative of modernity ... [and] corroborates the world view of the dominant class, by carving in stone their interpretation of their historical and cultural identity' (Heynen 1999b: 375). For many Victorian architects and politi-cians, architecture was a materialization of morality; with buildings 'only the visible forms above a more submerged order of beliefs and massing of knowledge' (Crinson 1996: 4). Dominant Victorian values concerning the hierarchical nature of different human 'races' became bound up with cultural forms (Malik 1996). Many public buildings such as universities and museums emerged as monuments to the progressive and civiliza-tional self-conception of Victorian elites, with the discourses centring on such architecture reflecting a self-assured, colonial nation that consid-ered its own society as the highest and clearest expression of 'civilization', but that nonetheless – in part due to its emergent character – was still in search of coherent cultural referents within which to materialize such values.

Indeed, as Mark Crinson suggests in the course of his definitive book on Victorian architecture and orientalism *Empire Building: Orientalism and Victorian Architecture* (1996: 38–71), architectural styles were actu-ally presented as products of more fundamental, racialized typologies by prominent critics of the day, including the hugely influential nineteenth-century critic John Ruskin (1819–1900) and James Fergusson (1808–86), one of the most prevalent Victorian architectural theorists. Ruskin's proclamations illustrate something of Crinson's argument. Ruskin saw two 'duties' to be carried out by national architecture: 'the first, to render the architecture of the day historical; and the second, to preserve, as the most precious of inheritances, that of past ages' (Ruskin 1992: 215); national styles of architecture are records of different geographical spaces and histories. His theory harbours a determinism at its core, with the sense that architectural forms could actually shape behaviour and morality prevalent in his work (Crinson 1996). Furthermore, proclamations around the 'correct' styles with which to represent the nation existed within a pseudo-religious, disciplinary fervour: Ruskin viewed Gothic as a 'celebration', and implored designers to 'render the architecture of the day historical ... to fill their buildings with historical reference and meaning' (1992: 215), and in *The Seven Lamps of Architecture* had suggested that the repertoire of feelings and values embedded in Gothic could express 'either symbolically or literally, all that need be known of national feeling or achievement' (1992: 48). Adamant that history was *the* most important legitimating value for contemporary practice and a crucial part of a 'civilizing' process, Ruskin believed that no new architectural styles should be developed, as existing – historicist – styles were sufficiently universalized and expressive to capture the whole range of human experience (1992: 272).[4] Ruskin thus emphasized the relationship between social meaning and architecture as a virtuous union, and believed that the state should create its reflection in those architectural forms strongly rooted in collective memory and in tradition. An essentialism that equates particular cultural form with stable social meanings is necessary to support this argument, which is reductionist inasmuch as it overlooks the contingencies and social struggles that exist around the construction, maintenance and mobilization of architects and their work; it is precisely the ways in which architects get drawn into political projects, and the ways they seek to position their architecture and discourse in this context, that are of sociological interest.

In the Victorian context, major political debates over the nature and form of the British state – and, by extension, 'Britishness' more generally – were refracted into the architectural field and imbued aesthetic choices with moral import. Initially, Victorian architects considered certain styles suitable for certain types of buildings; Wilkinson affirms that 'Gothic was the style of English patriotism' (2000: 144) and came to be considered by the British as a quintessentially British style (the conflation in

Victorian discourse of 'English' and 'British' is perhaps illustrative of a wider colonial politics). Attempting to reconcile the development of a distinct national culture with the ideal of the universality of European 'civilization' led to attempts to develop a distinct national cultural variant that reflected the cosmopolitan ideal of the universality of European 'civilization' (with the Eurocentrism in this conception of civilization reflecting the universalistic self-understanding of the Victorian state). 'Gothic' had become somewhat of a catch-all category within architecture, suggesting something of a 'universal' style that had played a key role in reflecting the achievements of the 'civilized' European nations.

It is interesting to note that, as a general rule, Gothic designs were favoured for religious buildings and a neoclassical style was favoured for public buildings (Wilkinson 2000). However, when Gothic *was* used on public (or, more generally, secular) buildings the moral dimension to the style was 'carried over' as it were, and the resultant association to the architects and the nation-builders was a desirable one. For example, Augustus Pugin (1812–52), designer of many of the most famous Gothic buildings in the United Kingdom, including perhaps most notably the Houses of Parliament (see below), considered the style to be 'morally uplifting', the aesthetic expression of a civilizing process through which barbarism and paganism had been defeated (again, perhaps in no small part due to Gothic's historical origins in twelfth- and thirteenth-century cathedral design). Between 1840 and 1870 there was a huge expansion of literature on Islamic architecture; Crinson charts the growth of 'a corpus that consisted of weighty multi-volumed works purporting to be of archaeological exactitude, batches of measured drawings and sketch-book studies, historical and theoretical overviews encompassing a subject in a comparative framework, articles in a scholarly or journalistic mode in various periodicals, and even built imitations of Islamic buildings' (Crinson 1996: 38).[5] Crinson suggests that these critiques and engagements with Islamic architecture existed to 'make cultural differentiation meaningful' (1996: 38): in other words, to embed ethnic and national cultural differences. Furthermore, knowledge of such 'exotic' architectural styles – whether they and the values they represented were only to be employed merely in a rhetorical binary with the Western canon – represented a form of cultural capital in the professionalizing architectural field of the day. Gothic, against a backdrop of Occidentalism, was positioned as a built testament to the age when the 'other' could be westernized (or Christianized) and assimilated (Crinson 1996). Ironically, the very incorporation of Islamic and 'Eastern' styles into European interpretations of Gothic, classicism and so on betrays the fact that cultures are never hermetically sealed, and are always open to dialogue, critique and contestation.

When universalized aesthetics do not allow for sufficient expression, problems of distinction abound, and it is clear that Gothic was a relatively 'universalized' architectural style until the development of a particularly 'English' or 'High Victorian' Gothic. The prefix 'High' was essentially a favourable adjective, 'if "High" is to mean for nineteenth century architecture relatively meritorious, "Victorian", a not-yet clearly defined style and/or period in the nineteenth century, and "Gothic", the architectural style dominant in the late medieval northern Europe' (Kornwolf 1975: 44). A more creative style of Gothic, High Victorian merged nationalized versions of Gothic from Italian, French and German Gothic influences to create this 'correct' English Gothic style (Kidson, Murray and Thompson 1965: 273) illustrating a dialectic relation between universalized styles particularized to reflect a specific, non-universal (national) identity. Given the contested nature of social meanings associated with architecture, what *did* vary from country to country were the associations Gothic had as a style. Illustrating the contested and constructed nature of the politicized values within which architectural styles are interpreted (Bonta 1979; Jones 2006), Sutton (1999) suggests that in Germany, for example, the style was squarely equated with Catholicism thanks to its use in cathedrals and in the work of August Reichensperger, a leading advocate of the style, who saw Gothic as a symbol of hostility to Prussian Protestantism. French architects who claimed Gothic as an originally French national style had emphasized the 'rationality' and 'functionality' of the style (Sutton 1999: 279), judgement that would perhaps seem strange to the contemporary, nonetheless so because such terms became central to the modernist project that sought to strip away the ornamentation of the type that characterized Gothic.[6]

As Umberto Eco notes, architectural theorists and historians debated the social meanings of Gothic architecture explicitly, with such struggles in the architectural field seeking to reveal the 'true' style of Gothic: 'the history of the interpretation of the Gothic teaches us that over the centuries the same sign vehicle, in the light of different subcodes, has been able to connote different things' (Eco 1997: 189). Eco uses the ogive (Fig. 7) as an illustration of this broader struggle, drawing attention to the debates that took place within the architectural field as to whether or not the ogive had a structural function or whether it was merely a facade.

Fig. 7. Ogive arch

Illustrating something of the 'field effect', the meanings associated with particular styles or buildings are not derived from anything inherent in the aesthetic but rather from a collective social agreement on any such symbolic associations, which develop in specific socio-political contexts and are consecrated or otherwise by the field itself (the 'force field' affect (Stevens 1998). It is important to note that the meanings attached to the Gothic style were highly contested *within* the architectural *battlefield*, and that one of the fascinating things about this debate was that the usually implicit judgements about the relationship between social meanings and aesthetics that characterize the architectural field were made explicit: 'battles' over style and meaning were fought from behind clear lines of engagement.

There was certainly a strongly historicist basis for this style, as the questions for the nineteenth-century state builders were centred on finding a style to suit the aims and aspirations of the state. It was only really in the nineteenth century that reasonably accurate knowledge of geographically or historically distant societies was available, which gave a 'storehouse' of historical styles to be mobilized to different ends: high-profile Victorian architectural theorists and critics were at the time 'torn between various doctrines which they could not reconcile' as '[t]he authority of historical precedent, the correct use of a national or local style in materials ... conflicted with the belief that history was a store-house to be raided at random' (Kidson, Murray and Thompson 1965: 272).[7] The classicists – although also obviously supporting the histori-cist approach – sought to emphasize the mutability and capacity to adapt this style to new social conditions and tastes and preferences. From the perspective of architectural theory, historicism amounts to giving precedent to historical styles and aesthetics over contemporary or future-oriented ones. However, it must also be noted that any such stylistic allusion to previous empires or regimes is intended to reflect something of that power on the state that commissions a building in this style. Reflecting on this dominant historicist frame, Göran Therbon has suggested that the

> European nation-builders' obsession with history was part of a much wider intellectual worldview. Historians were the great, the famous, and the leading scholars of the 19th century. Perhaps because soci-eties had started to move, timeless principles of religion and philosophy appeared less relevant, and because progress was young, uncertain, and not to be taken for granted, the past origins ... fasci-nated. (Therbon 2002: 40)

Against the backdrop of rapidly urbanizing population, the polarization of social classes and state expansion, these sets of values gave the illusion of a common history, of 'moving together' through history. Drawing heavily on the European civilizations – medieval Gothic, neoclassicism – the major architects of the day were actively creating this history rather than revealing it.

As suggested above, the English nation-builders felt a particular affilia-tion with Gothic, and this association was evident in the design competition for the Houses of Parliament.[8] After fire had destroyed the medieval Palace of Westminster in 1834, the competition to rebuild the damaged section of parliament specified a 'medieval' (i.e., a Gothic) style. The decision to rebuild in the 'inherently' English style of Gothic was controversial. As Vale points out, the decision to commission and design a parliament building is never made by a whole 'nation' or any other such reified collective, but a particular state or political regime in contract with an architect: 'no society is without its contradictions, and no [architect wants their] building ... to celebrate them – least of all in a government building' (Vale 1992: viii). In the rebuilding of parliament, one of the interesting facts in the debate about which architectural style should be chosen and who should be represented in that style was that the protagonists were not just those operating in the architecture field per se. Indeed, one of the major voices in the dispute belonged to Prime Minister Lord Palmerston, a central protagonist in the Battle of the Styles in general. A staunch opponent of Gothic, Palmerston felt that classical architecture 'best represented modern sentiments', and opined that

> The Gothic style was wholly unsuited to a public official building, and that ... whether in office or out of office, [he would] do all in his power to prevent its being adopted for that purpose ... though the Gothic style might be admirably suited for a monastic building, a monastery, or Jesuit college, it was not suited, either internally or externally, for the purpose to which it had now been proposed to apply. (Parl. Debs (series 3) vol. 155, col. 931; 4 Aug. 1859)

The competition was won by Sir Charles Barry (1795–1860), an English

Fig. 8. St Peter's Church, Brighton

architect who had travelled widely, touring Italy, France, Greece, Turkey, Palestine, Syria and Sicily (1817–20), and was in fact one of the first British architects to study ancient Egyptian architecture (Crinson 1996: 21). Up until his victory in the competition for the Palace of Westminster, Barry's most prominent designs had been for Gothic-style churches, such as St Peter's Church, Brighton (Fig. 8), but whose earlier work, including the Manchester Art Gallery (Fig. 9), had been neoclassical. Barry enlisted Augustus Pugin, the most high-profile British architect working in Gothic at the time and an expert in its origins in thirteenth- and fourteenth-century church design. In a debate on the technical parameters of the style, Pugin, a particularly vocal supporter of Gothic architecture, described the popular form of Gothic as incorrect, a translation of prior misreadings and misinterpretations. Debates over 'correct' versions of Gothic were made possible by the emergence of bodies of knowledge about previous societies and their architectural styles: from Pugin's reading of these transcripts and representations, Gothic should use only brick and stone building materials and should 'cement' the relationship between religious values and architectural form with the 'correct' style of architecture able to spearhead a religious revival (Crinson 1996: 34).

The new Palace of Westminster was designed by Barry – with the interiors by Pugin – specifically for British parliamentary use; the design and

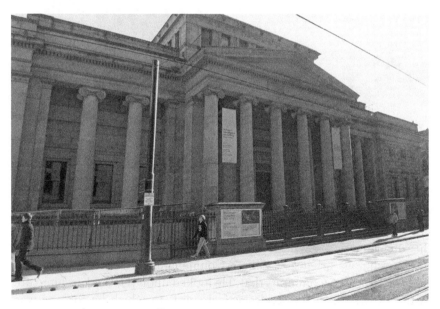

Fig. 9. Manchester Art Gallery

layout of the building were intended to serve the needs and workings of the British parliamentary system in general (for example, Barry located the Sovereign's throne, the Lords Chamber and the Commons Chamber in a straight line, thus linking the three elements of Parliament in continuous form, and his oppositional layout of the benches for MPs of differing parties is a spatial reflection of the adversarial nature of much of the debate in the House of Commons (Fig. 10).[9]

Why was it that in this industrializing nationalism historicism should have been such a dominant architectural and social discourse? The

Fig. 10. Interior of the Palace of Westminster (the House of Commons)

historicism of Gothic was explicitly designed to give the Houses of Parliament a lineage and gravitas, and a visible continuity with the past, although at the same time to represent a break with the medieval British parliament and its home in the ancient St Stephen's Chapel, which had burnt down in 1834. Capturing something of the tensions associated with this dual function – which was bound up with secularism and parliament's religious origins – William Coningham, then MP for Brighton, told the House of Commons that 'He looked upon [Gothic] architecture as the expression of the ecclesiastical spirit, to which he for one was strongly opposed, and which he believed to be opposed to liberty and the true interests and prosperity of a Protestant country' (Parl. Debs (series 3) vol. 28, col. 941; 4 Aug. 1859).

The Foreign Office was also a major public building around which the Battle of the Styles crystallized (Kornwolf 1975; Bremner 2005). After another open competition in 1857, George Gilbert Scott won the competition, and – despite a stated desire to design a Gothic building – came under substantial political pressure to design in a different style (Fig. 11). A fascinating, fractious debate (ironically, in the Houses of Parliament!) between different sides of the argument (all references from Parl. Debs

Fig. 11. The Foreign Office, Westminster

(series 3) vol. 28, cols 915–42; 4 Aug. 1859) clearly illustrates the interface of politics, culture and form. Peter Blackburn, MP for Stirlingshire, says he feared 'the same error' that had been made with the Houses of Parliament – that

> after an architect had been selected, instead of being left to attend to his own duty, he would be exposed to interference on the part of persons who proposed plans and schemes of their own. Without expressing any opinion as to the Gothic or classical styles of architecture, he thought that ... the best course would be to allow him to

erect a handsome building on the condition that it should be suitable for the purposes required, and should not exceed in cost the
amount of the estimate.

R. A. Cross, MP for Preston, chided other MPs for their 'ignorance ...
respecting the character of Gothic architecture', which, he contended,
'was not so monotonous in its character as had been stated by some hon.
Gentlemen'. Sir Joseph Paxton, designer of the Crystal Palace at the Great
Exhibition of 1851 (see next chapter), observed that Scott's building was
'beautiful' and suggested that 'Scott's design had been a little unfairly
treated' ... before it was rejected a stronger opinion should be given in
this House than had been hitherto expressed'.

Conclusion

Ulrich Beck has observed that 'architecture is politics with bricks and
mortar' (1999: 115), and certainly the affinity between political agencies
seeking to materialize their civilizational aims through the built environment and those architects operating in Gutman's 'natural market'
leads to explicit politicization of architectural practice and form.
Questions about the political construction of collective identities and the
cultural legitimation of power find a clear focus in those objects of state-
led architecture that are framed as symbols of national identities; rather
than simply reflecting an existing, authentic reality in an unproblematic
way, such state-led projects are active attempts to contribute to the
cultural construction and consolidation of communities such as the
nation. It is through such symbols that 'the state makes a decisive contribution to the production and reproduction of the instruments of
construction of social reality' (Bourdieu 1994: 13).

The challenge for architects engaged with nineteenth-century nation-
building projects was to make the nation state appear natural, historic
and continuous – in Clifford Geertz's words to make it appear 'indige-
nous' (1973: 318). Part of what makes the Victorian period so fascinating
in this respect is the explicit discussion of the strategies employed to this
end; the 'Battle of the Styles' was the site of struggles within and between
political and cultural elites about how best to represent their aspirations
for that particular nation. This struggle within architecture took place
against the backdrop of a rapidly professionalizing architectural field
in which new knowledge of other cultures and aesthetics was crucial,
both for the consolidation of the parameters of the field (for example,
distinction from related building professionals) and from within

(competition *between* architects for distinction and control of the field's aesthetic capitals).[10]

As per the observations made in Chapter 1 concerning the dynamic nature of the cultural field of production (Bourdieu 1993), it is important to recognize the 'internal' struggles over the nature of Gothic, which, framed in aesthetic terms within the architectural field and civilization-ally in the political field, led to a sociologically interesting political struggle around culture. From the example of Gothic architecture we can see that the past has proved to be a powerful legitimating force for the aims and aspirations of state definitions of the nation; much of the discussion that characterized the architectural field at this time proceeded as if styles of Gothic and neoclassicism had essential or fixed meanings that were more or less accurate descriptors of the Victorian state project, rather than highly contingent signifiers that reflected an ongoing construction of a political-cultural project. Of course, the connection of social meanings to buildings and styles contains an arbitrary dimension (Bourdieu 1992) inasmuch as it naturalizes a set of social values that express something of the capacity of one group to impose values over another. In the Victorian context, architectural style became synonymous with social meanings, and these connections between form (in this case, historicist) and previous civilizations were presented as immutable and rooted.

States actively seeking 'revolutionary changes in the internal structure of particular political units typically innovate architectural shifts' (Lasswell 1979: 13), and major public buildings give states the chance to situate themselves self-consciously with regards to the past. Architectural form is always 'political' in the sense that it emerges from particular political circumstances, and comes to represent social identities and events that help frame our understandings of the social world. The possibility of architecture provides a social space in which new ways can be found of seeing things and for new forms of social organization and distributions of power to be made manifest. The 'failure of pure and definitive ideological expression does not prove that there is no ideological component to architecture' (Rakatansky 1995: 10) but on the contrary directs our attention to the practices of those architects whose field position entails connecting their designs to politicized identity projects.

Notes

1 In Émile Durkheim's writing on integration in pre-industrial societies he discusses the role of totem, which he defines as 'the flag of the clan' (Durkheim 1985 [1915]: 220). In Durkheim's account, the totem 'stands in' for a social reality, namely

for the fundamental but intangible power of the social as manifest in the obligations and freedoms associated with social membership; worshipping a totem is a society's way of worshipping itself and of reminding individuals of their reliance on the group. In this sense, the totem operates as a synecdoche – a part that stands in for the whole – and is *in itself* an emergent 'social fact', a manifestation of wider social relations. This opens up important questions about materiality and representations of the social; as Neil Leach observes in a discussion of Homi Bhaba's work, 'if the nation is a kind of narration, it is never an abstract narration, but a contextualized narration *inscribed around certain objects*' (Leach 2002: 297).

2 The extent to which the Victorian period should be considered coterminous with a particular movement in architecture is debatable, and perhaps especially so given that Queen Victoria was not a particularly enthusiastic patron of architecture (Kornwolf 1975: 37–39). Illustrating something of the fact that the aesthetic preferences of the monarch are not necessary dominant in the field of cultural production, Hitchcock observes that Queen Victoria's 'personal tastes had in fact nothing at all to do with establishing the "Victorian" character of the architecture of her time [and] the private retreats of the Sovereign ... represent in their stylistic character a lag of a decade or more behind such architectural developments as were being patronized by the cultural elite' (Hitchcock 1954: 8).

3 George Mosse, in his wide-ranging discussion of the use of symbolism in German nationalist discourses (1994), briefly looks at the coterminous 'Battle of the Styles' in German architecture, with architects such as Schinkel, Gilly, Wallot and Klenze seeking to develop national architecture by mimicking famous buildings from the ancient world, including Rome's Pantheon and the Propylaem of Athens. The role of Berlin's Reichstag is this regard is discussed in more detail in Chapter 7.

4 The aforementioned tension between universalism and particularism is also alluded to by Ruskin, who saw significant architecture as that which carries universal messages in culturally specific ways. So Gothic as a style has universal 'messages' but vastly differing national interpretations.

5 As does Edward Said, Crinson (1996: 23–24) draws attention to Napoleon's invasion of Egypt (1798) as crucial for subsequent 'scholarly colonialism' such as in *Description de l'Égypte* (1809–28), which contained typologies of Egyptian architectural forms. Architects' knowledge of these forms was, in spite of travel tours, and resultant architectural sketches of the 'Near East', most frequently garnered from drawings.

6 Illustrating this point, Sir Alexander James Beresford Hope, the conservative MP and patron of All Saints, Margaret Street (1849) (designed by William Butterfield and identified by Henry Russell Hitchcock (1958) as the start of a distinct revival of High Victorian), suggested Gothic as 'the universal emanation of the mind of Christian Europe, or at least of its active portion' (cited in Crinson 1996: 140).

7 An eclectic approach to materials and historical styles was also to be a defining characteristic of postmodern architecture almost 200 years later.

8 There are many comparable examples of state-led Gothic architecture, with the most similar design to the Houses of Parliament perhaps Thomas Fuller's Parliament Buildings in Ottawa (1859).

9 The entry that succeeded in the competition was never fully realized, with the huge ceremonial gateway and the internal courtyard called for by the design brief not deivered. Their vision for the main block, however, was fulfilled.

10 On the latter point, the historicism of the aesthetic is interesting, because it should remind us that an avant-garde can at times be an *arrière-garde*, a defence and valorization of things past.

4

Modernity and Mega-Events: Architecturing a Future

It is right in the conduct of the nation's affairs every so often for nations to make a great statement of confidence, of great commitment to their own pride in the past and their optimism for the future.
Michael Heseltine, then Conservative MP responsible for the inception of the Millennium Dome project, in evidence to the Culture, Media & Sport Committee, 13 November 1997.

Introduction

States have long sought to embed their political-economic projects within socially meaningful forms, with the architectural field being mobilized to this end in a wide variety of socio-political contexts. As was discussed in the previous chapter, the desire to forge a sense of coherent national community with its roots in antiquity saw historical motifs and discourses as key frames for major British state-led architectural projects in the nineteenth century. But, quite aside from the mobilization of historicist architecture to stress lineage in this way, the latter half of the twentieth century saw nation states' repertoires of architectural representation characterized by the dominance of rationalist, future-oriented and technologically driven modernist forms. Seeking to benefit from the ostensibly progressive promises implied by modern architecture's broader social programme and aesthetic, many states in the post-Second World War period sought to use architecture to signify a self-conscious rupture with the immediate past. In short, the promise of modernist architecture, unencumbered by tradition, was to play a central role in symbolic and material social reconstruction of societies. This chapter is focused on the major modernist architectural projects at the centre of large-scale, state-led festivals. The British sociologist Maurice Roche has argued (2000) that 'mega-events' such as the Olympic Games, World's Fairs and Expositions reflect a 'performance complex' inherent in modernity through which states have sought to integrate mass populations into their

67

political projects and to make cultural statements of their place in the world to external audiences, including other states. Accordingly, the tensions surrounding representations of national cultural pasts and futures are often evidenced at such mega-events.

These events frequently centre on a piece of major landmark architecture. Such buildings can either house the festival itself or be those radical new spaces (often temporary structures such as pavilions) that are designed to offer a glimpse of possible futures, and the state's role therein. The architecture synonymous with mega-events is most frequently self-consciously modern, entailing a distinct break with older aesthetics and – crucially – politics. Indeed, the 'shock of the new' has been a defining characteristic of the architecture associated with mega-events since the middle of the nineteenth century, when iron buildings such as the Crystal Palace and the Eiffel Tower were conceived of as symbols of a radically new social and industrial age. After briefly assessing the role of the centre-piece architecture in these nineteenth-century mega-events, this chapter focuses on the Millennium Dome, the major architectural statement of the British state's project to mark the passing of the year 2000. This case is explored in the context of the New Labour government's broader project of modernization, which entailed sustained attempts to present a culturalized frame for economic activity (Hay 1999) and to codify a representative, 'multicultural' national identity. Given the intended aim of the project was to reflect a consensual and creative Britain united at the millennium, it is ironic that the Dome became mired in far-reaching social and political struggles that engulfed the project (McGuigan and Gilmore 2002) and which also revealed a number of deeper fault lines in the state-led construction of collective identities.

Celebrating the Machine Age: A Brief History of Mega-Events, 1851–1951

Although in the context of this chapter it is neither feasible nor desirable to rehearse the many and varied definitions of modernity, a sketch of some of modernity's central features – and their link to modernism – gives some context to subsequent discussion of the relationship between nation states and major mega-events. Jürgen Habermas, arguably the foremost contemporary theorist of the major social and political changes associated with modernity, identifies the end of tradition as a form of legitimation and a crucial component of modernity (see, for example, Habermas 1990). The forward-looking, progressive and frequently utopian dynamics of modernity are based – among other things – on enlightenment discourses of the application of reason to society through scientific knowledge (see also Toulmin 1992; Delanty 2000; Strydom 2000). Since their inception, modern states have colonized many different discourses in order to position themselves as progressive, dynamic institutions and best to exploit the hugely increased productive capacity associated with industrial advances.[1] Closely linked to modernity's reliance on knowledge as progressive and emancipatory discourses, the intellectualization of culture was crucial for its subsequent incorporation into the future-oriented discourses of the nation state (see, for example, Bauman 1989).

The embedding of state power in the cultural sphere is the backdrop to the ways in which World's Fairs and Expositions introduced state-led utopian visions of the future, to both internal publics and other states. Maurice Roche (2000) develops this line of enquiry through an assessment of the spectacular events that have characterized modernity. Roche suggests that what he calls mega-events reflect a 'performance complex' inherent in modernity. For him, the Olympic Games, World's Fairs and other major exhibitions originated with the aim of securing the participation of emerging mass publics. Roche sees such mobilization as necessary to states and elites because they needed to 'win the "hearts and minds" of the newly enfranchised working-class citizens for projects of economic growth and nation-building' (2000: 34).

A contention of this chapter is that architecture has had, and continues to have, a significant part to play in the incorporation of mass publics into the state via these 'discourses of belonging', and that as such these events and the buildings at their centres – regardless of the conceit – represent a highly partial and politicized representation of the nation. The tendency for political institutions to align themselves with radical modernist cultural form is clearly observable in the architecture that states commission in the context of mega-events, which provide them with the opportunity to situate themselves with reference to visions of the future. Modernism's promise was in the combination of social and aesthetic programmes with the radical forms emerging from the technological experiments incorporated enthusiastically into some state projects.

Seeking to make a virtue of what David Frisby (1985) has referred to as 'the newness of the present', modernism was to be unencumbered by tradition and what was expressed was not only to play a central role in the material reconstruction of post-war societies but to be at the vanguard of a new social order. At the core of the modern architectural movement were the efficiencies afforded by the mass production and the scientism of the Machine Age. Use of reinforced concrete (which could be prefabricated off-site and assembled quickly and efficiently), glass and steel characterized modernism, which also saw historical ornament, decoration and stylistic motifs (until then the definitive component of architectural production) eschewed in favour of strictly geometric shapes and forms. Claiming a rationality and, crucially in the current context, universalism, the radical architectural forms emerging from the early modernist experiments in Bauhaus and elsewhere in the 1920s and 1930s became key reflections of the aspiration to develop modern social projects based on a less classed, more egalitarian social organization.

As Crawford points out (1994: 34), engineering technology was at the heart of the modernist architectural project, with many of the 'brilliant symbolic gestures' of modernism, such as Mies van der Rohe's skyscrapers, contingent on the technological affordances of the steel frame. Somewhat counter-intuitively though, this led to a retreat into aesthetics by architects keen to retain distinction from allied building professionals; it was in part this project of distinction that led to the decoupling of modernist form, discourse and politics (Crawford 1994). It is interesting that in this way modernist architecture, which was based on the quest for an objective, disinterested aesthetic, should ultimately descend into Stevens' internal *battlefield* and a struggle over aesthetics. The modernist programme was to be one stripped of ornamentation and detached from questions of personal preference, with architects' skill in identifying and delivering the function that the form should follow. The modernist architect Adolf Loos was a staunch advocate of the removal of any 'unnecessary' decoration from architectural form, which he thought should be based on designs centred on objectified scientific knowledge. Loos felt strongly that anything in the built environment that could not be legitimated by reason was, by definition, superfluous and should be excluded. He was echoing the connection of moral meaning to architectural form of the 'Battle of the Styles' discussed in Chapter 3: that the very negation or repression of decoration is necessary for the regulation of social disorder more generally. Indeed, Loos even went so far as to claim that progress is the result of the renunciation of passions and to suggest that to revoke ornamentation brings with it a pseudo-spiritual power. It was for this reason Loos saw mass-produced ornamentation for general consumption as a trashy and culturally low form. He believed that as cultures 'evolved' ornamentation should be progressively phased out of architecture, with good taste becoming synonymous with a lack of ostentation and embellishment.

Regardless of the radical aims of such projects, the disjuncture between the theory and practice of modernism relative to social change and social justice became so great that the whole modernist project was compromised. Crawford argues that the 'successful appropriation of modernism's forms by the dominant political and economic order made the gap between theory and practice too large to contain within the existing modernist ideology' (1994: 37). As with any discourse, without some connection with social reality, it can lose its resonance, and if modernism was to retain credibility as a vehicle for social change it needed to connect the architectural field closely to political action, which – by and large – it failed to do. Indeed, the ideological commitment to social change actually gave a more forceful symbolic charge to the commissions, giving the corporations and states commissioning leading modernist architects extra credibility.

The modernist discourse – encapsulating both the progressive social engagement of the modernist architects and the forms they ushered in – has long been a hallmark of mega-events, as it provides a useful frame for those states keen to represent their capacity for economic innovation and social advancement. The Great Exhibition of 1851, which was housed in the Crystal Palace, a glass and steel structure whose radical aesthetic captured the exhibition's motif of 'newness', became a defining point of the nineteenth century and illustrates this wider contention. Enjoying strong political backing, the Exhibition's patrons included the future Prime Minister William Gladstone, who was a member of the Exhibition's organizing commission, and Queen Victoria's husband Prince Albert, who was Honorary President and a staunch supporter of the project, which he suggested should have 'exhibition, competition and encouragement' as central aims (Pearce and Stewart 1992: 17).[2]

The winning competition entry for the building to house the exhibition was a quick to erect, prefabricated structure designed by Joseph Paxton, who until that time had designed greenhouses.[3] Paxton's structure utilized the most modern architectural techniques and building materials available to an aesthetically radical end; this was an engineering-led building, around which claims for the virtue of its modernism and 'newness' were made. Reflecting a vision of mid-nineteenth-century Britain as a rapidly industrializing nation state, the modular construction of the Crystal Palace made extensive use of iron and glass, a technique that was still new in the building professions; indeed, it was only advances in machine technology that permitted the panels of glass to be cut so accurately as to allow reliable calculation of the weight to be borne by the repetitive pattern of the structure – a central feature of the Crystal Palace (Figs. 12 and 13).

It was in part through the radically modern nature of the design of the Crystal Palace – the central architectural statement that enclosed the exhibition – which the Victorian state sought to align itself with the affordances of new industrial technologies. The exhibition was organized under the auspices of the Royal Society for the Encouragement of Arts, Manufactures and Commerce (interestingly, today usually abbreviated to the Royal Society for the Arts) and it is highly significant that the Crystal Palace merged engineering and architecture, which since the professionalization of architecture had been two distinct professions, often defined in contradistinction (see, for example, Pevsner 1968, and for a problematization of the tendency, see Stevens 1998). This technologically inspired architecture captured the modernization themes of the exhibition perfectly. As with the function-led designs of railways sheds,

Fig. 12. Exterior of the Crystal Palace from the south wing

Fig. 13. Exterior of the Crystal Palace from the 'Water Temple'

docks, warehouses and factories that had emerged in the technological firmament of the industrial revolution, the Crystal Palace blurred the previously jealously guarded boundaries between architecture and engineering: in other words, as he had not received an architect's training, Paxton was not constrained by the architectural 'force field', since he had not been socialized into the stylistic and aesthetic preferences of the profession and the arbiters therein (Bourdieu 1996; Stevens 1998). While this gave him the freedom to experiment with radical technologies and materials, it also meant that his building served to disrupt many of the taken for granted parameters in relation to architecture. This contention is illustrated by the fact that whether the Crystal Palace could properly be considered 'architecture' was the topic of much controversy. The widely influential architectural historian Nikolaus Pevsner (1902–83) expressed his distaste for the Crystal Palace in particularly strong terms, referring to the building as 'colossal ... abominable ... wrong from any point of view ... unpleasantly realistic ... incongruous ... bulging ... overdone ... monstrous ... [revealing] failure, coarseness, barbarism, atrocities, vulgarity, [and] insensibility' (cited in Kornwolf 1975: 39). In other words, for Pevsner the Crystal Palace was a building but did not qualify as architecture; it was more akin – in his famous distinction – to a bike shed than to Lincoln Cathedral. This distinction can be seen as part of a wider struggle to maintain the distinction between the field boundaries of architecture and engineering, and to emphasize the different capitals and values at stake in one field as opposed to the other.

A similar distinction between the 'proper' architecture consecrated by the field on the one hand and some other form of 'non-pedigreed' building on the other was also at the heart of the critique emerging from the socialist reformer and author William Morris (1834–96) – a staunch supporter of historical reference in architecture and design and a key figure in the arts and crafts movement – who saw the exhibition's architecture as a celebration of the triumph of alienated, machine-led mass production over meaningful human craft. John Ruskin was also highly critical of the industrialized architecture of the Crystal Palace and its modernist exhibits; as briefly touched upon in the previous chapter, Ruskin saw the best architecture as drawing from nature, and 'losing touch with nature was a sign of losing touch with morality' (Crinson 1996: 59). The Godliness of nature should be reflected in architecture; the technological form of the Crystal Palace was considered by Ruskin and Morris as being as far removed from this as could be imagined.

Certainly the gains afforded by the advanced industrial building technology and materials used on the Crystal Palace allowed some notable developments – for instance, the possibility on a building this size for the enclosed volume to be significantly greater than its mass; these new spatial potentials offering new sites of social interaction as well as a functional interior space for display.[4] Although the Crystal Palace offered a clear challenge to history and antiquity as a source of legitimation, it would be a mistake to overlook continuities with the past altogether. Robert Stern suggests that as well as a radical modernity the Crystal Palace represented a recasting of historical ideals. He compared the Crystal Palace to a 'grand Roman public building of the imperial era translated into glass, metal, and wood' (1994: 51–52). For Stern, the Crystal Palace was significant not only as a vast shelter for such educational and industrial objects but as 'an internalization of public life on an unprecedented scale,' as 'the first building realized on the scale of mass democracy' (1994: 52). Similarly, a Habermasian reading of such exhibitions would be that they act as a space – both symbolic and material – in which national public cultures were forged (albeit a highly conscribed notion of 'public', with participation in such spheres of involvement not equal or 'undominated' (Habermas 1989b)).

Despite the self-conscious construction of the national community central to the Great Exhibition, the international dimension of the exhibition should not be overlooked. The full title of the 1851 event was 'The Great Exhibition of the Works of Industry of All Nations', with the official exhibition guidebook suggesting that 'to make the rounds of this palace means literally to circle the earth. All peoples come together here, and those who are enemies, here live side by side' (cited in Crinson 1996: 68). However, since such ostensible universalism was designed to allow favourable comparisons between the industrial achievements of Britain and the British Empire, to which half the exhibition space was given over (Crinson 1996: 68), this dimension of the project cannot be discounted. Nonetheless, what goes inside an exhibition is a significant part of its broader social production, and although the Crystal Palace itself has come to be remembered more than the contents of the exhibition it enclosed, the items and exhibits do reveal something interesting about the colonial state's self-image. There was a Turkish Court, with silks, hookahs, coffee sets, and Turkish Delight for sale; a Tunisian Court complete with an attendant with whom to haggle over the prices of carpets, guns and ostrich feathers; and many other stalls under Owen

Fig. 14. Representation of the Crystal Palace interior, at the opening ceremony (led by Queen Victoria)

Jones' Alhambra-inspired coloured silks and swags (Crinson 1996: 35; 62) (Fig. 14).

Edward Said's work has been particularly influential in revealing how the construction of a generalized category of 'others' was crucial to the self-definition of western colonial power (Said 1985). Although Said's work is more interested in addressing textual representations than the built environment, considering the Great Exhibition within his framework would perhaps lead us to position it as a manifestation of a cultural hierarchy constructed explicitly to confirm Britain's status as an industrial power, as a hegemonic project. The artefacts and objects celebrated by the exhibition contained a disciplinary component, inasmuch as it created and/or sustained a hierarchical vision of national cultures and 'races' (Crinson 1996). The essentialism inherent in the displays – that were classified and exhibited by nation, in line with the vision of prominent cultural reformer and high-profile patron of the exhibition Henry Cole (Crinson 1996: 54) – was designed to reflect positively on the British nation's leading place in culture and industry. In short, the Exhibition can be framed as part of an imperialist cultural project, a legitimation of capitalist ideology through a cultural expression of the industrial revolution, and a celebration of secular bourgeois values. In common with many of the Victorians' cultural interventions, there was an exoticizing orientalism that characterized the exhibits, which were to be viewed through the lens of imperialism and colonialism (Crinson 1996). From this perspective, the capacity of the exhibition to consolidate and legitimate dominant national cultural understandings is crucial.

Harold Lasswell notes that the combination of such spectacular elements involves

> catering to the excitement of perpetual innovation and display, the 'strategy of innovation' plays down the overtone of threat associated with inspiring awe. It is a strategy whose principle object is the seduction of hostile elements. Therefore the aim is not to overwhelm with majestic displays of power, but to attract by putting up a fine show. (Lasswell 1979: 17)

From this perspective such spectacular exhibits can be seen as positioning Eastern cultures within a commodified and commodifying relationship, with visitors positioned relative to spectacular artefacts and 'theatrical' symbols of national identity that put 'ephemera and dramatization to the fore' (Heynen 1999b: 378). The emphasis on objectified versions of 'other' cultures in the Crystal Palace served as an incorporation of hitherto unknown societies into commodity exchange and imperial mode of production and consumption; certainly, a strong emphasis on visual consumption pervaded the exhibition space and its contents, with the showcasing of spectacular 'exotic' objects '[b]eginning a trend whereby the international exhibition would aim to present produce in the most overblown proportions possible' (Greenhalgh 1988: 12). Drawing on Michel Foucault, Greenhalgh positions the 1851 exhibition as a disciplinary project, designed to quell dissent and to create a compliant populace, arguing it was 'a giant counter-revolutionary measure ... conceived of as an event to foster fear as well as pride in the minds of the British public' (Greenhalgh 1988: 30). A cynical Disraeli also spoke of the hegemonic component of the projects when suggesting the Exhibition as 'a boon to the Government, for it will make the public forget its misdeeds' (cited in Pearce and Stewart 1992: 11).

Architects, Modernism and the State

The Congrès internationaux d'architecture moderne (CIAM) (or International Congresses of Modern Architecture) was a coalition of modernist architects and planners who sought to codify modern architecture's aesthetic and social programme, and was operative between 1928 and 1958. Although having a fluid membership and varying criteria for entry (Munford 2002: 4), a group of leading European architects, including Sigfried Giedion, Le Corbusier, Ernst May and Walter Gropius, were prominent in CIAM and became associated with its programme of rationalized urbanism. They sought to place architecture at the core of a radical avant-garde and to put architects and their work at its centre and in a socially transformative role. Flexible in terms of a willingness to collaborate with politicians and regimes from across the political spectrum (a pragmatism underpinned by a faith in design-based solutions to provide more social, more 'rational' cities and to transcend such prosaic squabbles), members of CIAM were in fact a self-conscious cultural elite in the service of political authority (Munford 2002: 6). The advance of international modernism through CIAM and the 'morality' of 'correct' design created a set of associations between architectural modernism and a particular brand of progressive, state-led politics, which coincided with the need to rebuild European societies materially and symbolically after the Second World War.

The UK context provides a clear illustration of how modernist architecture was inserted into broader utopian discourses. The Festival of

Britain in 1951, although it emerged in a very different social and political context from its mid-nineteenth-century predecessor, was a continuation of the trend expressed by the Great Exhibition a century earlier. The aims and objectives of the 1951 Festival were broadly the same as those in 1851, namely a pride in national achievement and a celebration of free trade and industrial strength. While the impulse to rebuild British society both physically and symbolically after the Second World War was strong, the Labour Party Deputy Prime Minister Herbert Morrison believed that the purpose of the Festival should be to 'illustrate the British contribution to civilization, past, present and future, in arts, in science and technology, and in industrial design': the post-war British state had neither sufficient financial power nor the cultural assurance legitimately to claim any sort of triumphalist monumental expression (Frampton 1990). Insecurity about cultural expression is reflected in the origins of the project as well as in the architecture the 1951 Festival produced. The Festival of Britain was initially suggested by the Royal Society for the Arts, as was the Great Exhibition; early discussions in 1943 culminated in a 1946 exhibition called 'Britain Can Make It' (appropriately held at the Victoria and Albert Museum) that articulated a spirit of renewal and optimism; indeed, a phrase the media frequently used to describe the Festival of Britain was a 'tonic to the nation'.

The post-war period saw the British state in the process of relinquishing elements of its imperial identity (Frampton 1990: 262) and found a general public more cynical than in 1851 about the ability of free trade, industrialization and science to deliver a better social order. The cultural content of the Festival, for which the overall budget was £12 million (Frampton 1990), further reflected changing patterns of leisure – there was a less 'educational' tone to the Festival than a hundred years previously, with the 1951 celebration oriented more towards consumption than in the Great Exhibition. An early expression of the post-war consensus relative to welfare and housing, a group of new buildings demonstrating avant-garde principles to design was erected as a celebration of and an encouragement to British culture. Spectacular architectural statements such as the Dome of Discovery and the Skylon were aesthetically radical temporary buildings celebrating the potential of technology. The central, permanent architectural symbol of the Festival of 1951 was the Royal Festival Hall (designed by London City Council architects).

Modern architecture had ushered in an era in which historical ornament or decoration was outlawed – the central modernist dictum is that form should follow function, and this led to a renouncing of historical reference and a universalized aesthetic (supposedly) driven solely by function (see Ghirardo 1996 for a problematization of this conception). The Festival marked the start of a utopian vision of the place of modernist architecture relative to society; for example, elements of what was eventually to become the post-war housing project were introduced through the festival. The modernist architectural project is a clear illustration of this contradiction associated with the incorporation of a seemingly radical architectural form into dominant social imaginaries. Modernism's claims to transform the built environment and the social order were reliant on overcoming a dualism at the heart of the field itself, in connecting a political practice to a radical aesthetic and technological programme. Although a thorough discussion of modernism is beyond the limits of this chapter, a brief description of some of its ideal typical features allows us to situate the debates about critical architecture (for more extensive surveys of architectural modernism see, for example, Habermas 1989a; Frampton 1990; Ghirardo 1996; Heynen 1999a). The modernist vision was posited on the tranformatory potential of radical architectural programmes, with claims made for the potential of architects to be at the vanguard of revolutionary cultural activity directed at facilitating social justice. Modernism saw a confluence of 'progressive' aesthetics, political and social values within a mass-produced, engineering-led architecture that provided the basis for a technical solution to social problems.

The Millennium Dome: The Contested Mega-Event

While in many respects a continuation of the traditions of the earlier mega-events, the Millennium Dome project was intended as a celebration of Britishness at the millennium, but proved both difficult and expensive to deliver, and hard to legitimate with reference to any coherent national identity. The sense of crisis engendered by the scheme is of particular significance in the context of this book, as it revealed many broader tensions in the state's role in defining fragmented, divided nations through cultural discourses of collective identity. Making a strong claim to being the most politically charged piece of architecture Britain has ever seen, the discourses that surrounded the project were so disparate and complex that they could never be resolved in one architectural project or mega-event. The extent to which a range of contradictions around the nation state and Britishness were revealed by the project is a crucial consideration.

Although the project spanned both Conservative and Labour terms in office, the Millennium Dome and its contents became inextricably associated with New Labour's attempt at 'rebranding' Britain as 'Cool Britannia', a creative, dynamic nation that 'led the world' in creative industries (Blair 1998). The building was explicitly inserted into a neo-liberal political discourse stressing 'newness' and economic competitiveness. Steven Bayley, the Dome's original Creative Director, described the project as a bungled party-political advertisement 'managed by demoralized public servants in thrall to politicians who, in turn, were blown this way and that by gusts from the latest opinion research' (Bayley 2001: 2). However, despite coming to be strongly associated with the New Labour project, it was originally the Conservative government under John Major who in 1996 decided to commit National Lottery money to a year-long celebration of the millennium; the incoming New Labour government continued what had originally been a Conservative-initiated project. After parliamentary debates about whether or not the money should be spent elsewhere, the new government decided that the project should go ahead, albeit with the following provisos: 'no extra burden on the public purse; its content would inspire; it would be a national event; it would provide a lasting legacy; and the project management would be strengthened' (Thornley 2000: 694).

As has been suggested previously, 'to the extent that the new elite of a body politic sees itself as distinctive, whether in reference to predecessors or contemporaries, structural changes occur. Hence, the elite of a nation state ... tries to create symbols capable of setting it apart' (Lasswell 1979: 14). Unsurprisingly, their desire to distance themselves from 'Old Labour' and the Conservative Party led to a determined focus on architecture and the built environment by New Labour. Within the Labour government, overall responsibility for the project was complicated as it straddled three ministerial areas: the Minister for Culture, Media and Sport was in charge of the Millennium Commission (which amounted to finances); the Minister for Environment, Transport and the Regions was responsible for transport; the Minister Without Portfolio – then Peter Mandelson – became the Labour politician responsible for overseeing the project,[5] and the sole stakeholder in the Millennium Experience Company, the organization ultimately responsible for the fulfilment of the project (Thornley 2000).

The Dome was part of a broader engagement with architecture that characterized the early years of the New Labour administration. In 2000, the government set up the Commission for Architecture and the Built

Environment (CABE), whose self-defined brief is to 'inject architecture into the bloodstream of the nation ... [to] encourage public involvement in its creation ... [and to] create local distinctiveness and foster people's attachment to places' (English Heritage and Commission for Architecture and the Built Environment 2001). CABE's first report (published in 2000) was entitled *Better Public Buildings: A Proud Legacy for the Future* (see www.cabe.org.uk/publications/better-public-buildings), and has a foreword from then Prime Minister Tony Blair in which he pledges that the government will radically improve the standard of public architecture to leave a legacy of 'iconic' buildings comparable to those inherited from the Victorians. The report is framed by the assumption that architecture is an important way both to attract inward investment to post-industrial cities and to reflect civic values. As well as the desire for materialization of a new regime, the change in the British policy climate towards architecture is explained by the emergence of National Lottery money that, albeit frequently in partnership with other financial sources, has released 'public' funding for architecture. The Millennium Commission, an independent body set up in 1993 under the National Lottery Act, has spent over £1.2 billion on more than 200 landmark buildings. A desire to symbolize the passing of the year 2000 was also a catalyst for the heightened profile of architecture in the United Kingdom, with much 'state-funded' – or, more accurately, lottery-funded – architecture commissioned to celebrate the millennium (there were twenty-six landmark buildings erected in the United Kingdom to celebrate the millennium, at a cost of around £8 billion).[6] The Millennium Dome must be understood against this wider backdrop: the House of Commons Select Committee on the project confirmed that the 'Dome is a creature of the National Lottery' and underlined that no taxpayers' money should go towards it. Overall, the Millennium Dome project cost £789 million over the period it was open, according to the National Audit Office.[7]

Prime Minister Tony Blair sought to position the Dome as symbolic of a dynamic, progressive nation, as an architectural reflection of a changing political economy and an advert for a 'New Britain'. He suggested that the project was

> A sign of a new and exciting cultural renaissance in Britain [that is] the envy of the world ... [because Britain] can boast of ... the finest architects. We are leading the world in creativity. [The Dome is an] opportunity to greet the world with a celebration that is so bold, so beautiful, so inspiring that it embodies at once the spirit of confidence and adventure in Britain and the spirit of the future [and] a

celebration that is good for British business ... a chance to demonstrate that Britain will be a breeding ground for the most successful
businesses of the 21st century.[8] (Blair 1998)

The design brief for the Dome commission reflected this mobilization
of architecture as part of a national cultural reconstruction. The competition brief included twenty-five 'stimulus questions' devised by Creative
Director Steven Bayley, and included the following prompts:

Question three: What are we like?

Question four: Is God dead?

Question eight: Who are we – body, mind and soul?

Question sixteen: What is Britain's place?

Question twenty-two: How many races make a nation?

In the more prosaic part of the design brief, the Millennium Commission
had asked architects to design 'an all-weather venue capable of accommodating a large audience for one-off events and entertainment'. The
competition winner was Richard Rogers – now Lord Rogers of Riverside
– whose interpretation of the design problem in his summary of the
Millennium Dome competition brief emphasized both the functional
element of the brief and the mega-event lineage, discussed above: 'what
was wanted was a place where everyone could have a massive participatory exhibition ... a festival if you like, [which] continues that festival
concept like the Crystal Palace or the Eiffel Tower or the Festival of
Britain in 1951' (*Architecture Australia* 2001). Mike Davis, a founding
partner of the Richard Rogers Partnership, also suggests that the
Millennium Dome provided 'a simple, honest, elegant and minimalist
answer to a very big, simple problem [of enclosing the exhibition]'
(*Guardian* 1999).[9]

The claim to a functional solution to the problem of enclosing a
national exhibition echoes Paxton's description of his Crystal Palace over
150 years earlier, but Davis's protestations that the Dome should not be
'over-read' as a political symbol ring hollow when we consider the function of the building (see below) and Richard Rogers' experience of
designing major buildings in contested social and political contexts. The
high-tech style pioneered by Rogers and Norman Foster in their Team 4
days, and developed by both subsequently, reveals the close links between
engineering, technology and architecture that were such a central tenet
of the Crystal Palace and also the modernism that characterized the 1951

festival. An exploitation of the advanced affordances associated with computer-aided design and new building materials (see Tombesi 1999), high tech is contingent on a close relationship between engineering and architecture; instead of being 'hidden', the construction of the building is revealed, with pipes and other functional elements exposed (Fig. 15). This approach is demonstrated for example in many of Rogers' high-profile buildings across the world, such as the Pompidou Centre in Paris (1971, with Renzo Piano),[10] Lloyds of London (1990), HSBC Bank headquarters in Singapore, significant parts of Potsdamer Platz in Berlin (1998), the Senedd (Welsh Assembly building) (2006), and Heathrow Terminal 5 (2008). Rogers has become a politically influential figure in the United Kingdom: until recently head of the Urban Taskforce, a think tank set up to advise government on the sustainable regeneration of British cities and regions, chair of the Architecture Foundation and former chairman of the Arts Council. As a result, Rogers has established close links with the New Labour project, having been proclaimed a

Fig. 15. Lloyds of London
Photograph by David Iliff. This work is licensed under the Creative Commons Attribution-ShareAlike 3.0 Unported Licence. To view a copy of this licence, see <http://creativecommons.org/licenses/by-sa/3.0>.

Fig. 16. The Millennium Dome, London

'visionary' by then Prime Minister Tony Blair (*Guardian* 2000).

The Dome was built on a 181-acre site on the North Greenwich penin-sula on the River Thames (Fig. 16). The site had been derelict for twenty years before it was bought from British Gas in February 1997 for £20 million; the potential to redevelop a surplus piece of land was one of the main reasons for the choice of this location (House of Commons Select Committee Report 2002). The Greenwich site was also preferable to other options as the Greenwich Mean Time meridian cut across the north of the site, fitting in well with the project's central theme of 'time'. Like the Crystal Palace, the Dome was organized around a vast central inte-rior, 'an open, flexible theatrical space' (Richard Rogers Partnership n.d.) to be ordered around a number of distinct visitor attractions divided into 'zones' (the building itself encloses an area of 100,000 square metres with a circumference of over one kilometre, measuring 365 metres in diam-eter and 50 metres at its highest point) (Fig. 17).[11]

However, despite the scale of the structure enclosing it, as with any mega-event, the nature of the exhibits – in other words what goes inside the building – is significant for the success or otherwise of the project. Peter Mandelson was adamant that he did not want the project to be a 'trade show or a theme-park', and – echoing something of his grandfa-ther's attitude to the event he had organized half a century earlier – it

Fig. 17. Central interior space of the Millennium Dome
Photograph by Chris J. Dixon. This work is licensed under the Creative
Commons Attribution-ShareAlike 3.0 Unported Licence. To view a copy
of this licence, see <http://creativecommons.org/licenses/by-sa/3.0>.

was to be educational. As with all major architectural projects, as much
as the building's style or its place within the broader programme of development, what goes inside the building is crucial (the Select Commission
Report into the Dome emphasized that the project must not be purely
'an exercise in monumental architecture' and that 'the impact of the experience will depend principally upon what is inside') (Culture, Media and
Sport Committee 1997).

It is significant to note, then, that the content of the Dome's zones were
highly contested in conception and execution, reflecting something about
the broader state project of which they were a reflection. In their paper
entitled 'The Millennium Dome: Sponsoring, Meaning and Visiting' Jim
McGuigan and Abi Gilmore argue that the 'experience of the Dome was
conditioned massively by corporate interests'; although 'sponsorship
eventually amounted to less than one-fifth in value (around £150 million)
of the public expenditure on the Greenwich Peninsula and the [New
Millennium Experience] (around £800 million) ... corporate sponsors

had a decisive impact on the New Millennium Experience's focal concerns, design and management' (2002: 2). McGuigan and Gilmore suggest that this reliance on corporate investment – which is recast in New Labour discourse as 'partnership' or 'stakeholding' (Fairclough 2000) – can be read as a comment on the New Labour administration more generally, and that the effect of corporate sponsorship was to articulate the 'infrastructural and, indeed, ideological coalescence of social democracy with neo-liberalism' (McGuigan and Gilmore 2002: 7). McGuigan and Gilmore conclude that the Dome represents an 'extreme case of the questionable impact of sponsorship on public culture, [which illustrated] the inordinate power symbolically as well as materially of corporations in liberal-democratic polities' (2002: 18).

However, McGuigan and Gilmore also suggest a potential for the cultural self-examination promised by the Dome when they conclude that

> For a small fraction of the public money spent on it, sponsoring corporations were allowed to have the loudest say at the Millennium Dome. The role of sponsorship was actually much more significant ideologically … the whole point of the project from a governmental perspective … was to represent Britain as a nation of corporations instead of a democratic people engaged in debate over our time and place in history. (McGuigan and Gilmore 2002: 19)

From this perspective, the colonization of public culture by economic interests compromised a potentially valuable cultural debate about the nature of Britishness.

Struggles aside from those concerning corporate sponsorship also characterized discussion over the content of other zones in the Dome. The Faith Zone was to prove particularly contentious, with issues centring on the role of a secular state in the context of a multi-faith society. The fundamental tension between the Millennium Dome project as a celebration of 2000 years since Christ's birth and the government's suggestion that it was a celebration of contemporary Britain was never adequately resolved. The Department for Culture, Media and Sport (DCMS), in association with the Inter Faith Network, published a paper entitled *Marking the Millennium in a Multi-Faith Context* in which they acknowledged that 'a significant dimension of life in Britain at the end of the twentieth century is the presence of communities of the world's major religious traditions' (DCMS 1999). According to the DCMS, the Millennium Dome and its associated celebrations provided 'an opportunity for people of *all* faiths to draw on the spiritual heritages of their own traditions to think together about the values that underpin our society and to reflect on the future of our society and our environment of ourselves, our children and generations to come' (DCMS 1999).

The DCMS also acknowledged that in Britain the 'Christian tradition has been rooted for many centuries and has had such a formative influence [that] many national and civic celebrations will have a specifically Christian framework' (DCMS 1999), a position stated rather more forcefully by the Conservative MP James Gray, who in a parliamentary debate asked the Minister for Tourism, Film and Broadcasting to acknowledge that the year '2000 and the millennium mean only one thing: the 2000th anniversary of the birth of Jesus Christ' (Hansard, HC Deb. 29 Mar. 1999, col. 722). Even the Church of England could not agree on what should make up the religious content in the Dome. The Archbishop of Canterbury opened the Dome with a Christian prayer and wanted a strong church representation in the 'Faith Zone' of the exhibition, regarding the millennium display as an 'exciting opportunity'. Another strand of opinion within the Christian Church was represented by the then Archbishop of York, Dr David Hope, who labelled the Dome a 'monument to arrogance', suggesting that '[a]ll the monies spent to celebrate the millennium will be of little value unless we attend to the values themselves – the values displayed in the crib at Bethlehem'. He also argued that Zaha Hadid's androgynous sculpture in the 'Body Zone' – the centrepiece of the Dome – reflected the 'confusions of the age' (BBC News Online 1998a).

Appropriately, representative state codifications of national identities become a major concern of elements of the government at such junctures, with the sense that 'symbolic gestures granting or denying recognition can have profound and continuing effects within a political culture in ways that directly affect the well-being and self-respect of citizens of minority cultures, as well as their enthusiasm to participate in the political life of the larger state' (Kymlicka and Norman 2000: 29). The 'symbolic gestures' made by the state through the Dome were highly ambiguous, and contested, often stemming from the problem of representing diversity or multiculturalism at the level of the state. 'Multiculturalism' or 'minority rights' 'go beyond common rights of citizenship ... [and] are adopted with the intention of recognizing and accommodating the distinctive identities and needs of ethnocultural groups' (Kymlicka and Norman 2000: 2). The ability of a small political and cultural elite to encompass and reflect such 'distinctive identities' is highly questionable and consequently any symbolic representation of national

88   *The Sociology of Architecture*

identity 'requires members of the majority to rethink their own group's identity and relation to the state' (Kymlicka and Norman 2000: 30).

The project certainly became a focus for many kinds of discourses and debates, and perhaps none less so than the antipathy of the right-wing tabloid press to the New Labour political project. The *Daily Mail*, a right-wing British newspaper, saw the Dome's shortcomings as mainly due to a lack of anything 'intrinsically British' in the architecture or general project:

> what the Dome has lacked from the beginning – and still lacks – is any driving vision or high purpose. That's why it has been so slow to win either public support or private sponsorship. People are not fools. They would never voluntarily have footed the bill for such an ephemeral folly. (Cited in BBC News Online 1998b)

In fact, the *Daily Mail* was particularly scathing about the Dome and referred to it as a 'monument to political vanity' and 'the great Greenwich white elephant', declaring that

> If there was ever a symbol of the Blair administration, this was it – grandiloquent talk, spindoctoring promises, a vacuously empty shell. The execution, epitomizing the triumph of style over substance, was bad enough. But the fact that almost £1 billion has been wasted for the sake of political vanity is a terrifying indictment of what happens when politicians are allowed to spend our money. (*Daily Mail* 2002)

Regardless of the veracity of these politically motivated attacks on the project, they remind us of some of the ways in which the materialization of discourses of belonging and political power that architecture makes possible also open up the possibility for such mega-events to become touchstones for wider resistances and struggles.

Conclusion

The architecture associated with mega-events, whether 'a success or a debacle, become[s] associated with a regime politically and perhaps iconographically' (Vale 1992: 51). The threads running through the Great Exhibition, the Festival of Britain and the Millennium Dome project remind us of the continuities between architectural landmarks and a variety of future-oriented political projects. The architecturally centred projects of 1851, 1951 and 2000 evidence a central claim of Maurice Roche's work on mega-events (2000), namely that such large-scale state-led events provide one means of constructing national culture in such a way that seeks to integrate mass populations into state projects. As we saw in the previous chapter, nations 'do not emerge naturally: the "people" have to be chiselled from the bloc of local customs and peculiarities by political projects from above, using state power, and from below, by patriotic organizations in civil society' (Hirst 2005: 36). The incorporation of groups of people into political identity projects by such spectacular festivals clearly opens up a problematic for social science, with key questions centring on who is being represented, how, and to what end. On this point, Lawrence J. Vale suggests that 'although there may be some well-intentioned search for a unifying national symbol, normally the choice of symbol, if examined, reveals other, structural, social and economic tensions' (1992: 49).

A wider question emerging from this chapter concerns the role of states in providing the material symbols connected to political projects. States' relationships to populations are embedded in, and become socially meaningful through, culture. Despite very different social and political contexts, 'progressive' ideals underpinned by economic activity – and reflected in a variety of modernist forms stressing innovation – have been dominant frames within this tradition of state-led architecture from the Great Exhibition in 1851 to the Millennium Dome. As Thornley argues (2000), the case of the Dome can be situated as an expression of a more widespread strategy to distance states from the decline of manufacturing industries. The capacity of Rogers' design to develop the *existing* national imaginary and to materialize the culturalized vision of the creative economy – as per the 'Cool Britannia' brand – was uncertain. Reflecting something of the general contention of the present book, the 'interlocking set of economic, political and ideological determinations on the construction of the Dome both materially and symbolically' (McGuigan and Gilmore 2002: 3) revealed many social struggles extending far beyond architecture centring on the project. Even setting aside crucial pragmatic issues of cost and management, the state was in a highly ambiguous position in terms of offering a strong definition of the nation in this context, and for many the Dome came to symbolize a crisis in state-led British identity, positioned by hostile press as a testament to the New Labour government, mismanagement and political 'spin'. The Dome project reflects many of the social tensions inherent in the codification of national identity projects by nation states.

Notes

1 The seemingly radical break with tradition as a source of legitimation within modernity has a dialectical character, with modernity's characteristic institution – the state – often seeking actively to construct traditions. See Habermas' *The Philosophical Discourse of Modernity* (1990) for an exploration of this tension.

2 A monarch's approval for the project was a hugely populist statement, and won Albert support from the general public. In fact, the Albert Memorial, designed by George Gilbert Scott (famous as the designer of the iconic red telephone box, and father of Gilbert Scott, who designed Liverpool's Anglican Cathedral), contains numerous references to the Great Exhibition. It is somewhat ironic that such a staunch supporter of a modernizing project should be remembered with a 'British' Gothic monument.

3 Paxton was supported in the design and build by Charles Fox, whose own background was in railway engineering, and the civil engineer William Cubitt, who had until that point been involved in 'functional' design (bridges and windmills).

4 Britain was far from alone in seeking to exploit the positive associations of future-oriented, engineering-inspired architecture at major nineteenth-century state-led festivals. Another example of a state-sponsored radical iron structure comparable with the Crystal Palace was the slightly later Palais des Machines, built to house the World Fair in Paris in 1889 to celebrate the centennial of the French Revolution. As with the Crystal Palace, the external shell of this structure accentuated the huge open space of its interior, again a construction technique made possible by the great technological advances in the industrial production of steel and glass, developments that would usher in the modernist 'machine age' of architecture over the following hundred years. Again, as with the Crystal Palace, the fifteen-acre site enclosed by the Palais des Machines housed hundreds of industrial inventions (including some of Thomas Edison's) and many other items from industrial production. The other, now far more famous, architectural symbol of the Paris World Fair of 1889 was the Eiffel Tower, designed and funded by Gustav Eiffel. This is another example of highly modernized girder construction, albeit on a less 'functional' building. The tower illustrates the radically modernized processes of design that, in common with Paxton's girder construction, was a showcase for the innovative techniques so central to architectural modernism. The Eiffel Tower, although a centrepiece for the 1889 Expo and thus 'state led' to some degree, was in fact a private commission that ultimately, in the face of large capital outlay, proved to be very profitable for Gustav Eiffel. The tallest building in the world at the time of construction, the tower – in common with much of the architecture at World Fairs – was initially intended as a temporary structure, which would pass into state control after twenty years, when they planned to tear it down.

5 It is perhaps fitting that Mandelson should have taken on the project on Labour taking office; his grandfather was Herbert Morrison, the Labour MP charged with overseeing the Festival of Britain in 1951. Mandelson was the sole government shareholder of all the stock in the 'New Millennium Experience Company Ltd' (his own coinage), the 'company' charged with the management of the project.

6 These include: the London Eye (Markus Barfield); the Gateshead Music Centre (Norman Foster); the Centre For Life in Newcastle (Terry Farrell); Michael Wilford's Stirling Prize winning Lowry Centre, and Daniel Libeskind's Imperial War Museum (both in Salford); Peckham Library, again a Stirling Prize winner (Alsop and Stormer); and the New Art Gallery in Walsall by Caruso St John.

7 For a detailed breakdown of these figures, see McGuigan and Gilmore 2002. Despite the large overspend on the project in general, the structure of the Millennium Dome itself cost approximately £42 million, and was handed over 'on schedule and

under budget, on 30th September 1999' (Richard Rogers Partnership).

8 After the Millennium Dome had closed, Prime Minister Tony Blair admitted in a television interview that the project had 'not been the runaway success we had hoped', but added 'neither has it been the disaster that's been portrayed in some parts of the media'. Blair was speaking days after cabinet minister Clare Short called the Dome 'a flop', and said, if he had known in 1997 what he knows now about governments trying to run big 'leisure' attractions he would have considered the project 'too ambitious' (BBC News Online 2000).

9 Attempting to distance the Rogers practice from the gathering controversy generated by the project, Davis suggested, six months before the Dome was to open, that the building 'should not be over-read. In fact, it is not an architecture project at all. It is a lightweight, loose-fit, friendly cover … [i]t is no accident that it does this [showing how the yellow masts of the Dome resemble outstretched arms]' (*Guardian* 1999). Aside from the rather tenuous reading of inclusivity into the Dome's masts, it is interesting that Davis sustains the distinction between 'architecture' and more functional responses.

10 Tzonis and Lefaivre see the Pompidou Centre as illustrative of how landmark state-funded buildings convey multiple meanings. Certainly the Centre must be considered in terms of the wider debates that surrounded the competition for its building; architecture since 1968 had come to be perceived as a fundamental carrier of bourgeois ideology, to be viewed with suspicion. Tzonis and Lefaivre believe that the only acceptable message in that particular climate was a purely populist iconography which would function 'in the manner of a billboard' or as a space for people to operate and play out aspirations and revolutionary ideals (1992: 178). Rogers himself has said of the Centre that '[a]s a populist urban magnet designed to narrow the gap between culture and everyday life it has been a success beyond our dreams' (cited in Davies 1991: 10). As is the case with the Millennium Dome, the flexibility of the museum's functions is reflected in its design; as with the Dome, facades and parts can be taken apart and reassembled. Clearly the Pompidou is in the high-tech style. Piano and Rogers thought of the centre as a 'dynamic communications machine … a university of the street reflecting the constantly changing needs of users' (Rogers, cited in Tzonis and Lefaivre 1992: 86).

11 Large architectural projects tend to attract nationalized size comparisons: the government's website claimed that the Dome could contain twelve full-size football pitches, 1,100 Olympic-sized swimming pools or 18,000 London double-decker buses. It would also take Niagara Falls about fifteen minutes to fill the Dome (statistics from www.culture.gov.uk/millennium/Dome.html (no longer current)). Should you want to, you could also lie the Eiffel Tower – the nineteenth century's iconic architectural mega-event structure – on its side in the Dome, which is also capable of housing thirteen Albert Halls or two Wembley Stadiums (though not at the same time).

5

Architecture and Commemoration: The Construction of Memorialization

> Every period has the impulse to create symbols in the form of monuments, which, according to the Latin meaning are 'things that remind', things to be transmitted to later generations. This demand for monumentality cannot, in the long run, be suppressed. It tries to find an outlet at all costs.
> Sigfried Giedion, 'The Need for a New Monumentality' (1944), 553.

Introduction

Landmark building projects have a complex relationship with broader social forces. This contention is clearly evidenced by the major architectural projects the world over that in addition to their primary function also serve a memorial purpose. In such cases architects seek to reconcile a range of competing contingent functions and meanings, with their work taking on characteristics akin to monuments in an early modern age, a period of time when the built environment was one of the few spaces in which socially significant memories could be communicated widely across society (see Heynen 1999b; Tonkiss 2005). The desire of states and other polities to communicate social messages across rapidly expanding nineteenth-century urban citizenry led to the ascription of messages onto the built environment via a whole range of monuments and statues and major public buildings designed to have a memorial function; the countless monuments and plaques that characterize capitals and other large cities the world over are testament to this tendency (Therbon 2002) (Ruskin's notion of buildings as 'storehouses of memory' (1992 [1849]) is to be understood in this context).

However, ethnocentric associations – including, but not limited to, the close links with the nationalisms and fascisms of the twentieth century (Young 1992; 1993) – became bound up with the forms and functions of such traditional monuments, a context that has led to states and memorial designers to pursue increasingly reflexive approaches to commemoration in the built environment. But far from leading to a decline in the monumental impulse, this shift has seen the commemoration of significant losses of life in wars or other socially significant events increasingly transposed onto major architectural projects. As we have seen with cases in previous chapters, architecture not only provides an important space for 'remembering' but also, just as crucially, for 'forgetting'. In other words, certain memories become prominent in the 'city of collective memory' (Boyer 1994) while others are hidden. Indeed, the emphasis on the *social* meanings of large-scale architectural projects has meant that architects operating in the 'restricted' part of the field are well versed in positioning their high-profile buildings relative to discourses of belonging, loss and remembrance.

Because the commemoration of loss is such an inherently contentious process, it is a good yardstick against which to assess some of the broader questions raised in the course of *The Sociology of Architecture*. What memories are fit for commemoration? What form should such materialization take? And how should they be positioned politically? These are all crucial questions with regard to the broader social production of architecture. While much research has focused on the intersubjective meanings of such monuments and spaces, this chapter addresses attempts to insert architecture within nationalized, state-led discourses of commemorialization. The relationship between politics, commemoration and the built environment also reminds us that architecture has limited capacity to function as an uncontested medium for mass communication. Developing earlier claims about the growing centrality of architects' discursive role, it is also important to assess how social meanings are ascribed to the built environment, and to think about the ways in which political power shapes this process. With this in mind, Daniel Libeskind's master plan for the rebuilding of the Ground Zero site in New York expresses the contestation and ambiguity associated with commemoration in complex and contested political-economic contexts. The architect's material and symbolic attempts to position this project as a nationalized site of remembrance is controversial, not least because it reflects a highly nationalized symbolic response to the question of commemoration, closely linked to the state. The 'discursive construction' of this architecture also reinforces key claims concerning the centrality of architects' discourse in positioning their work relative to collective identity; the memorialization of the Ground Zero reconstruction is assessed with these questions in mind.

Commemoration, Remembering, Forgetting

As has been suggested throughout *The Sociology of Architecture*, the communicative potential of the built environment provides a material and symbolic space for those seeking to mark socially significant events. The nation state project (Gellner 1983; 1987) saw the construction of a huge range of monuments, memorials and buildings designed to help materialize broader cultural and historical narratives of belonging; on this point Göran Therbon observes that from the mid-nineteenth century European capital cities embarked upon a 'politicization and monumentalization of urban space ... a construction and an affirmation of national identity by collective national memory' (2002: 36). The monuments that emerged in this context can be understood as codifications of wider state-led identity projects, directed at constructing and consolidating the boundaries of national publics.

The creation of built expressions of social memory is contingent on the successful imposition of a standpoint on events, and so is bound up with broader questions of politics and social power relations, making the social values represented by monuments worthy of sociological attention. Revealing the self-understanding of the political elites commissioning these works, and reflected in the choice of images, people and events celebrated in memorial forms,[1] those forms are also symbols of wider state projects to codify national publics. Bourdieu's aforementioned (1977) concept of symbolic violence is pertinent in this context, as monuments and other commemorative elements of the built environment serve to present certain values and standpoints as unproblematic. The social construction of collective memory and memorialization is a burgeoning research agenda in social science (see, for example, Boyer 1994; Spillane 1997; Olick and Robins 1998; Heynen 1999a; 1999b; Mistzal 2003). Generally speaking, this work has questioned which memories are to be objectified and how, with the aim of drawing attention to the highly partial nature of any collective remembering, which is always and everywhere equally dependent on a kind of collective forgetting. This tension is often in evidence in major architectural projects, and, commenting on the absent voices in such narratives, Hilde Heynen has noted that 'memory and amnesia seem to operate in conjuncture rather than in opposition' (1999b: 369), with memorialization requiring 'that a restricted set of meanings be abstracted, a process that necessarily implies that other meanings be forgotten' (Kerr 2002: 71).

Monuments are a significant expression of states' desire both to engage in a politics of recognition and also to position themselves relative to pasts and futures. In previous chapters it was argued that the tendency towards either modernist, future-oriented aesthetics on the one hand or historicist styles on the other must be understood not only in regard to architects' aesthetic preferences and 'rules' of the architectural field at a particular point but also in relation to the nature of the commissioning political regime's broader identity project. In the eighteenth and nineteenth centuries, the nature of commemoration meant that memorialization was, almost by default, historicist in style. On this point, Lewis Mumford said that 'if it is a monument it is not modern, and if it is modern, it cannot be a monument' (cited in Young 1992: 272), while Therbon nuances this sentiment with reference to the connection between social meanings and aesthetics, suggesting that

> The official European idiom of the 19th century and the first half of the 20th was predominantly historicist, intensely preoccupied with the origins and predecessors of the present and with the conservation of the latter in a continuous line of memory. The period was also one into which the masses of the population was entering, and that wherein compulsory schooling was generally established. The often frenetic monumentalization of public space had high didactic intentions and ambitions, of framing the memory and the social perspective of the people of the nation. (Therbon 2002: 39–40)

Such aesthetic historicism clearly represented a powerful statement of intent from those nineteenth-century European states that used monuments not only to commemorate major figures in national histories but also to position themselves relative to previous civilizations (see Chapter 3).

Contrarily, new states or regimes, or those that want to distance themselves from a previous power, may be expected to construct a great many monuments;[2] it is also a reasonable hypothesis that such monuments may adopt a distinct (modern) aesthetic so as symbolically to distance the commissioning regime from others in different times/spaces. Many formerly Soviet societies have attempted materially and symbolically to reshape their built environment so as to re-imagine the cultural legacies of the communist period – with the negotiation of this legacy one of the major cultural tasks for post-communist states as they attempt to forge new national identities (Leach 1999). It is against this backdrop that, since 1989, commemoration in many former communist countries has become tied to new definitions of city spaces, which can often taken the form of renaming streets, squares and monuments (Leach 1999).[3] A recent reflection of the contentious nature of such changes can be found

Fig. 18. The Bronze Soldier of Tallinn

in the huge unrest that surrounded the removal of the Bronze Soldier of Tallinn (Fig. 18). The statue was erected in 1947 and – simplifying a complex controversy for the sake of illustrative brevity – came to symbolize national liberation and the defeat of Nazism for many of the country's Russian-speaking minority, while for the Estonian majority the statue became associated with Soviet occupation. Accordingly, many struggles centred on the removal of the monument to a different site, and when Estonia's parliament passed legislation outlawing Nazi and Soviet symbols this resulted in the Soviet-era statue being moved to a war cemetery on the capital city's outskirts, along with what are believed to be the remains of thirteen Russian soldiers. It is in part through the controversies around the statue that Estonia, one of the first former-Soviet states to move outside the Kremlin's control when they joined the European Union in 2004, has seen issues of wartime pasts, and state relationships with Russia, centring on these monuments.

Remembering Together: Collective Memory

A related focus within the scholarship on memorialization has been addressed towards the *collective* claims that underpin commemoration. The etymology of the word itself expresses a fundamental tension in this regard, as it is derived from the Latin *com* (together) and *memorare* (to bring to mind), a basic definition that opens up a central problematic for

social scientists: the claims to a distinctly *collective* basis to commemoration. Any suggestion that a monument represents a collective –
'community', 'society' or 'identity' – raises key questions concerning who
is making the claim and to what ends. Any such claim is always political,
as such collective invocation often reifies a diverse group as coherent,
glossing over the heterogeneity, power relations and struggles inherent
in any group. As has been pointed out by numerous authors (for example,
Hall 1996; Brubaker and Cooper 2000; Jones and Krzyżanowski 2008),
the idea of a distinctly *collective* memory can seem an implicit reification
reminding us of one of the fundamental problematics of sociology: how
can a group be said to have a *collective* existence over and above its
members?

On the other hand, without achieving some collective resonance,
commemoration is in danger of falling back on highly individualized,
intersubjective accounts of memory dependent on standpoint and narrative at the expense of any meaningful account of the social. While we
usually associate memory most closely with individual consciousness and
with our own intersubjective and personal recollections of the world, the
social basis to reality cannot be overlooked by social-scientific research.
Of central concern here then is the relationship, 'imagined' or 'real',
between the individual's subjectivities and the codifications of the collective. Maurice Halbwachs, whose *The Collective Memory* (1980) is one
of the definitive contributions to research on collective memory, was concerned to show that (as opposed to psychoanalytical and socio-cognitive
accounts) memory cannot be understood outside of distinctly social
contexts. In linking internalized memories and standpoints to broader
collectives, Halbwachs sought to develop a sociological approach to the
seeming paradox of collective memory. In the present context it is relevant that he also drew attention to the materialization of collective memory
in the 'stones of the city', drawing attention to the sense of personal loss
that is felt, for example, with the destruction of buildings and spaces. In
so doing, Halbwachs usefully recast questions of collective identity as
both a temporal and spatial social process, drawing attention to the
dialogue between past and present that exists in city spaces:

> [E]ven if stones are movable, relationships established between
> stones and men are not so easily altered. When a group has lived a
> long time in a place adapted to its habits, its thoughts as well as its
> movements are in turn ordered by the succession of images from
> these external objects.
>
> Now suppose these homes and streets are demolished or their

appearance and layout are altered. The stones and other materials will not object, but the groups will. This resistance, if not in the stones themselves, at least arises out of their long-standing relationships with these groups. (Halbwachs 1980: 33)

In setting up such a problematic, Halbwachs developed the social construction of memory research agenda, by seeking to account for the internalization of such memories through practice.[4] Although he can be criticized for assuming an unproblematic or relatively consensual translation of the collective into space, which sometimes verges on essentialization, Halbwachs did set up a useful framework within which we can seek to make sense of architecture's relationship to collective memory.

Working in Halbwachs's tradition, the architectural theorist Dolores Hayden has also positioned the built environment as a 'storehouse for social memories', but has suggested that rather than focusing on specific, designated monuments, the whole of the urban fabric should be considered in this light (1996). Here Hayden's argument recalls the notion of palimpsest, the suggestion that traces of social histories of cities can be read in the layers of the built environment.[5] Hayden's research is concerned to show how urban spaces in contemporary western societies reflect structures of patriarchal dominance, and for her monuments have an important twofold role: literally, in terms of shaping urban landscapes, and also in terms of a broader symbolic definition of society. Hayden draws particular attention to the highly gendered histories that prevail in major city centres, with prominent monuments depicting the achievements of dead white men in the city spaces and streets that often also bear their names. Hayden's work articulates a desire that places should express a range of gendered, classed and racialized histories that would equate to a public recognition of diverse cultures and memories. Other feminist scholars have also drawn attention to the highly gendered nature of modern monuments and spaces (Wilson 1992; Coleman, Danze and Henderson 1996; Yuval-Davis 1996; Borden et al. 2002). Sustained criticism from post-colonial researchers has also drawn attention to the limitations of the classically conceived monument, including the highly racialized assumptions of the narratives within which such monuments are frequently positioned (Nalbantoğlu and Wong 1997). One of the central themes of both traditions of work has been to reveal the misrecognition/partial appropriation/ignoring of a particular community's history in urban space. In this sense, material forms of commemoration are codifications of the narratives by which collective memories are organized, and as such are sites where power and collective identity are inextricably linked (see Halbwachs 1980; Giesen and Junge 2003): 'collective memory not only reflects the past but also shapes present reality by providing people with understandings and symbolic frameworks that enable them to make sense of the world' (Misztal 2003: 13).

Certainly such narratives are actively constructed by those agents and institutions that are sufficiently powerful in the public sphere to have capacity to frame what should be remembered and how it should be remembered. Uncovering the institutional actors responsible for such inventions, and their motivations for doing so, can reveal something of a political project's attempted cultural embedding. For example, the proliferation of monuments reflecting highly gendered and ethnocentric histories in an earlier modernity was closely bound up with broader projects of nationalization and imperialism. Fascist governments adopted these types of messages in the built environment and in large part owing to these critiques (which were also sustained by political action from nongovernmental organizations and other lobbyists) there has been a decided shift away from this form of commemoration in the built environment. The shift away from memorials needs to be understood in the context of broader political and cultural moves away from the immutable, fixed messages that the early monuments were supposed to achieve. In the process, a general aesthetic has been discredited owing to the political associations that have been attached to it. The crisis of representation implied by challenges to coherent readings of memorials and other materializations of collective memory has not led to the decline of commemoration, but on the contrary has led to the emergence of new political discourses about the memorialization of important social events. In the European and American contexts, at least, state-led commemoration is now far more likely to represent a disempowered community or individual than to be a celebratory representation of a leading politician, a long-dead military leader or a monarch.

This shift in commemoration practice has seen nation states adopting an increasing reflexivity towards the public recognition of cultures as expressed through their monuments. Sustained critiques of elite representations and colonizations of public space has made them – on the surface at least – more circumspect about monumentalizing political power as ostentatiously as in an earlier modernity. Indeed, earlier on I suggested that in the nineteenth century colonial states' self-understanding led them to assert their self-image onto the built environment, these strategies completely overlooking questions about the partial and exclusionary nature of the cultural and political discourses into which these constructions were inserted; the desire for a materialization of state power was most frequently unreflexive and unabashed. Contrarily, a significant concern of states today – ostensibly at least – lies in making their architectural expressions and monuments 'representative' (Kymlicka and Norman 2000) and suitably 'diverse' (Martin and Casault 2005), with political discourses reflecting a broader shift towards concern with representation and cultural citizenship. This is reflected in a noticeable shift from commemoration by and of elites in earlier modernity – monarchs, war leaders, prominent politicians and merchants – to the many recent monuments that have ostensibly been more 'democratic', or at least more populist in sentiment (Lowenthal 1985).[6] As a result, exactly who is being commemorated, and how, have become major issues for scholars concerned with public recognition of cultures (see, for example, Boyer 1994; Kultermann 1994; Jameson 1997b; Jones 2006). Public debates about commemoration today are about the meaning such events have for particular groups, rather than just for the state; and for this reason they are related to different standpoint positions – the subject as a victim, a spectator, a perpetrator etc. (Gray and Oliver 2004).

This increasingly reflexive approach to memorialization is further evidenced by some of the large architectural projects and monuments across Europe today that remember 'victims' rather than celebrate 'heroes' (as was frequently the case in past commemorative practice: Evans and Lunn 1997; Winter and Sivan 2000) (Fig. 19).[7] The ostensibly increased emphasis in architecture on discourses of participation and community engagement may have resulted in superficially broader forms of cultural representation, but ones that raise new questions (to which the aforementioned contestation around meaning in the built environment is a pertinent backdrop). Commemoration provides a further way for the state to situate itself vis-à-vis citizens. As was evidenced in Chapters 3 and 4, a major concern of states' 'discourses of belonging' – including national identities – is to connect the past to the present in a way that is meaningful for citizens and that presents the state as an unbroken unity with a coherent and progressive project. While commemorative spaces tend towards the 'out of the ordinary', in some regards they are also often 'everyday' spaces in which commemoration can become part of a routinized relationship with city spaces and state-sanctioned discourses of commemoration. It is important to question how such memories are transposed into materialized statements, as the architecturing that leads to their tangible public representation reveals

Fig. 19. Eisenman's Memorial for the Murdered Jews of Europe
Photograph by Ralf Schultze.

something of the contested nature of these memories, while they also expose a clear attempt by states and other polities to create a coherent narrative of collective memory and history.

It is in this context that architecture has increasingly become a space for the memorialization of socially significant memories, including loss. Rather than being in decline, the category of the monumental has 'recoded in the contemporary context of a voracious and ever-expanding memorial culture' (Huyssen 1996: 181). Paradoxically, the turn away from conventional monuments has not led to a decline in popularity of state-led memorialization in the built environment; indeed, at the present there has been an expansion in the numbers and ranges of memorials in Europe and the USA. James E. Young's influential work (1992; 1993; 2000) has drawn attention to 'counter-monuments', those monuments and memorials that seek to deconstruct the pretensions to universalism and essentialism that characterized their modernist predecessors. Hélène Lipstadt gives a precis of Young's perspective when she highlights the traditional monument's 'immutability, pretence to permanence, and complicity with fascism [that] disqualify it for service to memory and render it very much the moral inferior to *countermonuments*, those "memorial spaces" that "challenge the very premise of the monument"' (2000: 45). Of course, it should be noted, contra reification, that it was never the monuments themselves that showed 'complicity with fascism', regardless of their styles or messages, but the practices of designers and architects who worked with fascist regimes to position their work relative to values (including memories and futures).

Such memorial discourses are inextricably bound up with states' attempts to reposition themselves via such self-representations. Again, from this perspective, architectural commemoration is inseparable from the wider question of state politics, with the cultural discourses into which political regimes embed themselves revealing a great deal about their aspirations and self-image. Owing to the contradictions and tensions that always exist in such discourses, the potential for semiotic resistances always exists (subversions in the form of 'culture jamming' are attempts to do just this: Klein 2000). Such strategies seek to reveal the partial nature of representations of collective identity and memory, and expose the contingency of meanings as reliant on social action. In this regard, and if they are to be conferred a legitimacy, states' cultural forms must always seek to mediate between the 'meaningless infinity' (Weber 1951) of individual intersubjectivities and the objectified or reified category of the social, claiming legitimacy to define the collective and colonize definitions of the social (again, what Bourdieu would refer to as symbolic violence).[8]

The tendency for major architectural projects to take on features akin to monuments in an earlier age means that such buildings should not be considered reflections of long and enduring traditions or of underlying collective sentiments but as part of 'invented traditions' (Hobsbawm and Ranger 1983) that reveal much about political power and the often fragile coupling of meaning to form. Such buildings are always contested artefacts of process whose meanings are subject to challenge and change. There is also the suggestion that the so-called 'icon impulse' assessed in the previous chapter has filtered through to memorial architecture, where sometimes collective memory is 'processed, transformed and reduced to a good-looking, but superficial image of itself' (Heynen 1999b: 369–70), with the market-seeking nature of self-conscious icons more attuned to the aesthetic and political concerns of a tourist class than the ostensibly universalized – or even populist – sentiments and forms. Commenting on this shift, Göran Therbon suggests that

> a global(istic) iconography and monumentality are oriented towards

impressiveness and attractiveness in areas of international competition and to international visitors, rather than to expressions of
national or popular identity. Such globality characterizes not only
the cityscape of multinational corporations, but also new public
buildings and monuments. (Therbon 2002: 46)

An important question from this perspective is the degree to which these
types of 'commemoration by icon' are primarily commodified experiences inherently connected to a commodifying 'heritage industry'
(Hewison 1987). Christine Boyer's *The City of Collective Memory*
(1994) makes an important contribution to these debates. Speaking of
the 'flaunting' of city spaces and images as if in a photograph or in the
cinema (1994: 491), Boyer reminds us that the extraction of surplus
capital – as well as surplus symbolic value – is a major concern for those
marketing cities (see the next chapter for more on this discussion).
Certainly, the popularity of buildings such as the Jewish Museum in
Berlin, the Imperial War Museum in Salford and the Holocaust Museum
in Washington, DC illustrates not only the fact that architecture is readily
incorporated into state-led discourses of commemoration but also that
it is frequently packaged for a 'tourist gaze' (Urry 2002).

Architecture as Memorial: The 'Discursive Construction' of Ground Zero

Many of the aforementioned tensions surrounding architecture as memorialization are expressed in the rebuilding, including the crucial symbolic
reconstruction, of the Ground Zero site in New York. This site has
witnessed a wide range of struggles concerning the social meanings that
should be attached to the architecture that replaces the 'Twin Towers' of
the World Trade Centre that were destroyed by the attacks on 11
September 2001. The ongoing reconstruction of the site has been characterized by attempts to position these spaces within a state-led
nationalized discourse of commemoration, but the tensions between
architects' and politicians' memorial discourses and those material
economic considerations associated with bringing the once hugely profitable commercial space back into use have become pronounced. The
numerous competing interests – including those of economic capital –
reveal much about the tensions of positioning architecture as memorial.
Accordingly, rather than focus too narrowly on the exact form of the
architecture on this site, my intention in this section is to illustrate how
this architecture has been positioned within the frame of a nationalized

political memorial, drawing attention to the process associated with doing so. In this particular case, universalized discourses, including memory, democracy and freedom, have framed the architect's 'discursive construction', but coexistent attempts to situate the architecture within a nationalized repertoire of cultural artefacts have contradicted these attempts at a number of levels.

Echoing many of the debates that have taken place concerning the rebuilding of other sites that have witnessed large-scale loss of human life, the architecture at Ground Zero has become mired in a range of debates that go far beyond architecture and that resonate across a number of political and economic fields. The intense scrutiny that has characterized the rebuilding of the site has contributed to making these buildings the most politically charged pieces of architecture in the world today. Given the nature of the 9/11 attacks, calls for the nationalization of the site are unsurprising. Nonetheless, the collection of architecture suggested for the site (including commercial buildings, memorial spaces and religious buildings – none of which bears any ostensible architectural symbols of the nation, such as flags or particularized national styles) has become situated within a nationalized, and often emotive, cultural discourse. The highly contested competition process reflects something of this context.[9] The architectural competition for Lower Manhattan Development Corporation contract no. A40327 for the rebuilding of the site made it clear that the buildings erected in place of the fallen Twin Towers should have a single-function memorial component.[10] This stipulation is interesting given that, as well as a memorial (assessed below), the rebuilt site is also to contain a number of buildings having primarily retail and office functions, which clearly have an ambiguous relation to any nationalized memorial frame of meaning.

As was suggested earlier, the competition stage is an event that makes it incumbent on the architect to situate their architecture relative to dominant political and economic imaginaries; in this particular case the pressure was to incorporate the architecture at Ground Zero into a repertoire of nationalized symbols of loss. Libeskind, the Master Planner of the site, has suggested that the architectural symbolism associated with the Ground Zero site is 'too powerful' to be appropriated by any one political party or specific lobby group – 'I never thought anyone should appropriate the true images of America for one group's consumption as the right wing has done. Patriotism belongs to everyone' (*Observer* 2003b). But, given the capacity of states to incorporate such memorial symbols, this statement, and his symbolic attempts to 'nationalize' the towers, is naïve at best.[11] Given the tensions between architectural form and discourse, the rebuilding has ultimately reflected much of the contested political context in which the project has been conceived.

Claims that such spaces need to capture something of the traumatic loss of human life, found a champion in Libeskind, who embraced the public and political demands placed on the new architecture at Ground Zero. He suggested that any new architecture at the site should 'inspire New York, America and the entire world with the ideals of liberty and democracy' (*Guardian* 2004b). Such hyperbole places huge demands on what is possible with architecture, but Libeskind set to this task with characteristic engagement, with the discursive element of high-profile architects' practice. A further stipulation of the competition was to 'increase public understanding of the work and to build broad-based support' (cited in Nobel 2005: 190), and Libeskind met this part of the remit with enthusiasm, engaging in many interviews, public meetings, question and answer sessions and other public discussions about his role and the rebuilding.

In attempts to balance the complex, deconstructive architectural aesthetics with more populist statements, appearances on the Oprah Winfrey Show, Cable News Network (CNN) talk shows and participation in many other television, radio and internet interviews was vital in allowing him to disseminate some of the discourses that he sought to frame the reconstruction within. In one such interview the architect explained that when working on a project of such symbolic charge and magnitude 'you have a civic responsibility, you are not just an architect, you are also a member of the public' (*Observer* 2003a). While ostensibly difficult to reconcile with abstract architectural symbolism, this public facing allowed Libeskind not only to win the architectural competition but also further to situate his building 'in' a place and 'for' a people. As Master Planner of the Ground Zero site, Libeskind was responsible for assembling and overseeing a team of architects to rebuild the site.[12] Libeskind's original plan for the rebuilding was to contain significant swathes of memorial space, albeit not in the shape of traditional memorials and monuments. As was also the case with his design for the extension to the Jewish Museum in Berlin, he embraced the communicative capacity of architecture to the full; in this case the theme of memory was the prevalent frame that Libeskind sought to attach to the site (there was also a process of future orientation too, with the buildings positioned relative to a 'common' future for citizens of New York and the USA).

Various lobbying groups were quick to engage with Libeskind's symbolism, with the suggestion that 'Ground Zero mandates an urban gesture of mega national significance. What eventually rises from Ground Zero must reflect the best of what we are as a people, exhibiting our aspirations, our creativity and our industry' (signed by 'The American People') (Which Future for Ground Zero? 2003). Politicians also echoed such calls, with New York's Governor Pataki describing the rebuilding as a 'new symbol of this country and of our resolve in the face of terror' (*Guardian* 2004b) that would 'defiantly reclaim our skyline with a new beacon symbolizing all that makes our nation great' (cited in Nobel 2005: 205). As well as the general remit associated with Master Planner, Libeskind has also designed the centrepiece structure, a trademark silver-clad, angular building that incorporates a number of nationalized referents. Although not an exclusively memorial space, Libeskind has ascribed a number of nationalized discourses onto this building, in the process aligning the 'Freedom Tower' with USA national identity and values. The Freedom Tower was to stand 1,776 feet, which not only would have made it the tallest building in the world but also containing an allusion to the date of the signing of the Declaration of Independence. In common with the other narrative symbolic architectural references central to this building, the role of the architect in disseminating this information is key. Without the architect informing us of the exact height of the tower it is highly unlikely that one would consider 541.1 metres of any 'national' significance at all, but when provided with this narrative account the building becomes symbolically incorporated into an 'Americanized' discourse (Jones 2006). That the Freedom Tower suggests the form of the Statue of Liberty is perhaps also not immediately evident to the viewer or user, but this piece of nationally referential symbolism has been expressed explicitly through Libeskind's interviews and writings and the effect of further linking the new building into an ongoing narrative construction of the nation and the city. However, it can be suggested that given the subsequent war on Iraq, and violations of human rights in Guantanamo Bay associated with the 'War on Terror' following the attack on the Twin Towers, the Freedom Tower is a singularly inappropriate name.

Given the context of the rebuilding – including the coterminous US military campaigns in Iraq and Afghanistan – there was a strong argument to be made for a building less in keeping with such discursive and material nationalization and more in line with the 'post-national' frame employed by Libeskind on his extension to the Jewish Museum in Berlin.

However, in this case the highly charged and highly politicized discourse into which the building was inserted meant that such a strategy was neither expedient nor sustainable. Attempts to link architectural form to nationalized discourse are also in evidence in many other aspects of the site rebuilding. Describing the slurry walls, one of the few parts of the building – the foundation-cum-dam wall – to survive the attacks, Libeskind suggests that his plans for the expression of these walls are a way of 'revealing the heroic foundations of democracy for all to see' (2004: 169). The numerous allusions to democratic values underline exactly why discursive links between architecture and the event it purports to represent are so important. In fact, the decision to retain these walls has proved hugely controversial, with the *New York Times* architecture critic Herbert Muschamp, a powerful figure within the field, suggesting that this part of Libeskind's design is 'astonishingly tasteless, emotionally manipulative and close to nostalgia and kitsch' (*Observer* 2003b). Larry Silverstein, the site owner, has also expressed the opinion that the slurry wall is unsightly and would be off-putting to the commercial tenants he hopes to attract to the rebuilt site, which previously housed the USA's most profitable retail space (*Observer* 2003b). In defence of this memorial aspect of his design, Libeskind has argued that 'it is important to embrace the reality of the terrorist act, not bury it. You can't say nothing happened there. That day changed the world' (*Observer* 2003b). The memorialization of the Ground Zero site can be recast as tensions between the competing commemorative and other political-economic imperatives and imaginaries; attempts to reconcile these often contradictory agendas situated the architect in a highly ambivalent position and placed a great deal of expectation on his capacity to balance a range of discourses. The resonance of the social elements of the architect's discourse must be understood in the context of the huge loss of life witnessed at the site. At the same time, the economic imperatives of the scheme still resonate through the governance and positioning of many parts of the rebuilding. Commenting on this tension, Phillip Nobel suggests that 'though they soon tired of Libeskind's rhetoric, the political powers knew they needed it. His ability to mask the ugliness of the process was so important' (2005: 189). In other words, the symbolic capital brought by Libeskind to the project was crucial in sustaining the ideological resonance of the rebuilding.

James E. Young, whose influential work on 'countermemorials' (1992; 1993) is discussed above, acted as one of a panel of jurors to help LMDC decide on the memorial design for Ground Zero. Young noted that the panel had 'resisted the idea of the literal, that's why you don't get any Big Apples in the designs, or representations of airplanes, attacks, death, blood' (*New York Times* 2004); given that the representations would understandably not be literal, this serves to increase the importance, and the contestation, of the symbolic element of the architecture. Muschamp has bemoaned the surfeit of symbolism in Libeskind's Ground Zero design site, complaining of 'symbolic manipulation'. Certainly, with Libeskind investing the project with so much symbolism, critics will invariably attempt to challenge him on these grounds.[13] In actual fact, the exact aesthetic form that the rebuilding should take would prove (predictably) highly controversial. In this context of architecture as memorialization it becomes very significant to note the substantial lobby to rebuild the Twin Towers to the original plan. Team Twin Towers, a large lobbying organization with the restoration of the towers as their aim, has suggested that the Freedom Tower is 'replacing a symbol of world peace and human cooperation with a self-absorbed salute to America' (*Guardian* 2004a). Their interpretation of the Twin Towers, home to the World Trade Centre, as a symbol of peace and cooperation is surely only one reading of many, which further underlines the argument that landmark buildings have a whole range of possible associations and political discourses. The *New York Post*'s columnist Nicole Gelinas also supports the rebuilding of the original towers, suggesting that Americans 'understood' the Twin Towers because '[t]hey were us: stark capitalism, power and beauty without explanation or apology' (*Guardian* 2004a). Again, the exact constitution of this 'us' deserves further scrutiny.

Pre-empting the question of the appropriateness of the form for the Freedom Tower, Libeskind withdrew into a kind of mysticism:

> How do I know what to design? I listen to the stones. I sense the faces around me. I try to build bridges to the future by staring clear-eyed into the past … inspired by light, sound, invisible spirits, a distinct sense of place, a respect for history. We are all shaped by a constellation of realities and invisible forces, and if a building is to have a spiritual resonance, it has to reflect all these things. No one knows how body and soul are connected, but connect them is what I try to do. (Libeskind 2001: 16)

However, for all that the populist aspect of Libeskind's narratives suggests that representative architecture should 'speak directly' to the citizens it represents ('It's not about prescribed things you should know about. People discover things on their own, discover architecture on more than one level' (*Observer* 2003b)), this is frequently at odds with the detailed and complex narrative of symbolic association the architect has designed for this site. As with Libeskind's other work, the discursive element of this practice is hugely important.

One illustration of this highly referential symbolism is to be found in the design for the Wedge of Light, a triangular piazza whose boundaries are delineated by the angles of sunlight on the ground between the times of 8.46 a.m. (the time when the first plane hit the first tower) and 10.28 a.m. (when the second tower collapsed). The design was meant to ensure that no shadows would fall on the site between those times on 11 September, but the fact that this did not actually work in practice led to Libeskind being hoist by his own (symbolic) petard. Opening a critique of Libeskind's uncertain foothold on this slippery terrain, Philip Nobel suggests that a 'veil of language was cast over Ground Zero to bridge the great gap between form and message ... [paradoxically] language was so central to Libeskind's efforts that he literally refused to discuss the project's architectural basis' (2005: 195–96). Significantly for the present concern, Libeskind rejected stylistic and aesthetic comparisons for his work on the site, choosing instead to frame his work in terms of questions of memory, democracy, identity and loss. The danger is when the words become divorced from form; coupling the two is key if architects are to maintain the impression, crucial to the field, that architectural form has profound social meaning.

Hélène Lipstadt has been scathing about the elitist, field-specific assumptions concerning the expertise required to read such symbolism, suggesting that

> architects can continue to arrogate to themselves an expertise about memory that is so self-serving as to be ultimately convincing only to those who are equally inexpert in memory, that is to say other architects. Or ... they can take the long interdisciplinary detour that will allow them to be credible spokespersons for architecture in the ever-widening field of memory studies. (Lipstadt 2000:45)

Such critique is comparable to the arguments suggesting the necessity of a move beyond solely aesthetic understandings of architecture in order to reconnect the political dimension of architectural practice (see, for example, Dutton and Mann 1996; Dovey 2009).

Another part of the Ground Zero site that has attracted a great deal of attention, not to mention controversy, is Michael Arad's and Peter

Walker's memorial, which features two pools situated within the 200 ft × 200 ft footprints of the fallen towers.[14] This part of the site was subject to a separate open international competition – the World Trade Center Site Memorial Competition – distinct from Libeskind's master plan. In contrast to the Freedom Tower it is a single-function memorial space. In the preface to the competition document the then Governor of the State of New York George Pataki, and Michael Bloomberg, the Mayor of the City of New York, suggested that memorials 'give us a context for remembering the past, engaging the present, and reflecting on the future … The values of liberty and democracy transcend geography and nationality, and they must be given physical expression' (Lower Manhattan Development Corporation 2003: 2). This design gained qualified praise from Muschamp, who suggested that the monument has the 'greatest potential to be the least' (this critic's missive against over-embellishment is reminiscent of the postmodernist Charles Jencks' (1980) argument that the most effective architecture for symbolizing diversity is that in which the meanings are left 'open' to better represent a plurality of identities and voices). However, even within this context, the exact manner of the representation is controversial, as is illustrated by the debates around the listing of names of people who died in the 9/11 attacks. Arad, who is designing the memorial with landscape architect Peter Walker, has suggested that '[a]ny arrangement that tries to impose meaning through physical adjacency will cause grief and anguish to people who might be excluded from that process' (*New York Times* 2004). With symbolism already so prominent and highly politicized in the project in general, it is difficult to convince people that names with insignias next to them – as was suggested by Governor Pataki and Mayor Bloomberg for victims who were police officers, fire fighters, workers from other emergency services and court officials – are of equal symbolic 'worth' to those names that are unembellished. Some have interpreted this call as an attempt to impose an inappropriate hierarchy of victims, or an equally undesirable hierarchy of heroes, among those who lost their lives.

Conclusion

The abstract struggles over which social memories and events should be recognized and represented find a material reflection in struggles over which memorials and buildings should be preserved, destroyed or commissioned anew. The shift away from the ethnocentric narratives that characterized the proliferation of monuments in the nineteenth and early twentieth centuries has been supplanted with an increasingly reflexive approach to memorialization, where (in some cases) a universalization of the frames into which monuments are inserted is evident (also see, for example, the case of the Reichstag, as discussed in the next chapter). Of course, broader secularization, and those sometimes opened, sometimes closed dialogues with colonial/post-colonial histories that characterize many states' national cultural representations, are a vital backdrop here. James E. Young, an influential voice in research on commemoration and memory, has identified 'countermemorial' spaces and forms that seek to undermine the fixed meanings and ethnocentric associations that characterized the materialization of collective memory at an earlier point in modernity, and it is in part this practice that has led to architecture having a renewed significance in commemoration. The reflexive practice of those high-profile architects well-versed in public discourse chimes with the more ambiguous approach characteristic of state commemoration (which is in stark contrast to the celebration of ethnocentric and narrowly defined values that characterized earlier commemoration practice).

The project to rebuild the Ground Zero site reflects much of the ambivalence inherent in state-led commemorations in contested social contexts. Any project here was always going to prove highly controversial, and the range of struggles that have centred on the architecture clearly illustrates some of the broader contentions of this book relative to architecture, power and identity. While many European states find themselves engaged in broadly 'post-national' identity projects (Kastoryano 2002), since 9/11 the United States government has been engaged in a nationalizing project comparable to those undertaken in an earlier modernity. Cultural symbols such as flags, anthems, institutions – and in fact the very notion of 'community' itself – have all been re-evaluated and reinterpreted along national lines since 2001.

Libeskind's initial appeals (that the building should represent post-nationality, emptied of symbolically nationalized charge) have been superseded by appeals to the American people, with the universalized symbols of absence Libeskind employed in his post-national Jewish Museum seemingly inappropriate for a polity (and society) seeking to memorialize this recent tragedy. While ongoing attempts to situate the rebuilding of the Ground Zero site within a nationalized framework remind us of the close links that have always existed between states, national identity and commemoration, the extent to which such an architectural response should be part of the cultural discourse of a nation state waging war in the aftermath of the attacks is highly questionable.

In general, the legitimation strategies architects use when situating their work in the context of state-led narratives of belonging should always be approached from a critical perspective. The intention here has not been to single out Libeskind as some kind of apologist, but rather to draw out the inherently politicized nature of high-profile architecture and politics, which in this case existed against a backdrop of highly complex governance and economic arrangements. Libeskind has sought to balance both a number of conflicting interests and – crucially for this chapter – a range of competing and contradictory identity discourses in his plan. Perhaps above all, though, this architecture reminds us of the importance of narrative and discursive construction, where the role of the architect is crucial. As is ever the case, this particular response can only be understood by engagement with the political and economic contexts in which the project was conceived and into which the architect tries to connect it. While technical architectural debates have centred on the fact that some of Libeskind's symbolic measures – such as that at the Wedge of Light – express a tension, as their built form is not accurately aligned with his discourse, the more general point to observe concerns the ongoing contradictions in the material and social and political positioning of the rebuilding.

One encouraging tendency that can be observed about the rebuilding also reaffirms earlier claims apropos the frequently dissenting position adopted by citizens vis-à-vis the symbols that states develop in their name. While not advocating a pluralist position that would see resistance everywhere, this mobilization around the politics of identity has led to further contestation around state-led architectural-memorial projects; revealing the politicized and contradictory nature of some of the discourses into which the architect and politicians have situated the building is a crucial social function of this architecture. The sociological significance of such contestation is due to the fact that debate goes far beyond what is actually built, and frequently articulates abstract discourses pertinent to collective identity. The always-contested basis of the construction and maintenance of collective memory can thus be revealed through analysis of such projects.

Notes

1 Other material expressions of this tendency are visible in the currency, flags, stamps and cultural events – such as festivals, national holidays and celebrations – that characterized the emergence and development of the modern nation state and have been important sites of commemoration in this regard (Spillane 1997).

2 Therbon (2002: 41) notes that 150 statues (as distinct from other monuments) were erected in Paris from 1870 to 1914, compared with only twenty-six in the period 1815–70 and sixty-four from 1914 to 1940.

3 The Europeanization of collective memory is an interesting development here, and is bound up with the European Union's ongoing project to foster a sense of 'Europeanness' among citizens of member states (see Chapter 7 for a discussion of attempts to create Europe as an 'imagined community').

4 In so doing he arguably foreshadowed those theorists such as Anthony Giddens (1985) and Pierre Bourdieu (1989a) who explicitly sought to transcend the agency/structure dichotomy in the social sciences with their concepts of 'structuration' and 'habitus' respectively.

5 Hayden's research connects with Walter Benjamin's in this respect.

6 Monumental statements can also express tensions between elitist 'high-cultural' versus populist approaches to memorialization. This is illustrated by Marc Quinn's sculpture of Alison Lapping, the disabled artist, which was previously atop the hitherto empty fourth plinth at London's Trafalgar Square (named in 1830 in celebration of Lord Horatio Nelson's victory over the French navy in 1805). As Therbon points out (2002: 33), it is significant that Nelson's Column, completed in 1842, is far greater in size than the previously dominant monuments to Charles I, James II and George IV; from the perspective of the present book this is significant as it can be read as reflecting a shift towards celebration of military figures away from royalty. Designed by the architect Charles Barry in 1841, Trafalgar Square was explicitly a celebration of empire. Gormley's fourth plinth project – *The Public*, which invited members of the public to use the space on top of the plinth alongside celebrations of Britain's imperial past for (almost) what they saw fit – reflects a major shift in commemoration practice.

7 Fig. 19 illustrates another state-led architectural project engaged with the problem of representing the Holocaust: Peter Eisenman's Memorial for the Murdered Jews of Europe. Designed as a memorial for only the Jewish victims of the Nazis – in itself a contentious decision – this project is one of many state-funded Holocaust memorials in Berlin that use space in a stark way, with '4,000 concrete slabs arrayed like a vast burial ground, or an undulating bed of nails for the German conscience' (Wise 1998: 153). This is clearly a monument to victims and not, as was the case in the age of nation-building, to 'heroes'.

8 An interesting feature of many of landmark buildings with a memorial function is the extent to which the states responsible for their commission attempt to situate themselves as 'post-national', a development explored later on in this chapter and in more detail in Chapter 7.

9 An interesting dimension of the contestation around the competition process concerned the $40,000 that each competing architectural firm was offered for participation in the competition for the redesign of the site. As was suggested earlier, the high opportunity costs associated with competition entry both limits mass entry while also reaffirming the distinctive aesthetic foundation of architecture. Frank Gehry invited the wrath of some colleagues, and the media, by drawing attention to the limited budget available for entry into the competition (Nobel 2005).

10 'The Lower Manhattan Development Corporation was created in the aftermath of the September 11, 2001 attacks, by Governor George E. Pataki and then-Mayor Rudolph W. Giuliani, with the specific brief to help plan and coordinate the rebuilding and revitalization of Lower Manhattan, defined as the geographic area of Manhattan south of Houston Street. The LMDC is a joint State-City corporation governed by a 16-member Board of Directors, half appointed by the Governor of New York State and half by the Mayor of New York City. LMDC is funded by $2.78

billion in grants from the United States Department of Housing and Urban Development' (Lower Manhattan Development Corporation 2003: 2).

11 George Bush used images of the Ground Zero site in his successful campaign to be re-elected President in 2003.

12 Libeskind's response to the competition, and the political storm that engulfed his role as master planner, is documented in some detail in Philip Nobel's *Sixteen Acres: Architecture and the Outrageous Struggle for the Future of Ground Zero* (2005).

13 Make New York New York Again, another team advocating rebuilding of the Twin Towers, has suggested that while the 'average person' does not want to have to engage with complex architectural theory to understand a building, 'Libeskind's building is twisted. It seems to imply something bent out of shape, destroyed' (*Guardian* 2004a). It is significant that this statement, ostensibly populist and 'anti-symbolism', engages with the symbolism of the building, albeit bringing to bear a very different interpretation from the architect's. Such conflicting interpretations raise pertinent questions about the power of the architect's interpretation relative to those with less audible 'voices'.

14 Another of the more conventionally memorial spaces is the 'Matrix of Heroes', a series of intersecting lines in the pavement that trace the paths of the arriving emergency services on the day.

6

Iconic Architecture and Regeneration: The Form *is* the Function

Put me on the map, give my industrial city a second chance, make me the centrefold of the Sunday supplements, the cover of in-flight magazines, the backdrop for fashion shoots, give me an iconic land-mark, give me – architectural – shock and awe.
Charles Jencks, *Iconic Buildings: The Power of Enigma* (2004), 18.

Introduction

Political agencies' recent embrace of what has come to be known as 'iconic' architecture can be understood as a continuation of longstanding attempts to mobilize major building projects, first, to materialize wider discourses of major social change, and second, to generate surplus value from urban space. The desire to commission sufficiently persuasive and socially resonant architectural forms with which to attract various forms of mobile capital – especially from the private sector and tourism – while at the same time symbolizing an upward trajectory for a place, has seen iconic architecture incorporated enthusiastically into UK cultural policy strategies. The 'visually consumable' (Urry 2002) nature of such atten-tion-grabbing buildings, allied to a hope that iconic forms will help create instantly recognizable 'brand images' for places, has led Charles Jencks to claim a renewed function for statement architecture. He has observed that in 'the last ten years a new type of architecture has emerged. Driven by social forces, the demand for instant fame and economic growth, the expressive landmark has challenged the previous tradition of the archi-tectural monument' (2004: 7). This chapter suggests that the attempts to embed particular urban regeneration projects within socially meaningful components in the form of iconic architecture mean that a major chal-lenge for academic research lies in connecting the aesthetic forms and social and political discourses that characterize icons to broader strategies of capitalist accumulation (Jones 2009). The suggestion is that such build-ings are a reflection of a particular moment in regeneration discourse and

115

practice which resonated with the emergence and consolidation of a subfield of 'starchitects', whose celebrity transcends the parameters of the architectural field and whose reputation adds weight to place marketing initiatives that their buildings are designed to symbolize.

That iconic architectural projects are a fertile ground for sociological analysis is illustrated with reference to an ultimately unrealized development project with an iconic building at its centre: the 'Fourth Grace' project on Liverpool's waterfront was intended as a symbol of – and catalyst for – the city's renaissance, but a number of tensions eventually led to its collapse. The tokenistic consultation process by which Will Alsop's Cloud scheme was chosen, the form of the building and its funding, all proved hugely contested, with the struggles centring on the project revealing much about the material and symbolic volatility of the iconic building in the context of wider urban regeneration strategies. The general contention is that the emergence and collapse of this iconic architectural project reflected a particular moment in the political-economy of local urban regeneration strategies.

Defining an Icon: Architecture Selling Places

The 1997 opening of the Guggenheim Museum in Bilbao, a post-industrial Spanish city, marked something of a watershed in reminding those political agencies 'selling cities' (Hall and Hubbard 1998) of the potential of landmark architectural statements to create surplus value from urban space. Designed by high-profile Canadian architect Frank Gehry, the Guggenheim Museum is by now a very familiar case study for a particular model of urban regeneration. The museum opened in 1997 and attracted 1.3 million visitors in its first year, 70 per cent of whom reportedly went to see the building itself, rather than the art it housed. By 2000, visitor numbers were up to 3 million a year and 87 per cent of these visitors were from outside the Basque area, with the local state claiming that, since the museum's opening, over £300 million has been injected into the local economy from more than 4 million visitors (DCMS 2004: 12). Away from the headline figures there is much evidence to suggest that this museum – the definitive case of place branding through iconic architecture – has not been the unqualified success for local people as is often represented, with 'local residents, whilst recognizing the economic impact and value for a middle class minority, [finding] little value attached to the museum in terms of quality of life, social cohesion, regional identity or governance' (DCMS 2004).[1]

While the (perceived) gains associated with the Guggenheim have encouraged other political agencies to commission spectacular buildings in the hope of reproducing the 'Bilbao Effect', the initial economic benefits produced by large-scale iconic architecture projects are not always distributed across a range of social groups (Evans 2003; DCMS 2004). This makes it problematic to legitimate icon-led regeneration with inclusionary discourses, and – more broadly – raises pertinent questions about the 'ethics' of such major projects (MacLeod 2011) relative, for instance, to the environmental sustainability of the structure and the labour process that lead to its realization or – more symbolically – about the equity of the political-economic structure that gives rise to such an icon.

The incorporation of iconic architecture and the respective 'brands' of the famous architects responsible for the design of such buildings into the place marketing projects so central to recent UK urban regeneration strategies presents a rich research agenda for sociologists interested in the ways in which regeneration agencies seek to mobilize urban space and culture to produce surplus value. The symbiotic relationship between 'starchitects' and those agencies governing cities means that any latent assumptions of neutrality with regard to architecture commissioned and delivered in these contexts must be banished, as it is 'fully incorporated into the ideological apparatus of place-marketing [and plays] a major role in mediating perceptions of urban change' (Crilley 1993: 231). A central challenge is in getting to grips with the political economy of local elites and their relationship to architects, and interrogating architecture's capacity to embed political and economic change in a socially resonant form.

This challenging research agenda has been developed by Leslie Sklair, whose work (2005; 2006) uncovers the links between the transnational capitalist class, internationally high-profile architectural practices and iconic architecture. Sklair positions the emergence of contemporary iconic architecture as an expression of the long-standing desire of economic elites to materialize their power in urban space via attention-seeking buildings that are 'resource[s] in struggles for meaning and, by implication, for power' (Sklair 2006: 21). Sklair's approach identifies the temporal, spatial and aesthetic component of icons, which he presents as three related questions: 'iconic for where, iconic for whom and iconic for when?' (2005; 2006). These fundamental questions sensitize us to related-but-distinct sociological concerns about the role of icons in the entrepreneurial place-making strategies (iconic for where?); the differential reception of architectural aesthetics and meanings by different

118   *The Sociology of Architecture*

publics, including architects, economic investors, the general public and the architectural and general media (iconic for whom?); and the capacity of such buildings to capture a zeitgeist or major social change with an appropriate aesthetic (iconic for when?).

Furthermore, Sklair's work addresses the important question of how iconic architecture contributes to the global imagination, both via the aesthetic consolidation of a transnational corporate class (Sklair 2005) and also in the consolidation of a global 'imagined community' (Anderson 1983), more broadly. Iconic architecture is one 'space' in which political and economic institutions seek to present a socially meaningful, culturalized narration of the transformation of local economies associated with urban regeneration. This starting point necessitates engagement with the specificities of architecture as both form and practice, including reconciling (i) the definitive aesthetic and semiotic components of the architectural object with (ii) a sense of architects' position within the architectural field of production (Stevens 1998) while (iii) situating both within broader political-economic shifts (Harvey 1990). However, given that the aim of icons is to foster distinctiveness, 'icon inflation' and the semi-formalization of an icon aesthetic is ironic. Architectural critic Deyan Sudjic points to an 'architecture of diminishing returns in which every sensational new building must attempt to eclipse the last one ... designs, cutting edge when they were commissioned, are not any more. Architecture is characterised by long periods of intellectual inactivity, followed by moments of sudden movement' (2004).

This notwithstanding, the widespread desire to benefit from the raised profile and related inward investment opportunities associated with landmark buildings has led to a proliferation of iconic architecture across Britain, with the assumption that 'if a city can get the right architect at the right creative moment in his or her career, and take the economic and cultural risk, it can make double the initial investment in about three years ... the tertiary economy of the culture industry is a way out of Modernist decline' (Jencks 2004: 19). Such an approach to architecture positions the visitor to the site as a visual consumer, with architecture high on the list of commodifiable 'must-see' tourist sites in cities the world over. The role of sections of the public, especially the internationally mobile tourist class, as a constituent 'outside' of architecture is important in this regard. It is in large part the 'visually consumable' nature of iconic architecture that explains its centrality to place marketing strategies, as these buildings provide a tangible, marketable brand in keeping with the broader consumption of place. Iconic architecture is one manifestation of a long-established symbiosis between politics, economy and culture; explicitly designed to spatialize a moment in a city's projected transition, iconic architecture has proliferated in the UK over the last decade, with projects driven by coalitions of actors keen to rebrand post-industrial cities better to attract tourists and other forms of inward investment. The last decade has seen iconic architecture enthusiastically incorporated into culture-led regeneration strategies. The Department for Culture, Media and Sport suggests that 'by virtue of their outward appearance [icons] are immediately attractive as destinations and as marketing tools ... iconic buildings can contribute to the economic, as well as the physical, social and cultural regeneration of an area, bringing in new investment and creating jobs and opportunities for local people' (DCMS 2004: 11, 18).

Over the last ten years, a consensus in British cultural policy discourses has been that the 'presence of striking architectural landmarks on the landscape adds significantly to an area's cultural heritage and sense of place. By virtue of their outward appearance buildings ... are immediately attractive as destinations and as marketing tools for their localities and regions' (DCMS 2004: 18). Within such policy discourses there is an acute awareness that such buildings need to be part of a broader regeneration strategy; the DCMS challenges iconic architectural projects 'to be relevant, supported by and rooted in their local communities, rather than serving only outside visitors and the affluent' (2004: 12). Given the clamour for iconic buildings in Britain over the last decade, it can be hard to remember that it is only relatively recently that the British state has viewed such architecture as a cultural form with great potential to rebrand cities. While other European states have a long track record of commissioning iconic architecture with the explicit aim of rebranding and regenerating cities, Britain's governments have been slow to embrace the icon. France, on the other hand, has a long tradition of erecting high-profile buildings with the expressed aim of renegotiating identities and generating interest in a city or region –with the *Grands Projets du Président*, French landmark architectural projects commissioned by President Mitterrand, for example. These twelve, high-profile Parisian buildings, which include the Pompidou Centre (Rogers and Piano, 1971), the Pyramid at the Louvre (I. M. Pei, 1989) and La Grande Arche (Otto Von Spreckelsen 1990), can be seen as an attempt to situate Paris as a post-industrial city, while also consolidating the Paris-centric nature of French national identity.[2]

This enthusiasm for distinctive icons has certainly impacted heavily on the restricted part of the architectural field, whose reliance on the capitalist economy for major commissions (Larson 1994) has meant an enthusiastic embrace of place marketing agendas by high-profile 'starchitects', an emergent designation for the group of international architects who define the field (McNeil 2009). Reflecting on this changed status for architects and their attention-grabbing designs, Rem Koolhaas has observed that the 'idolatry of the market has drastically changed our [architects'] legitimacy and status even though our status has never been higher ... It is really unbelievable what the market demands [from architecture] now. It demands recognition, it demands difference and it demands iconographic qualities' (Koolhaas, cited in Jencks 2004: 101).

The Iconic Aesthetic: The Form *is* the Function

The relationship between aesthetics, semiosis and political-economy is contingent and necessitates careful, historicized empirical engagement on a case-by-case basis (see below). Whether a building necessarily needs to be tall or to dominate the skyline to be 'iconic' is an empirically open question and one contingent on this architectural field, the demands of those commissioning the building, and wider publics. Icons, while maybe or maybe not physically dominating the surrounding landscape, are explicitly positioned relative to a visual consumer – either the visitor in front of the building or more likely the viewer of a mediated image in press, television or film – and, a 'successful' building will necessarily develop a strong association to place through an instantly recognizable form designed to be both distinctive and widely disseminated in this mediated form. The 'gazes' of a mobile tourist class are overwhelmingly concerned with the facades and surface appearances of prescribed sites of objectified cultural interest, emphasizing the spectacular and 'out-of-the-ordinary'. Positioning architecture relative to visual consumption – as a form of what has been called 'architainment' (Fernández-Galiano 2005) – means that the 'surface appearance and visual effect is paramount as buildings are designed from the outside in, from the vantage of an external gaze ... "the public" are positioned as consumers of visual imagery' (Crilley 1993: 237).

In *The Tourist Gaze* (2002) John Urry argues that travel and tourism have become comparable to conventionally economic transactions such as shopping, with places and cities 'consumed' by tourists and other visitors. Urry argues that, owing to their quasi-economic nature, these tourists' gazes are directed towards spectacular buildings and other officially sanctioned, prescribed sites of objectified cultural interest.[3] As a result, such gazes are primarily concerned with surfaces and facades, and iconic buildings are readily incorporated into this broader consumption of place; icons are a product of this emphasis on externality, with an aestheticized approach to architecture – emphasizing surfaces – prevalent. Interestingly, the sociologist Leslie Sklair, the prominent architectural theorist Charles Jencks and the architectural critic Deyan Sudjic all use the term 'icon' as a proxy for an aesthetic: Jencks defines an icon as a building that can 'survive being shrunk to the size of a TV screen, or smaller, to a letterhead or stamp ... which allows it to become a brand image (2004: 23); Sklair sees the icon as having an aesthetic component, while also drawing attention to the question of historical icons in a way not common in other literature on the subject (2006: 38); and Sudjic sees the desire for bombastic, eye-catching brands as having led to the popularization of architecture "that looks best reduced to a logo on a letterhead or to the confined spaces of one of those Eiffel-Tower-in-a-snow-storm paperweights" (2004).

We can see linkages between certain regimes of accumulation or 'economic imaginaries' (Jessop 2004) – such as those associated with urban regeneration – and the form and meanings attached to architecture. In the context of aggressive place marketing initiatives, while iconic buildings may or may not *physically* dominate the surrounding landscape, successful ones necessarily develop a strong association to place through an instantly recognizable, distinctive form. The emergence of distinctive, eye-catching buildings needs to be situated within a wider political-economic configuration that sees cities competing with one another for 'brand recognition' and mobile capital (Harvey 1989); this context has implications for the aesthetic form and the semiotic component of major architectural projects. How architects respond to the intensification of the visual and aesthetic component of their work is interesting from the perspective of Bourdieu's concepts of field and autonomy, as it allows the high-profile architects who win such iconic commissions to embrace the artistic component of their work, with the overwhelming focus on form a vehicle for framing practice in this way. The 'force field' effect that sees architects developing the attention-grabbing aesthetics that characterize icons must be understood relative to a valorization of certain field positions and related values. As was noted in Chapters 1 and 2, there exists a dominant tendency within architectural theory to understand the high-profile architect's work as somewhat asocial, primarily as a development of their own oeuvre, relegating this

122   *The Sociology of Architecture*

field effect and the external constraints. Highly aestheticized notions of architecture as objectified commodity have become prevalent in that part of the field responsible for the design of such commissions. At particular junctures, these forms are as different as the imperatives of politics, economy and architecture itself. In the case of contemporary designs, such as Norman Foster's Swiss Re: Tower in London, Jean Nouvel's Torre Agbar in Barcelona (Fig. 20), or Adrian Smith's Burj-al-Arab Hotel in Dubai, the aim is to dominate both media coverage and the physical landscape (see the work on skyscrapers by Domosh (1988; 1992), Throsby (2006), Charney (2007) and McNeill (2009: 114–35)).

In their article 'Form Follows Power' (2006), Maria Kaika and Korinna Thielen chart the shift from the domination of the landscape by religious buildings to state buildings and then to those 'urban shrines' celebrating capitalist production. Reminding us that the exact architectural form that icons take varies much across time and space (see also Bonta 1979), they observe that early 'icons' were typically religious shrines characterized by 'sheer volume', further emphasized by location 'on a hill, in the centre of town, or in front of a public square … purpose built to host functions related to the building' (Kaika and Thielen 2006:

Fig. 20. Jean Nouvel's Torre Agbar, Barcelona

59). The attempt of early religious regimes to use buildings such cathedrals and town halls to capture the 'skyline and the public imagination' is an interesting counterpoint to the form of contemporary icons, which may or may not *physically* dominate the landscape, but that do necessarily develop a strong association to place through an instantly recognizable image that is explicitly designed to be widely disseminated in mediated form through the printed press, TV and film.

Mona Domosh (1988) has suggested that the progressive values implied by advanced construction techniques and radical aesthetics have long been meanings with which modernizing states and corporations have sought to align themselves. A desire to stress disjuncture with the past – including a symbolic distance from previous political regimes – often motivates a transformation of the built environment in general (Therbon 2002), with the aesthetic paramount in this regard for contemporary icons. The desire for a materialization of forward-looking change goes some way to explaining the aesthetic of the icons associated with selling places. The historicism discussed in Chapter 3 is at odds with the forward-looking aesthetics of the architectural icons that emerged in the context of regeneration strategies, which are explicitly designed to spatialize a moment in a city's (projected) transition, to give a socially meaningful form to a shift in a political-economic programme.

Recognizable silhouettes are often very important for the 'landmark' status of buildings (Lasswell 1979), and the stylistic component is crucial to any analysis of what makes an icon (including the capacity of 'great' buildings to shape the field judgements (Bonta 1979)). Commenting on successful capitol (parliament) buildings, Lawrence J. Vale identified 'a memorable and easily reproducible silhouette ... not openly derived from any one architectural source, unless it is a source that the sponsoring government wishes unabashedly to represent' (1992: 285). The close connection between iconic architecture and place marketing initiatives means that the 'function' of any such building is primarily to renegotiate a place's image; beyond this the actual *function* is frequently an unresolved ambiguity. It is the emphasis on aesthetic form 'which allows [the icon] to become a brand image, [but that] also threatens to make it a cliché or a one-liner' (Jencks 2004: 23).

Reinventing Liverpool: The Cloud on the Horizon

The Fourth Grace project was conceived as an architectural centrepiece for Liverpool's Capital of Culture celebrations in 2008, but proved highly contested from its inception. In keeping with one of this book's central arguments, the project served a valuable function in acting as a touch-stone of local opinion about the culture-led regeneration belatedly taking place in the city, revealing a number of important tensions, with questions of community participation, symbolic representation and part-nership-working all finding a tangible focus in this scheme. Before addressing such issues explicitly, I will situate the Fourth Grace project in the context of the prominent role assigned to the built environment in the rebranding of Liverpool, a city that, although boasting a proud archi-tectural history, has not witnessed the (re)emergence of iconic architecture in the way other comparable UK cities have, such as Glasgow, Manchester, Leeds and Sheffield. While there have been no proposals for landmark buildings in Liverpool for decades, the city's architectural heritage was a major focus in the successful bid to be European Capital of Culture 2008, with the famous waterfront – desig-nated a world heritage site by UNESCO on 2 July 2004 – featuring prominently. The waterfront architecture of the existing 'Three Graces' (the Liver, Cunard and Port of Liverpool Authority buildings) (Fig. 21), as well as the pioneering Albert Dock, are architectural reminders of Liverpool's previous role as a port (Lane 1999) and, relatedly, as a 'world city' in the nineteenth-century economy (Wilks-Heeg 2003).

Like many other governments and agencies engaged in place marketing

Fig. 21 'The Three Graces', Liverpool waterfront

projects, Liverpool City Council identified the waterfront (Marshall 2001) as 'the key image and gateway for the city [that offers an] opportunity to make a major public statement with a world class architectural statement of renewed city confidence' (Liverpool City Council 2004a).[4] In keeping with the hyperbole common in the early stages of large-scale architectural projects, the building was to provide both 'a focus and catalyst for the next stage of Liverpool's renaissance [and] an eloquent image for a resurgent city. The Fourth Grace will express Liverpool's 21st century aspirations as powerfully as the Three Graces articulate the civic and mercantile ambitions of a former age' (Liverpool Fourth Grace). Equally bold claims framed the project as an 'architectural signature that would be read by the world, a landmark that would become an eloquent symbol for Liverpool's renaissance' (Liverpool Vision 2003: 1).

Such hype is understandable given the aforementioned 'inflation' surrounding iconic buildings; pronouncements from the project leaders such as '[the Fourth Grace] must be iconic in style and represent an attraction in its own right' (Liverpool Fourth Grace) illustrate both the weight of expectation placed upon the project and also the concomitant 'talking up' of Liverpool as a resurgent 'world-class city' and European Capital of Culture (Jones and Wilks-Heeg 2004). Indeed, the Fourth Grace project proved crucial for the city's successful bid, with Mike Storey, the Leader of Liverpool City Council, situating it as 'one of the images that was key to the Capital of Culture bid. It symbolises the traditions of Liverpool and more than anything it represents the new Liverpool' (*Guardian* 2004c).[5] Aside from this contribution, other aims set out by the Fourth Grace Partnership (see below) for the development were to establish Liverpool as 'a premier European city' and to provide 'a recognised exemplar for design-led urban renaissance' (Liverpool Fourth Grace). Ultimately, the weight of expectation placed on the scheme by those rebranding Liverpool proved untenable, but the processes that led to the project's collapse reveal tensions inherent in situating iconic buildings at the heart of regeneration and rebranding strategies.

Participation, Consultation or Legitimation?

Given that those audiences who are the targets of icons – investors, middle-class tourists and shoppers – are a very conscribed 'public', contradictions abound between icons as 'transnational social spaces ... that could literally be almost anywhere in the world' (Sklair 2006: 22) and as place-markers that also connect convincingly with local residents' understandings of place/locality. The problem with positioning icons as reflections of localized identities is that it generates an 'arbitrary account of the social world that ignores the unacknowledged conditions of action as well as the many and varied emergent properties of action that go un- or mis-recognised by the relevant actors [and] ignores the many and varied struggles to transform the conditions of action' (Jessop and Oosterlynck 2007). Balancing such competing agendas, both in the discourses attached to the building and in its aesthetic, is a considerable challenge for those architects operating in the rarefied sub-field of practice. Anne-Marie Broudehoux argues that rebranding cities in this way is predicated on constructions of local identities that

> reduce several different visions of local culture into a single vision that reflects the aspirations of a powerful elite and the values, lifestyles, and expectations of potential investors and tourists. These practices are therefore highly elitist and exclusionary, and often signify to more disadvantaged segments of the population that they have no place in this revitalised and gentrified urban spectacle. (Broudehoux 2004: 26)

Struggles over the meanings associated with icons always exist, not least because these architectural discourses are always replete with tensions and contradictions (Jones 2006; 2009). In the case of the Fourth Grace, representativeness became a defining issue for the project; while regeneration practitioners are increasingly reflexive with regard to the participation of local communities, the promise of participation in regeneration to forge 'a "new" urban politics changing how citizens, including policy-makers, see themselves and others' (Jones 2006: 599) is tempered by the discrepancy between such participatory discourses and their operationalization (Atkinson 1999). So, while the Department for Culture, Media and Sport emphasizes 'community consultation and participation' as crucial in ensuring 'landmark cultural buildings achieve the right balance between maintaining cultural excellence and relevance to their local communities [as] innovation can be controversial and is often opposed by local communities' (DCMS 2004: 19–48), the proof of participation must be in the practice.

While the language of community participation is now ubiquitous in culture-led regeneration projects, it is not always clear what 'consultation' or 'community empowerment' actually mean in practice (Atkinson 1999). In the Fourth Grace project, there were major disjunctions between the participatory, democratic light in which the public consultation was framed and the way in which the decision was actually made. Many local cultural and media organizations felt that the public vote, far from empowering local people, made a clear statement about the true nature of community participation in the regeneration of the city.

Discourses of inclusion and community partnership/ownership were undermined by the public consultation exercise to help decide which of the four shortlisted development schemes should be awarded the Fourth Grace contract. The exhibition, held at Liverpool's Walker Art Gallery, showcased models and computer images of the proposed schemes, and included a public vote on which development should be chosen. Joe Dwyer, the then Chief Executive of Liverpool Vision (see below), who organized the vote, suggested that 'first and foremost the Pier Head and the waterfront belong to the people of Merseyside and that is why we want as many people as possible to come to the exhibition and tell us what they think' (*Liverpool Daily Post* 2002). People did: more than 15,000 local people visited the exhibition, over 9,000 of whom voted on their preferred design (*Liverpool Echo* 2002).

Despite polling fewest public votes (see Table 1), and amidst no small controversy, Will Alsop's scheme was chosen by Liverpool Vision to be the Fourth Grace (Fig. 22).[6] The success of Alsop's proposal led to accu-

Table 1. *Result of the public vote to help decide which of the four short-listed development schemes should be awarded the Fourth Grace contract*

Name of scheme	Architect	Percentage of public vote	Liverpool Vision's position
Ark	Norman Foster	29.5	'Included a huge amount of office space [that] could have meant a mammoth oversupply … would have dominated the skyline' (Henshaw, *Liverpool Echo*, 9 Dec. 2002)
Fourth Grace	Edward Cullinan	26.0	No public comment
Serpentine	Richard Rogers	26.0	'Not economically appropriate' (Henshaw, *Liverpool Echo*, 9 Dec. 2002)
The Cloud	Will Alsop	18.5	'Commercially viable' (Henshaw, *Liverpool Echo* 9 Dec. 2002); 'realistic option' in terms of size and scale (Liverpool City Council, 'Summary of Key Evidence – Fourth Grace', 2004)

sations that the public consultation was a legitimation exercise for a scheme that would have been selected regardless of the outcome of the public vote, the role of which was certainly ambiguous. Attempts to engender community participation in the scheme may well have been well intentioned but, in the context of a development funded primarily by the private sector, any decision-making power available to local citizens was to be highly conscribed. The coalition claimed legitimacy on the basis of empowering local populations in the decision-making process, and then effectively failing to do so created tensions between local communities and those running the project, raising Sklair's question 'iconic for whom?'.[7]

The tensions that can emerge when aesthetically radical architecture – designed primarily to attract the attention of external audiences – and a new building that is *perceived* by local citizens to reflect a meaningful sense of place are frequently at the fore in discussions over icons. I stress 'perceived' here, as any sense of an 'authentic' architecture should be problematized in light of the research that shows the contingent nature of the social meanings attached to the built environment (Bonta 1979). In this case, and even with financial concerns framing the inquiry into the project collapse (see below), the Cloud's aesthetic unpopularity within local public opinion was at the forefront of media and policy discussions alike.

Fig. 22. The Cloud, Will Alsop's design for Liverpool's Fourth Grace

The 'iconic urge' expresses a way in which the values of one rarefied part of the architectural field coincide with the interests and agendas of socially dominant urban actors and institutions. Drawing on earlier work by Weld Coxe and David Maister, Robert Gutman's typology of architectural firms positions ideal-type 'strong delivery firms' in contradistinction to 'strong ideas firms'. 'Strong delivery firms' tend towards an emphasis on functional buildings, which often express a close relationship to engineering technology, can be turned around quickly and are not primarily concerned with attracting the field's symbolic capital (such as prizes and favourable reviews in the architectural press). The ideal typical 'strong ideas firm' is based around a charismatic 'star' architect with a clear architectural 'signature'; these architects, who tend towards a strong stylistic code, are likely to position themselves as artists concerned with form-making rather than as technicians involved in engineering-led solutions (Gutman 1988: 50–59).[8]

For his own part, Will Alsop has been at the forefront of producing bombastic designs that embrace architecture's 'impact value', having 'self-consciously pursued the iconic building as a goal in itself' (Jencks 2004: 144). Alsop has an established record of designing publicity-winning buildings such as the Peckham Library (2000 Stirling Prize winner) (Fig. 23), a visually arresting structure that consolidated his reputation as a design maverick while delivering a socially engaged and commercially viable building. Regardless of the commercial or technical feasibility of schemes like the as-yet unrealized plans to make Barnsley a walled city or to develop a Northern English 'mega city' stretching the 125 miles from Liverpool to Hull, Alsop's projects typically embrace fully architecture's relation to place marketing and the generation of media interest. Robert Gutman's typology of architectural practices would position Alsop & Stormer – the firm responsible for the Cloud – as a 'strong ideas firm', which in its ideal-typical form is organized around a charismatic 'star' architect who adopts an aestheticized, artistic approach to architectural production (1988: 50–59). In the context of urban regeneration, those architects able to deliver an appropriate aesthetic response within a broader, economically driven development are internationally much in demand. Alsop's embrace of the iconic agenda can be understood as an opportunity to stress the artistic/aesthetic component of his architecture, through emphasizing drawing and the creation of distinctive form (reflecting this at the Fourth Grace competition stage, arguably Alsop's programme was more 'conceptual' than other shortlisted entries, which were more fully formed).

Fig. 23. Will Alsop's Peckham Library

Recalling Bourdieu's notion of autonomy, it is important to note that the aesthetic form any iconic building takes is not imposed on the architectural field in a determinist way; rather, iconic designs become part of the oeuvre of a particular group of architects consecrated not only by their own field but by the dominant from other fields. The notion of the 'field effect', namely the notion that fields exert force over those operating within them, is significant here as we can understand the emergence of a (relatively) coherent iconic style as a result of so-called starchitects being situated in a particular place within their field. In other words, an architect's 'production whether [s]he wants it or not ... always owes something to his [or her] position in this space' (Bourdieu 1988: 1). Those 'starchitects' whose fame resonates beyond the architectural field operate on the boundary between architecture – understood primarily as form making and the outcome of an aestheticized design process – and broader programmes of regeneration, place marketing and economic development.

In his book *The Global Architect: Firms, Fame, and Urban Form* (2009) Donald McNeill charts the intensification of elite architects' transnational practice in this regard, detailing the practice of the globally networked architectural firms that can run into thousands of employees and turn over hundreds of millions of pounds per annum. Such 'starchitects' are in themselves agents of the capitalist globalization they give material form to, with the media-savvy architectural firms ('brands') competing for major commissions, column inches and institutionalized capital in a parallel symbolic economy a significant part of the icon story (Sklair 2005: 487–88; McNeill 2005; 2009; Faulconbridge 2009) and the architectural field in general (Larson 1994; Gutman 1988; Lipstadt 2003). Those 'signature architects' with a strong stylistic code and a celebrity extending beyond the architectural field express a synergy with those high-profile building commissions bound up with place marketing, which have reinvigorated the profession for this elite band of starchitects.

The Fourth Grace was explicitly intended as a temporal and spatial reflection of a moment in Liverpool's regeneration trajectory, with the Cloud's forward-looking aesthetics explicitly designed to spatialize a moment in a city's (projected) transition and to resonate with the future-oriented discourses predominant in political debate (Sklair's 'iconic for when?'). An 'eloquent symbol for Liverpool's renaissance' (Liverpool Vision 2003: 1), the Cloud was to provide 'a focus and catalyst for the next stage of Liverpool's renaissance [and] an eloquent image for a resurgent city ... [and to] be iconic in style and represent an attraction in its own right' (Liverpool Fourth Grace).

Increasingly, those high-profile architects commissioned to deliver icons play a vital role in the 'talking up' associated with city rebranding (Sklair's 'iconic for where?'), and Will Alsop suggested his design would acknowledge

> the grandeur of the existing historic waterfront whilst at the same time creating a bold statement that looks to the future of the City ... The creation of a 21st century waterfront for Liverpool will indeed make the world stand up and take note. As an icon our building will always stretch the imagination and challenge preconceptions ... [and] contribute to a renaissance. (Alsop Architects 2002)

Such pronouncements illustrate the weight of expectation placed upon the project, but beyond place marketing the actual function of icons is often uncertain, as it was here. Iconic buildings often house art galleries, museums and concert halls – architecture that expresses an ambiguous notion of the 'public' limited to those consuming such urban spectacles. In the Fourth Grace this ambiguity was apparent, with allusions to middle-class consumption (Urry's 'tourist gaze') predominating. Given the decline of trade through Liverpool's docks Alsop felt that 'eating and living' were vital to the scheme. As iconic architecture commissioned for place marketing privileges the spectacular facade over function, buildings' users are considered primarily as those tourists and visitors consuming the architectural spectacle. Accordingly, an 'iconic building is about a silhouette, it's about what photographs well, not what it is like to use. The icon is the ultimate in media architecture' (*Observer* 2003c).

On this point, Graeme Evans has suggested that 'branding the city through cultural flagships and festivals has created a form of *Karaoke* architecture where it is not important how well you can sing, but that you do it with verve and gusto' (2003: 417). Many viewed the Cloud as exemplifying this strategy, with the building described variously as a 'deflated balloon', 'an abomination', 'an eyesore', a 'monstrosity', a 'cow pat' (*Liverpool Echo* 2002). While many questioned the aesthetic value of the winning design, David Dunster, Professor of Architecture at the University of Liverpool, suggested it is 'a common phenomenon for people to dislike modern architecture [...] the famous Guggenheim Museum in New York, the Eiffel Tower in Paris, and the Sydney Opera House were all universally condemned at the planning stage' (*Liverpool Echo* 2002).

What is considered 'good' or 'bad' architecture is interesting inasmuch as it reveals the learned nature of cultural taste and distinction (Stevens 1998). In this case, non-architect antipathy to the design was presented as an inevitable outcome of the Cloud's radical 'iconic' aesthetic. Jim Gill, then Liverpool Vision's Chief Executive Officer (CEO), suggested that the design 'was truly iconic and so produced a wide range of feeling' (Liverpool City Council 2004a), while Sir David Henshaw – then a Liverpool Vision board member as well as Council CEO – declared that as the architecture 'was truly iconic [it] produced a wide range of feeling' (Liverpool City Council 2004a). Architect Alsop echoed this point, suggesting that 'the instant response is negative because it challenges perception; it is the nature of the icon' (cited in Jencks 2004: 145). These responses reveal the tensions that can emerge when aesthetically radical architecture designed primarily to attract the attention of external media and a tourist audience are perceived to have been foisted onto city spaces in an undemocratic fashion. Leslie Sklair speaks of icons as 'transnational social spaces ... that could literally be almost anywhere in the world' (2006: 22), and points out that the extent to which such spaces can also connect meaningfully – in aesthetic or broader identity terms – to local visions of place is often a source of struggle around new projects (his 'iconic for whom?').

Formally, Alsop's design entailed three main elements: 'the Cloud' (the iconic component of the development, which was to be supported by stilts and clad in a range of eye-catching, bright and reflective materials), 'the Hill' (the space underneath the Cloud that was to afford access to the Museum of Liverpool and provide shelter for some of its exhibits)[9] and two seventeen-storey residential buildings. The Cloud, then, was a three-tier building made up of 'some' office space, a 107-room hotel and 50,000 square feet of unspecified 'community facilities' (Alsop Architects 2002). The Cloud was a quintessential Alsop design, what critic Charles Jencks has referred to as 'Blob Architecture' (2003; 2007) – formless and relatively undefined shapes, which in the case of the Cloud resembled 'a squashed donut on stilts', according to Alsop, who presented his aesthetically radical, ahistorical building as in keeping with Liverpool's social history:

> From its earliest days Liverpool has attracted people with an appetite for the new and the different – people with the courage to travel and explore: risk-takers, pioneers and investors. Only a genuinely daring and distinctive design will succeed in revivifying the spirit of Liverpool and capturing the imagination and attention of an international audience. (*Guardian* 2002b)

In an attempt to link the ahistorical and transnational aesthetic of the architecture to place, the building was to be decorated with hieroglyphics depicting Liverpool's 800-year history.

A Contested Partnership: Whose Building, Whose 'Brand'?

Given these issues about symbolic ownership of the building, it is instructive to map the agencies responsible for the funding and delivery of the Fourth Grace, and to chart the struggles within this coalition. The partnership's constitution reveals much about the ambiguous and frequently unstable relationships between the agencies responsible for the rebranding and regeneration of cities. The Department for Culture, Media and Sport concludes that 'strong leadership has been the key to driving through cultural innovation' (DCMS 2004: 6), but ultimately such leadership was lacking in the Fourth Grace project, where a 'strong lead was needed as the project required active management in view of its inherent difficulties and risks' (Liverpool City Council 2004a). In fact, discord *within* the regeneration coalition crystallized around the Cloud.

Liverpool's waterfront was initially identified as a suitable site for the Fourth Grace in the *Liverpool City Centre Strategic Regeneration Framework*, an influential document authored by Liverpool Vision, the country's first 'Urban Regeneration Company', whose self-defined role is to 'harness the entrepreneurial energies of the private sector and co-ordinate the activities and interventions of public partners ... Liverpool Vision is the custodian of the "big picture", and the guarantor of a focused and integrated approach that will deliver benefits and opportunities to all the communities of Merseyside' (Liverpool Vision 2003: 5). Liverpool Vision drew together a 'Fourth Grace Forum', a partnership between themselves, Liverpool City Council, Liverpool Culture Company Limited (leaders of the city's Capital of Culture bid), the Northwest Regional Development Agency and the two owners of the site: National Museums and Galleries on Merseyside and the Robert Smith Group (car dealers and management company). Liverpool Vision explained the partnership thus:

> Liverpool Vision identified the concept [for the Fourth Grace] ... promoted the opportunity, facilitated site assembly and we helped bring the Partnership together. We also acted as the facilitator for the various Steering, working and Project Group arrangements. Liverpool City Council's role was in respect of its interest in the regeneration of the City Centre and as planning authority. The Development Agency was a landowner and funding partner, the National Museums was a landowner and a potential occupier. (Liverpool City Council 2004a)

The last decade has seen Liverpool City Council belatedly move into line with many other local governments and embrace entrepreneurial regeneration strategies predicated on aggressive place marketing, with inward investment channelled through a range of public/private partnerships (Jones and Wilks-Heeg 2004).

The complicated cocktail of funding was central to many struggles. Given the public funding shortfall, private sector investment was always crucial to the success of the project. Significantly, Alsop's design required the lowest amount of public grant (*Liverpool Echo* 2002), which was to come from a £900 million, seven-year Objective One programme for regeneration on Merseyside. Sixty-five million pounds of this funding had been ring-fenced specifically for the development of the waterfront. The Fourth Grace Partnership had initially bid for £43 million of the grant towards the Cloud's estimated cost of £228 million (made at the design stage in July 2003). The developers originally put forward public fund estimates of £50 million, costs that, according to Liverpool Vision, had risen to £73 million when the project was eventually pulled (Liverpool City Council 2004a). However, in common with most architecture projects of this scale, the costs of the Cloud increased significantly from the proof of concept stage. Projected costs had risen to £324 million when the decision to drop the project was taken almost exactly one year later; this was alongside the increase of values of the project from £127 million to £155 million, leaving an overall funding shortfall (Liverpool City Council 2004a).

Henshaw, a Liverpool Vision board member as well as the council's CEO, said Norman Foster's Ark, although receiving most public votes, was not viable because it 'included a huge amount of office space [that] could have meant a mammoth oversupply or could have stripped office use out of other parts of the city' (*Liverpool Echo* 2002). However, given that insufficient public sector funding existed to build the Cloud,[10] the private sector's input was always crucial. Given the rising costs of the scheme, Neptune Developments and Countryside – the private development company responsible for the Cloud contract – needed to increase the profitable element of the development; the chosen vehicle for this was through three extra residential blocks. But, increasing the development's residential blocks ran counter to the original justifications for the choice of Alsop's design, namely that the residential – and office – space was a relatively small component of the overall plans (Fig. 24). In fact, Alsop had already been forced to decrease the size of the two *original* residential towers for planning reasons associated with the designation of the waterfront as a World Heritage Site. This was quite aside from the fact that the redesign of the residential building would have shrunk the overall size of the Cloud by 15 per cent, reducing the allocation of public space relative to the space used by the private sector (*Liverpool Echo* 2004). Crucially also, significant alteration to the scale or design of a scheme means being 'called-in' for investigation by the Office of the Deputy Prime Minister, which in this case would have created a two-year delay, thus jeopardizing the vital £65 million of Objective One funding for the waterfront. While the coalition driving the project claimed the Cloud was an appropriate symbol of a modernizing, regenerated city, such iconic architecture is by definition not 'in harmony with' with historic surroundings such as those at Liverpool's waterfront. CABE identified the Cloud's impact on the sightlines of the existing Three Graces as prob-

Fig. 24. Residential and office space in Will Alsop's design for
Liverpool's Fourth Grace

lematic in February 2003, but the issue was not addressed at the crucial
Proof of Concept stage, and the inquiry found a failure to resolve this
issues as 'a fundamental flaw in assessing the deliverability of the scheme'
(*Liverpool Daily Post* 2004c).

This contradiction eventually proved untenable. Liverpool Vision
highlighted the 'massive increase in the residential element of the scheme
– doubling the original number of apartments envisaged to 700, including
the challenging prospect of 200 apartments in the historic Canning Dock
area' (Liverpool Vision 2004) when explaining their decision to drop the
project. However, this was entirely predictable, given the profit-motive
of the private sector developers. In fact, these concerns had led to suggestions that the building would not go ahead as early as 2002; Dennis Brant,
chairman of the Fourth Grace Project Group, said that they knew 'very
early on' that it would be very difficult if not impossible to gain planning
permission for the residential component of the design. When asked why
the competition was allowed to proceed in this restricted planning
context, Jim Gill, Liverpool Vision's then Chief Executive, said 'at that
stage all the designs could be scaled down' (*Liverpool Echo* 2004). This
not only neglects the delicate balancing act between public and private
interests but overlooks altogether the huge risks associated with changing
initial plans, not least being 'called in' by the Office of the Deputy Prime
Minister.

Throughout these negotiations the council – publicly at least – framed the private sector as 'guarantors' who would 'insulate the public sector from some of the development risks'; the public sector was to 'support the quality "iconic" status' (Liverpool City Council 2004a). Arguably, viewing private sector investors as beneficent 'guarantors' neglects the pervasive logic of the capitalist market; such value-neutral constructions of the private sector were evident in the public sector's surprise at the developer's attempt to increase the profitable component of the project. Henshaw later acknowledged he 'would have liked to create a more formal joint partnership' (*Liverpool Echo* 2004), and he feared the scheme being dominated by the private sector with 'the nightmare scenario that the Cloud would became a residential tower block, a private building that we put X million of pounds of public money into' (*Liverpool Echo* 2004).[11]

The manner in which the decision to abandon the Fourth Grace project was made illustrates these concerns about the workings of the coalition. Somewhat ironically, given the city council's fears that the private sector was assuming control of the project (Henshaw, in *Liverpool Echo* 2004), it was actually Liverpool Vision that ultimately exercised decision-making power. The panel that made the decision included Gill (then Chief Executive of Liverpool Vision), Henshaw (the Chief Executive of Liverpool City Council and also a Liverpool Vision board member) and Council Leader Mike Storey, who were roundly criticized for making the announcement to the media before the Fourth Grace consortium had had the chance to argue their case and even before the architect had been informed of the decision.

The Cloud's architect, Will Alsop, learnt of the decision through the media and felt that the city council, and specifically its Chief Executive, had 'overrun local, regional and central government because he was afraid that people don't like the design' (*Guardian* 2004d). Similarly, in an open letter to Deputy Prime Minister John Prescott announcing his resignation from the board of Liverpool Vision, Labour Councillor Joe Anderson said 'Liverpool City Council exerts power and influence that means the regeneration company [Liverpool Vision] acts in the interests of Liverpool City Council, not in the interests of Liverpool or its citizens' (*Liverpool Daily Post* 2004c). Regardless of apportioning blame, we are left to reflect on a case where the overwhelming desire for an icon obscured the question of the true purpose of the building (other than a brand). The distinction between architecture and private-sector-led regeneration in the project was never clear, a common problem when iconic buildings lacking a clearly defined function are used as a place marketing brand.

Conclusion

Architecture's capacity to provide a material, socially resonant representation of economic and political change has left iconic architecture in an interesting but uncertain position in regard to materializing those urban developments designed to facilitate the extraction of surplus value from city spaces. These twin imperatives bring with them a challenging social terrain for those high-profile architects whose own celebrity and reputation add weight to the symbolic and material (re)construction of cities. As a result, architectural icons not only express much about the political economy of regeneration and – of central interest in this chapter – between the architectural field and a particular project of urban renewal[12] but also further reinforce the distinction between restricted and mass parts of the field (Stevens 1998). These 'icons' are not the work of the vast majority of architects, but are the product of a subfield of people whose work is positioned by them as symbolic and aesthetic rather than functional and technical.

Although regeneration practitioners have recently displayed enthusiasm for iconic architecture, it is clear that when imposed on communities without a mandate, the aim of developing forms to attract a tourist audience becomes difficult to justify, making these spectacular buildings a focus for local communities to voice their discontents about the regeneration process more generally. The quest for participation (or, from a less generous reading, legitimation) leads the coalitions responsible for such buildings to seek to engage local communities, but the inescapable realities of what are, to all intents and purposes, economically motivated developments constrain the decision-making power available to local residents. In the case of the Fourth Grace this tension led to the language of community participation looking like empty rhetoric or, worse still, an attempt to legitimate the decisions of the locally powerful groups driving these projects. Accordingly, disjuncture between how cities are branded and the social realities of the local population are often expressed through contestation centring on major architectural projects. It is significant to note that when incorporated into attempts to attract inward investment such iconic buildings have come to symbolize a whole range of tensions centred on efforts to position cities relative to external audiences; indeed, such building projects frequently provide a focus for a wide range of otherwise abstract and disparate struggles about the regeneration projects, of which they are a material reflection.

Notes

1 Gehry has said that the commissioning Bilbao government asked for a 'hit' comparable to the Sydney Opera House (Jencks 2004: 12), and this embrace of architecture's impact value has characterized a great deal of the recent practice of contemporary high-profile architects. Subsequent to the perceived success of the Guggenheim, Gehry has said he gets requests from clients to 'do a Gehry building' (Jencks 2004: 12).

2 Braunfels (1988: 309) suggests that, historically, 'France more than any other country regarded its capital as a monument to its greatness, to the state, and to the level of its culture'.

3 As Roy Coleman pointed out to me, lighting building facades further compounds this notion of architectural spectacle as visually consumable by directing gazes towards officially sanctioned 'sites of interest' and – crucially – away from spaces not in keeping with rebranded visions of the city.

4 Given the desire for an icon to supplement the existing waterfront architecture, it is interesting to note that the Deputy Chair of CABE, Paul Finch, suggested that the Three Graces 'weren't built to be seen as icons for the city, they were no more than middle-of-the-road office buildings, it was only later that they came to mean something else' (*Observer* 2003c).

5 The Fourth Grace was not actually due to be completed until 2009, with council executives suggesting this demonstrated Liverpool's plans for sustainable regeneration beyond the Capital of Culture year (2008).

6 Another poll, conducted by the Liverpool Architecture and Design Trust on their website, also placed Alsop's design in last place with 10 per cent of an open public vote.

7 The public inquiry into the subsequent collapse of the project confirmed this, with Alsop's Cloud found to be the only 'realistic option' in terms of size and scale; the worldwide competition to design a new icon for Liverpool had yielded one realizable bid (Liverpool City Council 2004b).

8 This distinction expresses something of the architectural field's 'unresolved contradictions' (Crawford 1994), revealing a tension between architecture as aestheticized programme and as important components of the 'hard' political economy of development (Ghirardo 1994).

9 A development containing a single-function Museum of Liverpool, restaurants, shops, 376 apartments and 13,000 square metres of office space is to open in 2011 (*Building Design* 2006).

10 National Museums Liverpool, whose Museum of Liverpool Life was to be a part of the Fourth Grace, had not yet secured capital funding. A bid was to be submitted to the Heritage Lottery Fund, or revenue funding, an application for which was to be sent to the Department for Culture, Media and Sport for when construction was due to start (*Liverpool Daily Post* 2004a).

11 In actual fact the pre-development costs were borne by the private sector alone, with Neptune instigating legal action to recover the roughly £4 million costs incurred (*Liverpool Echo* 2004), while the only cost for the public sector was the time of Henshaw and his colleagues (Liverpool City Council 2004a)

12 An interesting question – drawing on Bonta's (1979) work on the social construction of architecture's social meanings – concerns subsequent readings and

understandings of these buildings. In the case of the Fourth Grace, though, we are left to reflect on a never to be realized project that revealed much of the speculative and uncertain nature of one of the key planks of recent urban regeneration in the UK.

7

'European' Architecture:
Politics in Search of Form and Meaning

> In a living state organism, people are always trying to reinterpret
> political symbolism.
>
> Wolfgang Braunfels, *Urban Design in Western Europe:*
> *Regime and Architecture, 900–1900* (1988), 321.

Introduction

It has been argued in previous chapters that states' strategies to foster
belonging among their citizens have led to the built environment being
mobilized in a variety of ways in differing political contexts. The focus
of this chapter is on two distinct but related developments in contemporary Europe: first, the European Union's attempts to embed their political
project in cultural forms from architecture and the built environment
(discussed with reference to the Brussels Capital of Europe project), and
second, coexistent projects in member nation states to reposition and
'Europeanize' existing national architectural symbols (illustrated with
reference to Norman Foster's reconstruction of the Reichstag in Berlin).
An overarching concern of the chapter is to develop an understanding of
the role of architects in the cultural construction of what can broadly be
understood as 'transnational' European political projects. As such, the
focal point is not so much the emergence or otherwise of a distinctly
European style of architecture, but rather the extent to which the ongoing
work of high-profile architects to embed the 'imagined community'
(Anderson 1983) of Europe into socially meaningful forms reveals something about the wider politics of architecture in the contemporary
European context.

After a brief contextualization of EU cultural politics, the first substantive discussion in the chapter addresses the EU's Brussels, Capital of
Europe project, which drew together a number of high-profile European
cultural commentators – including the leading architects Rem Koolhaas
and Jean Nouvel – to suggest a range of interventions both in Brussels'

built environment and in the EU's 'branding' more generally in order better to reflect the institution's 'European' values. The spatial and architectural projects that emerged from the project meetings and the subsequently published report (European Commission 2001) are explicit engagements with the cultural form that political Europeanization, a highly contested project in search of democratic legitimacy and popular support, should take. As a result, the Brussels Capital of Europe project reveals a number of the tensions associated with both the political mobilization of architects and, more broadly, the ambiguous relationship between architectural form and social meaning.

Distinct but related from the EU's attempts to develop socially meaningful architectural symbols, state-led renegotiations of national cultural histories have seen some *existing* landmark buildings reoriented to within a more Europeanized, less nationalized frame. The potential for states to 're-narrate their nations' (McNeill and Tewdwr-Jones 2003: 738) via major architectural projects has seen the built environment becoming the site of much activity in this regard. Some EU member states and, indeed, aspirant member states, have commissioned high-profile architects to assist in 're-narration' away from the nationalized discourses emphasizing the particularism of a particular people, national culture or political regime and towards less particularistic, ostensibly more 'open' cosmopolitan Europeanized discourses (Jones 2007). The Reichstag, the German capitol in Berlin, expresses much of the ambiguity associated with such 're-narration': the cultural and political discourses into which the redesign of the home of the German parliament has been inserted reflects a conscious distance from the devices of the nationalized architectural forms and meanings of the nineteenth century. Norman Foster's self-defined 'critical reconstruction' (2000) of the building to mark the return of the German parliament to Berlin in 1999 was explicitly designed to embrace and materialize Germany's central role in a 'new' Europe. In part owing to the Europeanized discourse into which the architect sought to position the reconstruction of the Reichstag – a building with a turbulent and contested history – sociologically interesting tensions between national pasts and futures, and between form and meaning, centred on the building's reconstruction.

Constructing European Culture

Ever since the *Declaration of European Identity* (signed by the then nine member states in 1973)[1] the EU has been very active in attempting to shape a European identity through culture – seeking to codify an official European identity through culture. The overarching aims of this disparate project have been, first, to define the political structure of the Union in relation to the cultures of citizens of member states, and second, to reflect the connections between the EU and the rest of the world (Delanty and Jones 2002: 460–62). In the process of such attempts, definitions of an official identity have included a wide repertoire of symbols, including (but not limited to) an EU Flag, an official anthem (Beethoven's 'Ode to Joy'), the euro currency, EU passports, twinning arrangements, a range of sporting events and the European City/Capital of Culture award. Such forms and events have been developed in part in the hope that some recognition of a common European culture will take root in the popular collective imaginary and practices, thus providing the EU with at least a minimal European cultural identity that would go some way to legitimating their political project.

There is a considerable body of scholarship focusing attention on the politicized nature of these elite constructions of European boundaries. Generally speaking, a central concern of research in this area has been to question the extent to which these emergent cultural symbols of the European Union identity project can be defined in a way that avoids the ethnocentric, elitist and nation-centric/territorial assumptions that characterized the development of state-led cultural identities for hundreds of years, while retaining meaning and resonance within the lifeworlds of the diverse range of citizens that constitute European societies (for more discussion, see Delanty 1995; Roche 2001; 2002; 2009; Stråth 2002; 2008; Amin 2004; Delanty and Rumford 2005). It is fair to say that, in general terms, scepticism abounds about the extent to which contemporary EU-led European identity projects can ever be anything more than disengaged political construction, detached from citizens' collective belonging and lacking popular resonance or legitimacy.

Cris Shore's *Building Europe: The Cultural Politics of European Integration* (2002) is a definitive contribution in this tradition. Assessing the 'politics of elite-formation and the question of whether the EU has developed within its own institutions the embryo of a European identity and consciousness ... for diffusing the European ideal among the population at large' (Shore 2000: 206), Shore interrogates the politicized images associated with the emergence and maintenance the EU. Drawing attention to the ultimately contested nature of the cultural construction of European collective identity, Shore's work encourages a critical approach to both the development of symbols of Europe and the related claims of the EU to represent a meaningful social project. Shore is highly sceptical about any potential to forge a European identity through cultural policies; he has observed that 'The European Commission has invented a new repertoire of "post-nationalist" symbols, but these are pale imitations of nationalist iconography and have so far failed to win for the EU the title deeds upon which national loyalties and allegiances are claimed' (2000: 222). Ironically, it is the persistence of the national cultural identities actively constructed under the auspices of states over the last few centuries – themselves more often than not the outcome of elite-driven political projects (see, for example, Gellner 1983) – that has provided the EU with something of an intractable obstacle on their path to develop European modes of belonging. In an attempt to overcome this tension, the EU initially aimed to contribute to the development of members' existing *national cultures* while at the same time 'bringing the common cultural heritage to the fore' (Maastricht Treaty Article 151 (ex Article 128)) as part of its identity project. EU cultural policy has sought to develop the 'common cultural heritage' embedded in national cultural discourses and practices with reference to the ambiguous theme of *unity in diversity* (Delanty and Jones 2002). The capacity of the EU convincingly to incorporate national and regional cultural diversities into its own cultural discourse has been a crucial issue for the maintenance and legitimation of the political project more generally; in general it can be observed that the EU is in the ambiguous position of attempting to define a European cultural identity that is not so universal as to be meaningless and not so particularistic to be exclusionary, and against the complicating backdrop of entrenched, widely practised 'banal nationalisms' (Billig 1995).

As Shore's argument forcefully demonstrates, the Commission's reliance on culture is an illustration of a mistaken understanding about culture and collective identity. Using aspects of the cultural sphere – such as language, religion and history – in an attempt to unite cultural communities is doomed to failure as these are the very cultural practices that most divide Europeans today; recalling Bourdieu, the notion that the cultural sphere is one that tends towards consensus and agreement must be jettisoned. Rather, from his point of view, culture is a sphere of practice that creates and sustains social divisions. Instead of focusing on semiotic analysis of the symbols emerging from the European project (see Sayer 2001; Jessop 2004 for a critique of this tendency), pertinent sociological questions centre on the capacity of institutional political actors to embed a vision of a cultural community – regardless of the diversity of the discourse – without meaningful connection to the social practices and lifeworlds of citizens. These various EU-led attempts at the development of a cultural form are also reminiscent of Michael Billig's argument concerning '"flagging" as a continual background for political discourses' (1995: 8–9).

It is against this backdrop that the EU is increasingly concerned with what has become known as 'cultural policy' (Roche 2001), those 'symbolic initiatives' (Sassatelli 2002: 435) that seek to foster some sense of European identity. One example of this is to be found in the design of the euro banknotes, which have gained attention elsewhere (Shore 2000; Delanty and Jones 2002). These notes provide a clear example of how the EU has attempted to incorporate a degree of Europeanization into existing national cultural imageries and established Billig's 'banal' everyday practices. The seven different euro notes all use ahistorical, placeless representations of architecture and the built environment, including bridges, doorways, arches and so on, reflecting generalized architectural styles associated with periods of European cultural history.[2] These designs suggest symbols of 'openness', 'access' and 'transparency'; removed from particularistic national contexts, these vague resonances of European cultural history are interesting, especially in view of the fact that the euro coinage – unlike the notes – retains an identifiable national icon on one side.

To a similar end, the EU has also developed the European Capital of Culture (ECC) project (originally entitled European City of Culture) to foster 'Europeanness' in the cultural sphere. In 1983, Melina Mercouri, the then Greek Minister for Culture, envisaged the development of an award as an opportunity to express the various nationalized versions of a more universal European high culture; given this, the initial awards of the title to Athens (1985), Florence (1986), Amsterdam (1987), what was then still West Berlin (1988) and Paris (1990) were somewhat predictable from the point of view that all of these cities were sites of objectified 'European' high cultural capital. Monica Sassatelli has described the ECC project as a 'salient example of the attempts at awakening a European consciousness by diffusing its symbols, while respecting the contents of national and local cultures' (2002: 436). The ECC is thus also indicative of a broader shift away from national cultural identities and towards European and – just as crucially – local and regional identities.[3]

Architecture and Europe: The Search for a Spatial Form

What is the place of architecture and the built environment in such 'official' constructions of European identity? Given the established pattern of the commission and mobilization of architects and architecture by polities seeking to forge links with a public, it is unsurprising that the EU has used the built environment as part of the repertoire of symbols designed to legitimate its political project. Lawrence Vale has noted the 'curious, even bewildering disjuncture between the monumentality of most new national assembly complexes ... and the fledgling democracies they ostensibly signify' (1992: 51). In the case of the EU though, its cultural project has by and large been characterized by an aversion to bombast; this still-fledgling polity has trod carefully relative to the cultural symbols – including architecture – it has commissioned and disseminated. Nonetheless, the reflexive approach to questions of collective identity and its politicization has opened up some interesting sociological issues regarding the role of architects in socializing this contested polity.

Indeed, architecture and space have been significant in the wider repertoire of the EU's 'Europeanized' cultural forms. The EU commissioned the Brussels, Capital of Europe project to contribute to this element of symbolic construction; the published report was organized around a series of 'dialogues' between prominent European figures that were intended to reflect critically on existing EU cultural constructions and to project new possibilities for suitably representative and engaging European cultural forms. Of particular interest in the present context was the EU's vision of the report as facilitating effective communication 'through the physical substance and buildings of European institutions' (European Commission 2001: 13); this component of the report was organized around a discussion between the architects Rem Koolhaas, the leading but highly controversial Dutch architect, and Jean Nouvel, the high-profile French designer.

Introducing his discussion of Koolhaas, Donald McNeill (2009: 98–113) recounts the architect reflecting that at one point international CNN seemed to him like a 'private bulletin board', as he felt so personally bound up in the major global social and political stories of the day. Certainly, through his firm Office of Metropolitan Architects (OMA) and his own high profile, Koolhaas is a globally active figure, with current and recent projects including major buildings in Berlin, the Arab Emirates, Las Vegas and Beijing. In the course of these projects – many of them politically highly contested – Koolhaas has engaged directly with both the branding function of contemporary architecture and its critical function (Fraser 2005). He has provocatively suggested that '[t]oday's architecture is subservient to the market and its terms. The market has supplanted ideology. Architecture has turned into a spectacle. It has to package itself and no longer has significance as anything but a landmark' (Koolhaas 2006) (Fig. 25).

Fig. 25. Exterior of Rem Koolhaas's Seattle Public Library

Koolhaas came relatively late to architectural practice[4] and, in common with Daniel Libeskind, initially made his mark on the field with some widely influential theory, most notably the deconstructive urban design manifesto *S, M, L, XL*. First published by Monacelli Press in 1995, the book has become a much-cited contribution outside of architecture and urban design. As was observed in the early chapters of the present book, it is precisely, but counter-intuitively, architects' claim to critical autonomous practice that gives the architectural field its capacity to generate symbolic capital for corporate and state commissioners. Kim Dovey has shown how in this way 'autonomous formalism is a required condition for the production and renewal of symbolic capital in [the capitalist] field' (2009: 49).[5] He illustrates this argument with reference to the incorporation of the 'radical' work of Rem Koolhaas into corporate markets, observing that 'the success of the work of Rem Koolhaas and his firm OMA rests strongly on the implicit or explicit claim to be an architecture of emancipation' (2009: 103).[6] Koolhaas has embraced the impact value of architecture, and has taken highly contentious commissions – such as the state Television Cultural Center (TVCC) building in Beijing and a number of retail developments – while at the same time defending the spaces within such projects that engage in forms of discursive and spatial radicalism. Koolhaas's ambivalent approach is characterized as 'post-critical' by Murray Fraser, who suggests the architect can be seen as experimenting with the application of insights and critiques from cultural studies into architectural practice (2005: 318). Still, embracing the branding component of the job, Koolhaas hints at how the global capitalist context has shaped the aesthetic form of architecture when noting 'The idolatry of the market has drastically changed our [architects'] legitimacy and status even though our status has never been higher … It is really unbelievable what the market demands [from architecture] now. It demands recognition, it demands difference and it demands iconographic qualities' (Koolhaas, cited in Jencks 2004: 101).[7]

Despite his tendency towards hyperbole, Koolhaas's engagement with the contingencies and complicities of architectural production in the context of global capitalist conditions of action means that some of his projects (such as TVCC in Beijing, the EuroLille station, the Dutch Embassy in Berlin, commissions for Prada, his celebration of Lagos street markets – viewed from a helicopter – as part of the architect's role at Harvard Design School, forcefully critiqued by Matthew Gandy (2005)) remind us that the social engagements and pronouncements of globally mobile architects are often contingent on highly partial social connections and represent much of their elite cultural and economic position. Against this backdrop, serious questions relate to whether or not Koolhaas is simply aestheticizing the political regimes and capitalist corporations that commission him, including the incorporation of a pseudo-resistant, aestheticized radicalism and critique. In her thought-provoking work on the ethics of architecture, Suzanne MacLeod (2011) has sought to question the wider contexts that give rise to architecture – including the sustainability of the built objects that emerge from the field, the uses to which they are put and the extent to which they connect with local practices – and certainly situating the work of Koolhaas against this backdrop gives rise to some fundamental questions.[8]

Jean Nouvel is a similarly high-profile architect, whose work has gained the institutional capitals of the field but whose impact resonates beyond it. Like Koolhaas, Nouvel is a Pritzker Prize winner, with his designs (among others) for the Institut du Monde Arabe (IMA), or Arab World Institute, in Paris, the Torre Agbar in Barcelona and the soon-to-be completed Philharmonie de Paris and DR Koncerthuset or Copenhagen Concert Hall garnering attention from global mass media beyond the architectural press. Another architect who holds positions himself and his practice as harbouring some potential for social change (he has spoken on the 'ethics of architecture' (Baudrillard and Nouvel 2002)), the Brussels Capital of Europe project gave an opportunity for Nouvel to connect some of these wider discourses to tangible practice.

Charles Jencks (1980) offers the suggestion that the most effective type of architecture for symbolizing diversity is that in which the meanings are to some extent left open, giving buildings the ability to represent plural identities. This strategy offers an interesting counterpoint to that employed by Koolhaas and Nouvel, the architects responsible for the EU's Brussels, Capital of Europe project. Both architects suggested the development of a new 'Europeanized' aesthetic and sought to ascribe meanings to these forms. Koolhaas explained his work on the Brussels Capital of Europe project thus:

> [The] iconographic message about Europe needs to be reinforced and modernized, becoming less reticent. We live in an era of branding and in a certain sense it is admirable that there has been no branding of the European Union: this has helped to maintain a greater authenticity. On the other hand it is also sad because it leaves an important message misunderstood and ignored. (European Commission 2001: 21)

It is difficult to imagine such an explicit and reflexive dialogue about the cultural construction of earlier state-led national identities, but although Koolhaas was explicit about the aims of the project – 'we tried to make the EU's political message clearer, more attractive and easier to communicate' (*Der Spiegel* 2007) – the ostensible openness and reflexivity must be understood in the context of a polity in search of a legitimation.

In this project, Koolhaas emphasized openness and mobility as 'soft' options (European Commission 2001: 19) and suggested that such aspirations must be allied to what he describes as a 'hard' option, involving urban planning, the development of new buildings and monuments. However, and in line with Umberto Eco's favoured 'soft' option, which was organized less around a material transformation of Brussels' spaces and more around a transformation of the cultural symbols associated with the EU, Koolhaas proposed a new design for the EU flag. Resembling a brightly coloured barcode,[9] Koolhaas suggested that the new design better represented the diversity inherent in the member states and that the existing cultural representation of the European Union 'as one entity is often flat and without eloquence. It is possible to represent both the diversity and unity of Europe in a more attractive way' (European Commission 2001: 13). In his response to tabloid indignation in Britain, Koolhaas suggested that outrage reflected a loyalty to the old flag, which symbolized everything that Britons 'loved to hate' (de Graaf and Koolhaas 2004: 385), with this amusing and engaging provocation raising questions about the European project both in the context of more entrenched national identities and as a trading bloc. Koolhaas suggested that the lack of entrenched and established constructions of Europe were beneficial in this regard, arguing that 'we should be happy that we haven't had similar artificial constructs in Europe and no European chauvinist indoctrination has taken place' (European Commission 2001: 20). However, given the ethnocentricism that underpins many of the EU's cultural representations and self-conception, such as those from former President Romani Prodi (European Commission 2001), frequently bound up with attempts to align Europe to a Christian heritage, then the extent to which 'Europe' itself is an empty signifier is arguable.

Beyond this, though, such an aestheticization of politics is also evident in the report, which offers a reminder of the capacity of polities to absorb dissent and critical voices into the cultural components of their wider projects (what Bourdieu refers to as an 'aestheticism of transgression' (in Wacquant 1989)). Of particular interest in this regard were the attempts within the Brussels Capital of Europe project to incorporate dissent about the democratic deficit within the EU's political structure. The publication was replete with a range of images of protests and other forms of direct political action. The EU's response to the (perceived) need for an identity-building project is that the collective identity they have attempted to construct is paradoxically apolitical, in the sense that it avoids political conflict and stresses harmony with other collectives. Even the images of protest, featuring prominent EU buildings in the background, while alluding to the desirability for a vibrant civil society or a conception of Europe based on protest (Imig and Tarrow 2001), reflect a highly aestheticized vision of the political sphere and reveal something about the self-construction of an emergent political institution in search of a cultural community.

As well as images of architecture, the built environment also played a central role in some of the suggestions that emerged from the project. While Eco noted that 'constructing impressive buildings as symbols could be sending the wrong signal … international institutions start their decline at the very moment they make their definitive building' (Umberto Eco in European Commission 2001), Koolhaas suggested another strategy:

> Another way of communicating the European Institutions in Brussels is through its buildings. The European Union has asked for an enormous amount of buildings in the last 20 years. But this demand was expressed without influencing the choice of architecture or the meaning of those buildings. One would expect that the buildings in which the European Institutions are represented reflect the best ability and the highest quality. This is not the case. Brussels today is a European capital by default, a curious aesthetic landscape, sometimes generic and sometimes of such a scale that you can only talk about megalomania. In this condition it is unable to articulate any idea about Europe. (European Commission 2001: 13–14)

Here a focus on the aesthetics and meaning of architectural form as a replacement for engagement with EU (or Brussels)[10] politics is allied by the essentialism implied by ascribing values such as 'megalomania' to particular architectural styles (again, see Bonta 1979 for a problematization of this tendency). The use of architecture in the Brussels Capital of Europe project is what Manuel Castells would refer to as a 'legitimizing identity project' (1997), one where the appropriation of European cultural history and spatiality is mobilized by a political institution, in search of legitimacy, to serve an ideological end. Castells argues that much of contemporary architecture represents an 'end of meaning' in which any meaningful relationship of society to architecture has been obscured (1997: 418–28). Fundamentally, the Brussels Capital of Europe project returns us to the conclusion that challenging the existing aesthetic forms of the EU will not in itself challenge the existing democratic deficit.

The Reichstag: Designing a Post-National Discourse

While a Europeanized cultural agenda has primarily been driven by the EU, the mobilization of transnational cultural forms and discourses has also been taken up enthusiastically by some European member states. However, any such relationship between claims made for national cultures and European cultures is beset with tensions, especially when taking place in the context of a major state-led project; the entrenched nature of forms of national cultural belonging mean any such construction risks appearing as a political imposition, disconnected from the more established sets of signs and symbols associated with national identities.

Attempts to situate architecture in a post-national context are evident in a number of high-profile buildings that are situated within European frames of meaning. As some states seek to align themselves with less nationally bounded, more 'European' cultural and political motifs, what roles can architects and major state-led architectural projects play? Norman Foster's extension to the Reichstag is one of most symbolically significant architectural projects to have been built in the German capital since 1945, and reveals much of the ambiguity of EU member states appropriating or adopting more Europeanized, less nationalized, cultural forms. Baker suggests that on this particular building 'every stone, every wall, and every window has a story that is not just a matter of architecture but also a clue to who the Germans are, who they have been, and how they see themselves in the future' (2000: 192).

Certainly, Berlin's history is a complex and contested one, and its retelling was a major symbolic and material feature of the reconstruction of the Reichstag.[11] The claims made on behalf of the Reichstag as a literal redesigning of the state must be approached cautiously, especially in light of earlier discussions about anti-essentialism. As much as the outward appearance, or the architectural form that the building takes, the remarkable history of the Reichstag building is central to understanding its key role for recent reconstructions of German national identity. Indeed, as Foster suggests, the 'history of the Reichstag is the history of Berlin in microcosm' (2000: 208). Originally commissioned by Bismark in 1871, twenty years after Germany's second unification, the Reichstag was completed in 1894 and was funded from reparations from the war with France (Dovey 1999: 55). The building has been a backdrop to many of Germany's and Europe's major political events since: the formation of the German Republic was announced from the Reichstag's window in 1918; fifteen years later the building became the site of a number of struggles associated with Hitler's rise to power; the building was set on fire a month after Hitler's appointment as Chancellor, an incident that was capitalized on by the newly appointed government as evidence of communist insurgency, and was subsequently mobilized as evidence for the suspension of a range of human rights under the Nazis. (Those responsible for the fire are still unknown – although the Nationalist Socialists themselves are strongly suspected. Dovey notes that 'the razing of this national icon touched a deep nerve in the German people and unleashed a reservoir of power which Hitler harnessed' (1999: 56)).

The original Reichstag was designed by the German architect Paul Wallot, who, in an echo of the 'Battle of the Styles' taking place in Victorian Britain discussed in Chapter 3, bemoaned the lack of a strictly 'German' architectural style at the time and reportedly lamented 'we are building a national edifice without a national style' (cited in Ladd 1998: 86). Given the absence of a style agreed upon within the architectural field as unambiguously 'German', it is interesting that Wallot sought to draw on historical styles to present the newly established state with a sense of lineage and tradition. Using ostentatious ornamentation to this end and to underline the building's consequence, a composite of different historical styles characterize the building: neoclassicism, baroque, and rococo are all incorporated into the original piece of bombastic, monumental architecture.

The Reichstag was a heavy-laden symbol relative to national identities, and in its reconstruction Foster was negotiating an already existing piece of architecture that had a huge number of symbolic connotations. He was certainly not working on a literal or metaphorical 'clean slate', as it were. However, the wrapping of the Reichstag by Bulgarian artist Christo was intended to symbolize something of a 'clean slate' to the political associations of a building already heavily loaded with meanings. Christo's covering the building in over one million square feet of silver fabric was in many ways indicative of the German state's desire to present a democratic and progressive face to the rest of the world and to signal the rebirth of a 'new' Berlin. During a discussion on the controversial plan in parliament, the Green MP Konrad Weiss suggested that the wrapping 'enables us to see in another light and newly, perceptually experience this central and ambivalent place in German history', adding that 'the wrapping of the Reichstag will remind us of the limits of our perceptions and how uncertain our knowledge is ... it will cut into the history of this building and ... it will be a peaceful, a productive turning point' (1994: 1). The critic Martin Pawley saw this project as a success in these terms, believing that the Reichstag had become a 'strangely demythologized landmark', and celebrated the 'catharsis' (Pawley 2000: 57) that the wrapping had achieved.

Hinting at the contestation surrounding the reconstruction project, and the struggle between form and meaning, Chancellor Kohl and some other conservative ministers tried to prevent the wrapping, arguing that the Reichstag was too important a national symbol to treat in such a 'facetious' way. Wolfgang Schäuble, the Christian Democrats' parliamentary leader, underlined this perspective when he said 'State symbols, symbols in general, should unite people, bring people together. Wrapping the Reichstag would, however, not unite people it would polarize them. Too many people would not be able to understand and accept it' (cited in Ladd 1998: 94). During the wrapping over five million people visited the building (Ladd 1998). When the fabric was removed, Foster began, with the building becoming a material and symbolic reconstruction site.

Foster engaged with the question '[W]hat kind of official architecture is appropriate for a country whose past has rendered patriotism suspect?' (Wise 1998: 11) through distancing the reconstruction from the particularistic history of the German nation and connecting it to a broader European imaginary, making numerous claims in his discourse about how the renovation of the Reichstag is 'multi-layered and identifiably locked into the history and culture of its own times, the age of reunification and European integration' (Foster 2000: 208). Foster was well aware of the position that he and his architecture occupied in complex renegotiations of Germany's national identity and its place in the 'new Europe', and attempts to situate the Reichstag relative to such agendas are interesting. Well aware of the position that he and his architecture occupied in complex renegotiations of Germany's national identity relative to the past and to a projected Europeanized future, Foster claims he has attempted to codify the complicated history of the Reichstag architecturally through a 'critical reconstruction' that can be 'read' as a monument to its own – and more broadly to Germany's – contested identity.

Lasswell observes that 'the incorporation of foreign patterns is usually motivated by more complex value perspectives than the unconscious demand to remodel the self in the image of those who are perceived to be powerful' (1979: 53). While not necessarily a remodelling in the image of a more 'powerful' state, the German state's choice of a British architect is significant, however, given the wider attempt to distance the reconstruction of the Reichstag from ostensible celebrations of the nation. Indeed, Wolfgang Thierse, the then President of the German Bundestag, suggested that the choice of a British architect was hugely significant in this regard: 'the decision to choose Norman Foster demonstrates that Germany is serious in its attempts to unite Europe and its people, and sends out a signal against narrow-mindedness' (2000: 7). Thierse's predecessor Rita Süssmuth also saw the selection of a non-German architect as indicative of 'a world shaped less and less by national borders' (1999).

However, owing to the highly charged context surrounding the rebuilding, almost every decision relating to the reconstruction took on a highly politicized character. Commenting on this, Buchanan suggests 'the impossibility of avoiding the symbolic, especially on a building like the Reichstag. No matter what functional intention determined its forms, people will inevitably seek and attach meanings to them, and so the architect must anticipate and shape these too' (2000: 173). Certainly, and as was suggested in the earlier chapters of this book, architects in a particular position in the field of production often find themselves required to position their architecture relative to a collective identity, not just in form of their designs, but also in their public utterances about meaning; in other words, the structural positions of internationally renowned architects such as Foster require them to create discourse as well as buildings. Forging and retaining a meaningful relationship between the two involves a delicate balancing act; in the case of the Reichstag, Foster claimed a critical approach to the project, saying he did not want the building to 'keep any secrets', adding that the issue that emerged most strongly from initial meetings with the Bundestag's Building Committee was that the building should be 'open and transparent' (2000). Indeed the design brief for the building stated that the winning entry should 'express the joy of communicating and a closeness to the citizen'. The design competition also stated that to win the commission architects should engage with 'the changing historical fortunes of the building, its symbolic significance and its future function' (2000: 23).

The glass cupola (Fig. 26) has, according to Foster, connotations of transparency and democracy, and 'can be read at many functional and

Fig. 26. The glass cupola on the Reichstag, Berlin

symbolic levels. It signals renewal' (2000: 130). Although not in his original design, Foster came to conceive of his dome as 'communicating the
themes of lightness, transparency, permeability and public access ... a
"lantern" with all the architectural and metaphorical associations which
that term implies' (2000: 87). To exacerbate this effect of 'light' and
'democracy' beams were originally sent out 4 km into the Berlin sky,
'creating a new symbol of Parliament and an ethereal landmark that can
be seen all over Berlin' (2000: 143); this lighting proved to be confusing
for air traffic, so the dome is now lit in a more subdued fashion. Foster
referred to the glass dome as a 'lighthouse of democracy' (in Wise 1998:
129), reinforcing his claim that his rebuilding attempted to banish any
'secret domains' (Foster 2000: 86). Emphasizing the democratic
symbolism in the cupola, the dome is a viewing chamber that is open to
the public – people can stand above the politicians debating in chambers
below.[12] Foster's reasoning behind the viewing gallery was that he
wanted to reinforce the democratic ideal of the public as masters, politicians as servants. He did not want the public to feel detached from the
political debates in the parliament (2000). Even engaging with Foster on
these terms, it can be observed that such symbolism could be presented
as suggesting the public are spectators of – rather than participants in –
the political process (Vale 1992: 9). Some conservative MPs wanted
Wallot's dome to be replaced faithfully, but Foster called this an 'empty
historicist gesture ... [f]undamentally at odds with the whole ethos of
the scheme' (2000: 130). The symbolic architectural device of Foster's
dome is intended as a spatial reflection of a commitment to openness,

transparency and accountability, a 'non-elite' spatial device in contra-distinction to Wallot's original, bombastic and purposefully elitist construction. The public space above the politicians' heads is, Foster tells us, a spatial reminder to both politicians and the public of democratic principles, as citizens can look down on the politicians debating. Harold Lasswell has observed that 'where the dominant ideology is democratic, popular regard for human dignity is a factor that tends to eliminate many of the prestige devices used in despotisms and autocracies as means of widening the gap between elite and non-elite' (1979: 40).

The slippery terrain of the various symbolisms attached to glass is revealed in Annette Fierro's excellent book *The Glass State* (2003). Making the point that glass can be read as both democratic (owing to its transparency) and fascist (owing to its capacity in effect to collapse the public/private distinction central to any democracy), Fierro's work can be seen as an echo of Bonta's general point about the contingent social constructions within the architectural field that mean particular architectural styles (or in this case materials) are stabilized relative to particular meanings.

Other elements of Foster's reconstruction also demonstrated the tensions associated with the connection between architectural form and meaning. For instance, the Gothic script on a stone scroll directly above the Reichstag's entrance reading 'Dem Deutschen Volke' (to the German People) (Fig. 27) was only added in 1916, over thirty years after the original building was completed and in the course of the First World War, as a nationalistic call to arms. Supplementing buildings with text in this way is an interesting attempt to overcome the, again, slippery relation between architectural form and social meaning. But, as Lawrence Vale points out when describing the case of an inscription on Hogan's parliament building in Papua New Guinea, ambiguities can arise in the interpretation of supposedly straightforward textual messages.[13] Illustrating the point, a textual element in Foster's design that engages with the form and meanings of the original building is the re-laid flower garden in one of the Reichstag's courtyards, which is visible from the rooftop (Fig. 28). The Gothic script in the flower bed spells out 'der Bevölkerung' (the population), a statement that can be read in contrast to the explicitly nationalistic connotations of the 1916 inscription; the more recent dedication is a less particularly German dedication and can be considered part of a wider dialogue with the nationalist frame that surrounded the original building.

James E. Young, whose work was assessed in more detail in the

Fig. 27. Stone scroll above the Reichstag's entrance

Fig. 28. The
relaid flower
garden in one of
the Reichstag's
courtyards

previous chapter, has argued that '[w]hile the victors of history have long erected monuments to remember their triumphs, and victims have built memorials to recall their martyrdom, only rarely does a nation call on itself to remember the victims of crimes it has perpetrated' (1992: 270). The codification of national victories so central to nation building in an earlier period was frequently accompanied by a kind of forgetting, or a partial representation, of those politically uncomfortable aspects of the past. In the case of the reconstruction of the Reichstag, the architect was keen to reflect the state's desire for a transparency about the building's – and Berlin's – history. One manifestation of this desire is evidenced by Foster's decision to preserve the anti-German, Cyrillic graffiti chalked on the wall by the invading Red Army in 1945. Foster has called the graffiti 'visible memories of the building's past' (2000: 13) that evidence the German state's support of a 'non-sanitized' version of their national identity, a clear attempt to engage with a difficult past, as is the decision to leave bullet holes and shrapnel in the stone walls (Fig. 29). The preservation of such artefacts presents a certain aspect of a nation's history and, more than this, recalling earlier observations about historical memory, illustrates how decisions made about politically charged architecture cannot be considered neutral. For some, the conservation of the graffiti 'might be interpreted as verging on collective self-abasement ... to erase the past with a seamless restitution of historical detail is one thing; not to clear up what are merely territorial markings are another' (Buchanan 2000: 172); for others, it may be part of a 'state-supported myth' about the liberation of Berlin by the Soviet Red Army, central to legitimization of the East German communist regime (Fulbrook 1999: 234).

Commenting on the changing interpretative frames into which objects are understood, Ulf Hedetoft has noted that

> though political symbols may impress us as having 'always' had the same connotative signification and societal meaning – because their representational form (as signifiers) stays the same – it is nevertheless far from uncommon for the same symbolic material to change its functions and connotations over time, and even at the same temporal intersection to imply different meanings to different groups. (Hedetoft 1995: 122)

Illustrating this point about the social construction of symbolic values, the sculpture of an eagle that overlooks the Reichstag's debating chamber (Fig. 30) is another heavily loaded symbol that articulates some of this book's claims about the discursive nature of meaning in the built environment. Foster himself said that 'the story of the design of that eagle would fill a book by itself' (2000: 212). While I do not want to test that theory here, the symbolic value of the form of the eagle sculpture is worth some abbreviated discussion as it contributed to the construction of the state-led German nation code through its 'mood and character' (2000: 212), again reinforcing the point that 'architects emphasise the aesthetic and the semiotic' (Jones 2009). Foster observes that historically the design of the eagle – whether aggressive, with prominent beaks and talons, lithe, plump, turkey-like and placid – has mirrored the aspirations of the commissioning government (2000: 214). After much heated discussion, the 1952 design by Ludwig Gies stayed; before this was decided upon though Foster was asked to redesign the eagle, and during his research it became apparent that there have been hundreds of eagles used over the years, with each one projecting the specific aims and aspirations of the German state of the time (Foster 2000: 214).

Fig. 29. The Reichstag after the Allied bombing of Berlin and its capture by Soviet troops, 1945

Fig. 30. Sculpture of an eagle that overlooks the Reichstag's debating chamber

Conclusion

In his discussion of architecture and the French revolution, Anthony Vidler (1991) criticizes the predominant, essentialist approaches when he suggests that we should be concerned less with finding a definitive formal style *of* the revolution and more with studying the roles of architects and uses of architecture during the revolutionary period. Evgeny Dobrenko has made a similar argument in his book *The Political Economy of Socialist Realism* (2007). He suggests that socialist realism was not simply a way of aestheticizing the socialist movement; rather it was part of the way it was brought into reality, and became meaningful. Observing the various ways in which architecture, art, music, painting and other forms of cultural production were drawn into the socialist project, Dobrenko is sensitized to architecture's status at the interface of culture and politics.

Udo Kultermann has suggested that 'European architecture is a unique symbol of contemporary transformations typical of our time and possibly the near future' (1994: 286). Illustrating something of how polities have

historically sought to develop collective identities as a means of legitimating and naturalizing their political projects, the ongoing search for
European cultural forms that will be sufficiently persuasive to resonate
across a number of member states reveals broader tensions between
national cultural particulars and 'European' universals. The EU's mobilization of architects and their architecture to fill the cultural vacuum
that currently exists in 'European' cultural consciousness is problematic,
not least because any such attempt to create architectural or spatialized
symbols for an as yet non-existent community is what Manuel Castells
(1997: 8) refers to as 'legitimizing identity' projects designed to give
meaning to an institution lacking social resonance. Against this backdrop, it is significant to note the explicit nature of the ways in which the
mobilization of architecture in the service of politics is discussed in the
Brussels Capital of Europe project. Koolhaas and Nouvel embrace this
element of elite architectural practice. Pretences of critical independence
are being jettisoned in favour of an unambiguous attempt actively to
create cultural belonging for a disputed polity via deconstructive forms
and discourse.

While architecture can possibly contribute to the programme of
cultural Europeanization being spearheaded by the EU and, to a lesser
extent, member states, it is perhaps through revealing the fragility of
ongoing attempts to codify political projects. Discourses of diversity,
plurality and equality abound, but the extent to which these architecturally inspired visions of Europe are forms detached from the social
reality of Europe is a defining issue to date. In his discussion of post-colonial parliament buildings, Lawrence Vale concludes that 'Capital cities
and the parliamentary buildings constructed within them would seem to
be ready purveyors of national identity, since they are ostensibly built to
serve and symbolize a nation state' (1992: 48). The reconstruction of the
Reichstag provides a reflection of the ways in which national identities
can be cross-cut with other, less nationally bounded sentiments (a
reminder that culture and identities are not hermetically sealed but practised in real social contexts and open to mediation and influence from
other identity discourses).

Furthermore, the Reichstag illustrates something of the cultural and
political tensions that can emerge when internationally mobile architects
– and the regimes commissioning them – move away from grand
'national' designs in the positioning of their work. During the Reichstag
reconstruction, Foster, as would be expected of an experienced architect
in the position in the field he occupies, was well aware of the politically

loaded nature of almost every design decision he made – such as the
colour of furnishings, the type of stone used, the sharpness or otherwise
of the Eagle's beak or the shape and size of the cupola. What initially
may have been a pragmatic choice or an aesthetic preference became a
symbolic decision about a wider political discourse.

Such reflexivity is characteristic of architects working on such
contested social and political commissions, and Foster's capacity to
sustain a meaningful connection between form and meaning is one of the
reasons he is so successful. The social and political discourses into which
the design for the Reichstag has been inserted are of cosmopolitanism,
transparency and democracy that in turn reflect some of the dominant
motifs in contemporary European political culture; instead of epic
grandeur and pomposity, Foster's architectural discourses and form are
more inclined towards a reflexive approach to collective identity.
However, while Paul Wallot's ostentatiously national motifs and script
can be contrasted with Foster's more reflexive 'critical reconstruction',
we must keep in mind that the latter is still designed to resonate with a
particular political discourse at a particular moment. Although Foster
has attempted to avoid the ethnocentrism and the bombast that characterized earlier parliament buildings, the ability of the EU meaningfully to
represent the diversity inherent within national societies means that state-
led architectural projects are increasingly ambivalent. The reconstruction
of the Reichstag, precisely because it entailed a complex renegotiation
between nationalized and post-national discourses, expresses much of
this ambiguity.

Notes

1 *Bulletin of the European Communities*, 1973, No. 12, Section 5, Clause 2501.
The declaration states: 'The Nine member countries of the European Communities
have decided that the time has come to draw up a document on the European Identity.
This will enable them to achieve a better definition of the relations with other coun-
tries and of their responsibilities and the place which they occupy in world affairs'
(European Community 1973: 118–22).

2 The classical style is displayed on the €5 note; Romanesque and the hint of a
Norman bridge on the €10; Gothic on the €20; Renaissance on the €50; baroque and
rococo on the €100; iron for the industrial age on the €200; and, for the €500 (one
of the highest value notes ever printed), the minimalist glassy modern style with a
suggestion of the postmodern age. The designer, Robert Kalina, an engraver at the
Austrian National Bank, scanned computerized images of famous bridges and monuments such as the Rialto Bridge in Venice and the Neuilly Bridge outside Paris and
then removed all discernible signs that might identify them with a particular context
(Delanty and Jones 2002: 462).

3 The award of the ECC title to Glasgow in 1990 marked a decidedly different

turn for the ECC award. Glasgow became a paradigmatic case of a city that used the award as a catalyst for a broader 'culture-led' regeneration (see Mooney 2004 on the highly partial nature of this 'success'). The award of Capital of Culture to Liverpool in 2008 can be seen as a further dilution of the 'European' element of the award, with very little of the city's bid or subsequent programme emphasizing anything distinctly European of the city's heritage. The bid document was organized around the theme of 'The World in One City', which, quite aside from other material realities, hinted at cosmopolitanism and diversity – dominant themes in contemporary EU discourse (see Jones and Wilks-Heeg 2004 for a detailed discussion of Liverpool's bid). The extent to which such locally/nationally particularized projects stress a common European heritage is a moot point, as is explored in Katie Jones' ongoing comparative analysis of Stavangar and Liverpool's year as shared capitals of culture in 2008 (Jones – in preparation).

4 In a wry comment on the relatively late 'social age' of the practising architect, in 'The Hexx', Pavement's Stephen Malkmus sings: 'Architecture students are like virgins with an itch they cannot scratch. | Never build a building till you're fifty. | What kind of life is that?'

5 In his discussion of Mies van der Rohe, Dovey (2009: 44) draws attention to his depolitization of the Bauhaus School and project, and his subsequent public statement of support for Hitler.

6 Koolhaas formed Architectuur Metropolitaanse Officie (AMO) as a 'twin studio' to the Office for Metropolitan Architecture (OMA) to reflect the 'liberation of architecture from practice' (McNeill 2009: 100); this 'liberation' – contingent on the 'think tank' status of AMO – is an ambiguous one, as when separated from the context of 'real' political commissions what does architecture mean?

7 Interestingly, Fraser seems to hint that OMA's flirtation with bankruptcy in the 1990s encouraged Koolhaas to adopt an approach more conversant/engaged with contingencies and complexity; certainly this ostensibly critical approach does provide the firm – and Koolhaas – with something of brand distinctiveness.

8 In his critique of the Pritzker Prize – the most prestigious award in architecture, which he received in Jerusalem in 2000 – Koolhaas included a blurred image of two Israeli officers, captioned 'the architect "regretted that political obliviousness is now assumed to be part of the Architect's equipment"' (cited in McNeill 2009: 101).

9 See <www.guardian.co.uk/culture/2004/sep/15/2>.

10 Drawing on Will Kymlicka's work on the public representation of culture, Dirk Jacobs draws attention to the backdrop of tensions and disparities within the model of 'multiculturalism' in evidence in Brussels, a city that 'has over time evolved from a Flemish city into a metropolis in which French has become the lingua franca ... the capital is officially bilingual (French and Dutch) and there are a set of institutional measures to ensure political participation and power of both language groups [but where] ethnic minorities have no independent public recognition outside the dual Flemish-Francophone structure of the political field' (Jacobs 2004: 328).

11 Bonn was capital after 10 May 1949 and was 'a beginning, a city without a past', according to West Germany's first ever Chancellor, Konrad Adenauer (cited in Wise 1998: 23). A relatively small provincial city, Bonn was selected to be the seat of government immediately after the Second World War in large part because it had no particularly strong associations with National Socialism. Bonn was a 'capital of self-effacement' (Wise 1998: 23) in which the 'reformist impulse was powerfully reinforced by the widespread desire to suppress all possible links to the capital of the Third Reich, whether that desire was motivated by revulsion at the Nazis or a sense of guilt' (Ladd 1998: 177). The architecture of Berlin was a major concern for the Nazis, with Hitler's architect Albert Speer describing the city as a 'place of worship'

where 'the Nazi plans for Berlin envisaged nothing short of a preposterous shrine to power and nationalism' (Vale 1992: 23–25). Accordingly, many architects working on the physical reconstruction of Berlin were 'burdened with the responsibility of providing a legitimate passage from the past into an imagined future' (Grezner 2000: 220). Architecture figured very prominently in the reunification project, with Berlin's status as capital of the new Germany finding a tangible articulation in the many building projects that characterized the Berlin skyline in the late 1990s.

12 This is not the only example of this type of symbolism being utilized in the architectural design of parliament building. The 'Capitol' in Canberra allows the public to walk on top of the building on a grassy area while parliament sits.

13 Designed by Hogan and opened in 1984, the Parliament House in Papua New Guinea has the slogan 'All power belongs to the people – acting through their elected representatives' tiled onto its facade. However, the complexity inherent in communicating 'clear' messages through architecture, even textual messages such as this one, reveals tensions between culture and politics, with Vale suggesting that as well as raising serious questions about the linguistic tradition of cultures in Papua New Guinea the inscription is directed as much at the Western tourist gaze as that of the country's citizenry (Vale 1992: 165–89).

8

Conclusion:
Sociology, Architecture and the Politics of Building

> To make architecture is to map the world in some way, to intervene, to signify; it is a political act. Architecture, then, as discourse, practice, and form operates at the intersection of power, relations of production and culture, and representation, and it is instrumental to the construction of our identities.
> Thomas A. Dutton and Lian Hurst Mann, 'Problems in Theorizing "The Political" in Architectural Discourse' (2000), 117.

A central claim of this book has been that architecture should not be considered a neutral or free-floating cultural form, but rather as an inherently social production that reflects one way in which those with political power attempt both to materialize this status and to make it socially meaningful. Revealing the coincidence of interest between the architectural field and the socially dominant, what Kim Dovey (2000) has referred to as a 'silent complicity', means retaining a sense that architectural production is always and everywhere a political practice that has deep-rooted connections with social order. Doing this makes necessary challenging those dominant accounts that position architecture primarily as a practice characterized by autonomous form-making. A shift away from the architectural object at the centre of critique, to be replaced with engagement with the social function of architecture – including its wider politics and economy – would pave the way for a more critical architecture that, connected to wider social and political realities, could contribute to social action that challenges existing social relations rather than assisting in the legitimation of their reproduction. Capturing the essence of this argument succinctly, the architect Mark Rakatansky has surmised '[a]ll architecture is social architecture. All architecture is political architecture' (1995: 13).

The focus of this book has been on some of the ways in which high-profile architects' professional practice – including but not limited to the design of built forms – has been mobilized in the context of state and

166

wider political projects. Generally speaking, architects and their designs have historically had a key role to play in the construction, maintenance and mobilization of social categories such as the nation, with attempts to materialize national identities a hallmark of the major European state-led projects of the nineteenth century. Indeed, in this period, the 'elective affinity' (Weber 1958: 91–92) between political agencies seeking to materialize civilizational aims and national cultural distinctiveness and architects – a rapidly professionalizing group reliant on commissions for their practice and identity – led to a proliferation of major state and public buildings. Sustained attempts to situate these buildings within 'national' political and aesthetic frames revealed much about the nature of this affinity and about the cultural component of the state project more generally. Although shaped by 'internal' field shifts, including the emergence of bodies of knowledge about previously existing geographically distant built environments and 'external' interventions from powerful politicians, historicist architectural designs reflected the British state's self-conception and ongoing constructed myth of origin. The 'battle' over Gothic versus neoclassicism representations illustrates how architectural styles can be 'read' as a proxy for a wider sets of social and political values and arrangements.

The contestation around these historicist styles is thus significant, as it points to a much wider problem, namely the challenge for a sociology of architecture to maintain a sense of architects' position as a cultural elite working in definite political-economic contexts while also engaging with architecture's status as a socially resonant form loaded with social meaning (which is always contingent on the capacity for these to be made through practice). Indeed, the understanding of the values and practices of the state and the politics of particular administrations, are in part mediated by the built environment, a point that raises pertinent wider questions about the 'political' role of architects and their work in particular social contexts.

For instance, the cases of the Reichstag and the EU project suggest something of the interesting ways in which new European political refrains of openness, diversity and transparency have been refracted into architectural practices (forms and discourses). Any such positioning requires negotiating well-contested ground, and high-profile architects are extremely adept at drawing on highly reflexive social discourses when attempting to situate their work in relation to nations or other cultural communities; the danger of symbolically privileging one identity discourse over another is a constant threat in such projects, and architects' increasingly sophisticated social discourses – and attempts to connect these to what is actually built – reflect much of this sensitive context. Social scientists interested in architecture must approach the narratives architects, politicians and others attach to buildings not merely as part of reified histories and canonized objects but rather as part of a repertoire of cultural forms that add social meaning – and thus their own specific force – to the political-economic structures within which architecture is conceived, realized and subsequently mobilized. Architects working on prestigious state commissions are increasingly engaged in managing the competing symbolic claims and identity discourses that centre on the high-profile projects that characterize the practice of their firms. The argument has been that a focus on the symbolic element of architectural form and its capacity to support diverse social meanings is often at the expense of a deeper critique of the unequal power relations that underpin the social production of architecture and the practices and values of those that commission it.

As the work of cultural producers straddling system and lifeworld in this way, architecture is situated within social struggles that go far beyond the built environment. The displacement of material questions of inequality onto cultural meaning (a vestige of the cultural turn associated with postmodernism (Callinicos 1990)) has led to a paradoxical situation in which cultural identities are represented publicly but frequently with little engagement with the material inequalities that underpin the partial representation of public cultures in the first place (Sayer 1999; 2001). Architects working on highly charged commissions must embrace the obligations associated with the active construction of identities, and a participatory approach that is clear about both the limits of power available to consulted publics and the expertise of the architect is key in this regard. But if public recognition in the built environment is to go beyond mere tokenism, then architects must engage in a critical process in which conflict must be revealed rather than hidden; the question here does not so much relate to representing diversity 'accurately' but rather in revealing tensions. The extent to which critical architectural practice may 'defamiliarize' (Tzonis and Lefaivre 1992) or disrupt these categories – revealing their arbitrary nature – is a crucial way architects can open up questions about the complex relationship between architecture, power and the communication of social meanings.

Manuel Castells has argued (1997: 418–28) that much contemporary architecture is representative of a context in which a meaningful connection between society and the built environment is increasingly obscured.

Cynical about the potential of the buildings and spaces that are the products of global capitalist activity to connect meaningfully with the polarized social realities of the publics inhabiting major urban centres, Castells has suggested:

> The more that societies try to recover their identity beyond the global logic of uncontrolled power of flows, the more that they need an architecture that exposes their own reality, without faking beauty from a transhistorical spatial repertoire ... Either the new architecture builds the palaces of the new masters, thus exposing their deformity ... or it roots itself into places, thus into culture, and into people. (Castells 2010: 449, 453)

For Castells, this 'root[ing] into people' necessitates a move away from architecture that seeks legitimation for globalized capitalist and political projects. Although a somewhat romanticized call, Castells does remind us that social identities are social constructions that require active maintenance and 'flagging' if they are to survive as social realities in the minds of actors. An important role for critical architecture in this respect is to reveal the contradictions and tensions inherent in political projects, rather than simply aggrandizing them.

As the capacity of architecture to represent any order of values unambiguously is highly conscribed, revealing the constructed and contested nature of social projects is a valuable public function; in encouraging debate and dissent about social categories such as the nation, the potential for architects to create a space for this to happen implies an architectural practice less encumbered by celebrity, fashion and place marketing and more connected to community politics and other forms of critical social action. Ensuring that the 'language' of architecture is meaningful and connects to citizens' experiences means acknowledging the constraints and complicities of architectural production in capitalist societies while also retaining a sense of architecture's material function.

The extent to which landmark architecture can ever be 'representative' is highly conscribed, and, given that such buildings have always been shaped by the powerful, attempts to make them seem less so are ideological. On this point, Lawrence Vale has noted that 'if architecture is to retain or regain a position as an integrated and integral part of culture rather than a detached club for aestheticians, both architects and architecture critics must probe the dynamics of the relationship between a building and its society' (1992: 275). Any critical architecture would not so much seek to represent diversity 'accurately' in form, or reveal a preexisting 'authentic' identity, but rather aim at revealing the tensions and conflicts inherent in the active creation of the symbols and discourses that construct categories of belonging. In other words, while collective 'identity may be promoted through attempts to demonstrate architectural evidence of cultural uniqueness, such identity may be forged oppositionally as well' (Vale 1992: 51).

Deyan Sudjic has observed that the difficulties in establishing stable social meanings relative to architectural form have 'led today's generation of architects to claim that their work is autonomous, or neutral, or else to believe that if there is such a thing as overtly "political" architecture it is confined to an isolated ghetto' (2005: 7). To ensure a valuable public function of their work far beyond the boundaries of the architectural field, the irreducibly political component of architectural practice needs to be revealed; any such approach means actively puncturing the illusion of architecture as a neutral, independent or primarily aesthetic endeavour. Questions of politics and social justice should not be seen as impositions from other fields, as externalities that diminish what makes architecture special, but rather fundamental to socially meaningful architectural practice. A task for critical social science is to contribute to such a politicization of architectural practice, to reveal architecture to be not 'an autonomous, self-referential discipline interested in forms and form-making alone, but rather a larger institutional, cultural, and social field with important political considerations' (Bozdoğan 2001: 12).

Bibliography

Adcock, B. (1984) 'Regenerating Merseyside Docklands: The Merseyside Development Corporation 1981–1984', *Town Planning Review*, (55): 269–89.

Albrecht, J. (2002) 'Against the Interpretation of Architecture', *Journal of Architectural Education*, 55(3): 194–96.

Alsop Architects (2002) 'Alsop Consortium Wins Competition for Liverpool's 4th Grace'. Press release at <www.alsoparchitects.com/tempate_image/FourthGrace.pdf>. Accessed Dec. 2008 (no longer current).

Amin, A. (2004) 'Multi-ethnicity and the Idea of Europe', *Theory, Culture and Society*, 21(2): 1–24.

Anderson, B. (1983) *Imagined Communities: Reflections on the Origin and Spread of Nationalism*. London: Verso.

Archibugi, D. (1998) 'Principles of Cosmopolitan Democracy', in A. Archibugi, D. Held and M. Kohler (eds), *Re-Imagining Political Community: Studies in Cosmopolitan Democracy*. Cambridge: Polity Press.

Architecture Australia (2001) 'Interview with Richard Rogers'. <www.abc.net.au/arts/architecture/rogers.htm>. Accessed Mar. 2001 (no longer current).

— (2005) 'Interview with Frampton, Colomina, Wigley'. <www.architecture australia.com/aa/aaissue.php?issueid=200409&article=15&typeon=3>. Accessed Jan. 2006.

Arnason, J. P. (1990) 'Nationalism, Globalization and Modernity', *Theory, Culture and Society*, 7(2): 207–36.

Atkinson, R. (1999) 'Discourses of Partnership and Empowerment in Contemporary British Regeneration', *Urban Studies*, 36(1): 59–72.

Baker, F. (2000) 'Mythos Reichstag', in N. Foster (ed.), *Norman Foster: Rebuilding the Reichstag*. London: Weidenfeld & Nicolson.

Barthes, R. (1968) *Elements of Semiology*. New York: Hill and Wang.

Batuman, B. (2005) 'Identity, Monumentality, Security: Building a Monument in Early Republican Ankara', *Journal of Architectural Education* (Autumn): 34–45.

Baudrillard, J. and J. Nouvel (2002) *The Singular Objects of Architecture*. Minneapolis: University of Minnesota Press.

Bauman, Z. (1989) *Legislators and Interpreters: On Modernity, Post-Modernity and Intellectuals*. Cambridge: Polity Press.

— (1990) *Modernity and the Holocaust*. Cambridge: Polity Press.

— (2004) *Europe: An Unfinished Adventure*. Cambridge: Polity Press.

Baydar, G. (2004) 'The Cultural Burden of Architecture', *Journal of Architectural Education*, 57(4): 19–27.

Bayley, S. (2001) 'The Last Word on the Millennium Dome, North Greenwich', *Design, Community, Architecture, Discussion*. <www.designcommunity.com/discussion/18498.html>.

BBC News Online (1998a) 'Dome Branded "Arrogant"', 20 Dec. <http://news.bbc.co.uk/1/hi/uk/239185.stm>. Accessed May 2010.

— (1998b) 'Sun Shines on the Dome', 25 Feb. <http://news.bbc.co.uk/1/hi/uk/59996.stm>. Accessed May 2010.

— (2000) 'Blair Admits Dome Letdown', 24 Sept. <http://news.bbc.co.uk/1/hi/in_depth/uk_politics/2000/conferences/labour/939581.stm>. Accessed May 2010.

Beck, U. (1999) 'The Open City: Architecture and Reflexive Modernity', in Ulrich Beck, *Democracy Without Enemies*. Cambridge: Polity Press.

— (2002) 'The Cosmopolitan Society and its Enemies', *Theory, Culture and Society*, 19 (1–2): 17–44.

Becker, H. (1967) 'Whose Side are We On?', *Social Problems*, 14(3): 239–47.

Bhabha, H. (1990) 'Introduction: Narrating the Nation', in H. Bhabha (ed.), *Nation and Narration*. London: Routledge.

Billig, M. (1995) *Banal Nationalism*. London: Sage.

Blair, Tony (1998) 'Speech by the Prime Minister – "Why the Dome is Good for Britain"', Royal Festival Hall, 24 Feb. 1998.

Blau, J. (1984) *Architects and Firms: A Sociological Perspective on Architectural Practice*. Cambridge, Mass.: MIT Press.

— (1991) 'The Context and Content of Collaboration: Architecture and Sociology', *Journal of Architectural Education*, 45(1): 36–40

Bloomer, J. (1993) *Architecture and the Text: The (S)crypts of Joyce and Piranesi*. London: Yale University Press.

Bognar, B. (1989) 'Toward an Architecture of Critical Enquiry', *Journal of Architectural Education*, 43(1): 13–34.

Bonta, J. P. (1979) *Architecture and its Interpretation*. London: Lund Humphries.

Borden, I., J. Rendell, J. Kerr and A. Pivaro (2002) 'Things, Flows, Filters, Tactics', in I. Borden, J. Rendell, J. Kerr and A. Pivaro (eds), *The Unknown City*. Cambridge, Mass.: MIT Press.

Bourdieu, P. (1977) *Outline of a Theory of Practice*. Cambridge: Cambridge University Press.

— (1988) 'On Interest and the Relative Autonomy of Symbolic Power', *Working Papers and Proceedings of the Center for Pyschosocial Studies*, 20: 1–11.

— (1989a) *Distinction: A Social Critique of the Judgement of Taste*. London: Routledge.

— (1989b) 'Social Space and Symbolic Power', *Sociological Theory*, 7(1): 14–25.

— (1990 [1980]) *The Logic of Practice*. Cambridge: Polity Press.

— (1993) *The Field of Cultural Production: Essays on Art and Literature*, trans. R. Johnson. Cambridge: Polity Press.

— (1994) 'Rethinking the State: Genesis and the Structure of the Bureaucratic Field', trans. L. Wacquant and S. Farage, *Sociological Theory*, 12(1): 1–18.

— (1996) *The Rules of Art: Genesis and Structure of the Literary Field*. Stanford, Calif.: Stanford University Press.

— (2005 [2000]) *The Social Structures of the Economy*. Cambridge: Polity Press.

Bourdieu, P. and J.-C. Passeron (1977) *Reproduction in Education, Society and Culture*. London: Sage.

Bourdieu, P. and L. Wacquant (1992) *An Invitation to Reflexive Sociology*. Chicago: University of Chicago Press.

— — (2001) 'Neoliberal Newspeak: Notes on the New Planetary Vulgate', *Radical Philosophy*, 105: 2–5.

Bourriaud, N. (2002) *Relational Aesthetics*. Paris: Les Presses du réel.

Boyer, M. Christine (1994) *The City of Collective Memory: Its Historical Imagery and Architectural Entertainments*. Cambridge, Mass.: MIT Press.

Bozdoğan, S. (2001) *Modernism and Nation Building: Turkish Architectural Culture in the Early Republic*. Seattle and London: University of Washington Press.

Braunfels, W. (1988) *Urban Design in Western Europe: Regime and Architecture, 900–1900*. London: University of Chicago Press.

Bremner, G. A. (2005) 'Nation and Empire in the Government Architecture of Mid- Victorian London: The Foreign and India Office Reconsidered', *Historical Journal*, 48(3): 703–42.

Bridger, J. (1996) 'Community Imagery and the Built Environment, *Sociological Quarterly*, (37)3: 353–74.

Broudehoux, A.-M. (2004) *The Making and Selling of Post-Mao Beijing*. London: Routledge.

Brubaker, R. and F. Cooper (2000) 'Beyond "Identity"', *Theory and Society*, 29: 1– 47.

Buchanan, P. (2000) 'When Democracy Builds' in N. Foster (ed.), *Norman Foster: Rebuilding the Reichstag*. London: Weidenfeld & Nicolson.

Building Design (2006) 'Mann Island Go-Ahead Settles Waterfront Site', 10 Nov.

Burgess, J. P. (2002) 'What's so European about the European Union? Legitimacy between Institution and Identity', *European Journal of Social Theory*, 5(4): 483–98.

Burk, A. L. (2006) 'In Sight, Out of View: A Tale of Three Monuments',

Antipode, 38: 41–58.

Burton, P. (2004) 'Power to the People? How to Judge Public Participation', *Local Economy*, 19(3): 193–98.

Butterfield, A. (2003) 'Monuments and Memories: What History Can Teach the Architects at Ground Zero', *New Republic*, 3 Feb.

Calinescu, M. (1987) *Five Faces of Modernity: Modernism, Avant-garde, Decadence, Kitsch, Postmodernism*. Durham, NC: Duke University Press.

Callinicos, A. (1990) *Against Postmodernism: A Marxist Critique*. Cambridge: Polity Press.

Cameron, K. (ed.) (1999) *National Identity*. London: Intellect Books.

Castells, M. (1977) *The Urban Question: A Marxist Approach*. London: Edward Allen.

— (1997) *The Power of Identity*. Oxford: Blackwell.

— (2010) *The Rise of the Network Society*, 2nd edn. Chichester: John Wiley.

Charney, I. (2007) 'The Politics of Design: Architecture, Tall Buildings and the Skyline of Central London', *Area*, 39(2): 195–205.

Chisholm, D. (2001) 'The City of Collective Memory', *Journal of Gay and Lesbian Studies*, 7(2): 195–243.

Clarke, P. W. (2005) 'The Ideal of Community and its Counterfeit Construction', *Journal of Architectural Education*, 58(3): 43–52.

Coleman, D., E. Danze and C. Henderson (eds) (1996) *Architecture and Feminism*. Princeton, NJ: Princeton University Press.

Coleman, R. (2005) *Reclaiming the Streets: Surveillance, Social Control and the City*. Cullompton: Willan Publishing.

Colquhoun, A. (1997) 'The Concept of Regionalism', in G. B. Nalbantoğlu and C. C. T. Wong (eds), *Postcolonial Spaces*. New York: Princeton Architectural Press.

Comte, A. (2009 [1865]) *A General View of Positivism*. Cambridge: Cambridge University Press.

Crary, J. (1989) 'Spectacle, Attention and Counter-Memory', *October*, 50: 96–107.

Crawford, M. (1994) 'Can Architects be Socially Responsible?', in D. Ghirardo (ed.), *Out of Site: A Social Criticism of Architecture*. Seattle, Wash.: Bay Press.

Crilley, D. (1993) 'Architecture as Advertising: Constructing the Image of Redevelopment', in G. Kearns and C. Philo (eds), *Selling Places: The City as Cultural Capital, Past and Present*. Oxford: Pergamon Press.

Crinson, M. (1996) *Empire Building: Orientalism and Victorian Architecture*. London: Routledge.

Cuff, D. (1989) 'Through the Looking Glass: Seven New York Architects and Their People', in R. Ellis and D. Cuff (eds), *Architects' People*. New York: Oxford University Press.

— (1991) *Architecture: The Story of Practice*. Cambridge, Mass.: MIT Press.

Culture, Media and Sport Committee (1997) *Second Report: Session*

1997–98. 11 Dec. <www.parliament.the-stationery-office.co.uk/pa/cm199798/cmselect/cmcumeds/340ii/cu0202.htm>. Accessed May 2008.

Cunningham, D. and J. Goodbun (2006) 'Marx, Architecture and Modernity', *Journal of Architecture*, 11(2): 169–85.

Daily Mail (2002) 'Handed Over for Nothing at All: the Dome that Ate Up £1 billion', 30 May.

Daily Telegraph (2007) 'War of Words Over Bronze Soldier', 5 Feb.

Davies, C. (1991) *High Tech Architecture*. London: Thames and Hudson.

Davis, M. (1992) *City of Quartz: Excavating the Future in Los Angeles*. Vintage: London.

De Frantz, M. (2005) 'From Cultural Regeneration to Discursive Governance: Constructing the Flagship of the "Museumsquartier Vienna" as a Plural Symbol of Change', *International Journal of Urban and Regional Research*, 29(1): 50–66.

de Graaf, R. and R. Koolhaas (2004) 'E-conography', *Content*: 376–89.

Delanty, G. (1995) *Inventing Europe: Idea, Identity, Reality*. London: Macmillan.

— (2000) *Modernity and Postmodernity*. London: Sage.

Delanty, G. and P. Jones (2002) 'European Identity and Architecture', *European Journal of Social Theory*, 5(4): 449–63.

— — (2004) 'Europe, Post-national Identities and Architecture', in J. P. Burgess (ed.), *Museum Europe: European Cultural Heritage between Economics and Politics*. Oslo: Norwegian Academic Press.

Delanty, G. and C. Rumford (2005) *Rethinking Europe: Social Theory and the Implications of Europeanization*. London: Routledge.

Del Rosario Betti, M. (2006) 'Architecture as the Built Message of Power: Buenos Aires under Evita's Spell, *Journal of Architecture*, 11(2): 225–39.

Department for Culture, Media and Sport (2004) *Culture at the Heart of Regeneration*. London: DCMS.

— (1999) (in association with the Inter Faith Network) *Marking the Millennium in a Multi-Faith Context*. London.

Deutscher Bundestag (2006) *Facts: The Bundestag at a Glance*. Berlin: Deutscher Bundestag.

Dobrenko, E. (2007) *The Political Economy of Socialist Realism*. London: Yale University Press.

Domosh, M. (1988) 'The Symbolism of the Skyscraper: Case Studies of New York's First Tall Buildings', *Journal of Urban History*, 14(3): 320–45.

— (1992) 'Corporate Cultures and the Modern Landscape of New York City', in K. Anderson and F. Gale (eds), *Inventing Places: Studies in Cultural Geography*. Melbourne: Longman Cheshire.

Dovey, K. (1999) *Framing Places: Mediating Power in Built Form*. London: Routledge.

— (2000) 'The Silent Complicity of Architecture', in J. Hillier and E. Rooksby (eds), *Habitus 2000: A Sense of Place*. Aldershot: Ashgate.

— (2009) *Becoming Places: Urbanism/Architecture/Identity/Power*. London: Routledge.

Dovey, K. and S. Dickson (2002) 'Architecture and Freedom? Programmatic Innovation in the Work of Koolhaas/OMA', *Journal of Architectural Education*, 56(1): 5–13.

Dubord, G. (1992) *The Society of the Spectacle*. London: Rebel Press.

Durkheim, Émile (1985 [1915]) *The Elementary Forms of the Religious Life*. London: Allen & Unwin.

Dutton, T. A. and L. H. Mann (eds) (1996) *Reconstructing Architecture: Critical Discourses and Social Practices*. Minneapolis: University of Minnesota Press.

— — (2000) 'Problems in Theorizing "The Political" in Architectural Discourse', *Rethinking Marxism*, 12(4): 117–29.

Eco, U. (1997) 'Function and Sign: The Semiotics of Architecture', in N. Leach (ed.), *Rethinking Architecture: A Reader in Cultural Theory*. London: Routledge.

Eggener, K. L. (2002) 'Placing Resistance: A Critique of Critical Regionalism', *Journal of Architectural Education*, 55(4): 228–37.

Eisenman, P. (1995) 'Eisenman (and Company) Respond', *Progressive Architecture*, 76(2): 88–91.

Ellin, N. (1996) *Postmodern Urbanism*. Oxford: Blackwell.

— (1997) *Architecture of Fear*. Cambridge, Mass.: MIT Press

Engel, H. (2000) 'The Marks of History', in N. Foster (ed.), *Norman Foster: Rebuilding the Reichstag*. London: Weidenfeld & Nicolson.

English Heritage and Commission for Architecture and the Built Environment (2001) *Building in Context: New Development in Historic Areas*. London: English Heritage/CABE.

Erman, T., B. Altay and C. Altay (2004) 'Architects and the Architectural Profession in the Turkish Context', *Journal of Architectural Education*, 58: 46–53.

European Commission (2001) *Brussels, Capital of Europe*. Brussels: European Commission.

European Community (1973) 'Declaration on European Identity', *Bulletin of the European Communities* (Dec.), No. 12.

Evans, G. (2003) 'Hard-Branding the Cultural City: From Prado to Prada', *International Journal of Urban and Regional Research*, 27(2): 417–40.

Evans, M. and K. Lunn (eds) (1997) *War and Memory in the Twentieth Century*. Oxford: Berg.

Fairclough, N. (2000) *New Labour, New Language?* London: Routledge.

Fallan, K. (2008) 'Architecture in Action: Travelling with Actor-Network Theory in the Land of Architectural Research', *Architectural Theory Review*, 13(1): 80–96.

Faulconbridge, J. (2009) 'The Regulation of Design in Global Architecture Firms: Embedding and Emplacing Buildings', *Urban Studies*, 46(12):

2537–54.

Feldmeyer, G. G. (1993) *The Politics of Memory: The New German Architecture.* New York: Rizzoli.

Fernández-Galiano, L. (2005) 'Spectacle and its Discontents; or, the Elusive Joys of Architainment', in W. S. Saunders (ed.), *Commodification and Spectacle in Architecture.* London: University of Minnesota Press.

Fierro, A. (2003) *The Glass State: The Technology of the Spectacle, Paris 1981–1998.* Cambridge, Mass.: MIT Press.

Filler, M. (2001) 'Into the Void', *The New Republic Online.* <www.thenewrepublic.com/100101/filler100101.html>. Accessed Apr. 2002 (no longer current).

Firth, R. (1973) *Symbols Private and Public.* London: Allen & Unwin.

Flyvbjerg, B. (2005) 'Machiavellian Megaprojects', *Antipode*, 37(1): 18–22.

Foster, H. (1984) '(Post)Modern Polemics', *New German Critique*, (33): 67–78.

Foster, N. (ed.) (2000) *Norman Foster: Rebuilding the Reichstag.* London: Weidenfeld & Nicolson.

Fowler, B. and F. Wilson (2004) 'Women Architects and their Discontents', *Sociology*, 38(1): 101–19.

Frampton, K. (1983) 'Towards a Critical Regionalism: Six Points for an Architecture of Resistance', in H. Foster (ed.), *Postmodern Culture: The Anti-Aesthetic.* London: Pluto.

— (1990) *Modern Architecture: A Critical History.* London: Thames and Hudson.

— (1994) 'Reflections on the Autonomy of Architecture: A Critique of Contemporary Production', in D. Ghirardo (ed.), *Out of Site: A Social Criticism of Architecture.* Seattle, Wash.: Bay Press.

— (2000) 'Seven Points for the Millennium: An Untimely Manifesto', *Journal of Architecture*, 5 (Spring): 21–33.

Fraser, M. (2005) 'The Cultural Context of Critical Architecture', *Journal of Architecture*, 10(3): 317–22.

Frisby, D. (1985) *Fragment of Modernity.* Cambridge: Cambridge University Press.

Fulbrook, M. (1999) *German National Identity After the Holocaust.* Cambridge: Polity Press.

Fuller, S. (2006) *The New Sociological Imagination.* London: Sage.

Foucault, M. (1985) 'Space, Knowledge, and Power', in P. Rabinow (ed.), *The Foucault Reader.* Harmondsworth: Penguin.

Gandy, M. (2005) 'Learning from Lagos', *New Left Review*, 33: 37–52.

Gans, H. (1977) 'Toward a Human Architecture: A Sociologist's View of the Profession', *Journal of Architectural Education*, 31(2): 26–31.

García, B. (2004) 'Cultural Policy and Urban Regeneration in Western European Cities: Lessons from Experience, Prospects for the Future', *Local Economy*, 19(4): 312–26.

Geertz, C. (1973) *The Interpretation of Culture*. New York: Basic Books.

Gellner, E. (1983) *Nations and Nationalism*. Oxford: Blackwell.

— (1987) *Culture, Identity and Politics*. Cambridge: Cambridge University Press.

— (1994) *Encounters With Nationalism*. Oxford: Blackwell.

— (1997) *Nationalism*. New York: Weidenfeld & Nicolson.

Genestier, P. and R. Lapidus (1995) '"Great Projects" or Mediocre Designs?', *SubStance*, 24(1/2): 62–72.

Ghirardo, D. (1984) 'Architecture of Deceit', *Perspecta*, 21: 110–15.

— (1994) 'Eisenman's Bogus Avant-Garde', *Progressive Architecture* (Nov.).

— (1996) *Architecture After Modernism*. London: Thames and Hudson.

Giddens, A. (1985) *Structuration*. Cambridge: Polity Press.

Giedion, S. (1944) 'The Need for a New Monumentality', in P. Zucker (ed.), *New Architecture and City Planning*. New York: Books for Libraries Press.

Gieryn, T. F. (2000) 'A Place for Space in Sociology', *Annual Review of Sociology*, 26: 463–96.

Giesen, B. and K. Junge (2003) 'Historical Memory', in G. Delanty and E. Isin (eds), *Handbook of Historical Sociology*. London: Sage.

Glancey, J. (2002) 'Architects Compete to Give Liverpool's Waterfront Extra Grace', *Guardian* (12 Nov.).

Gloag, J. (1975) *The Architectural Interpretation of History*. London: A & C Black.

Gray, P. and K. Oliver (eds) (2004) *The Memory of Catastrophe*. Manchester: Manchester University Press.

Greenhalgh, P. (1988) *Ephermeral Vistas: The Expositions, Universelles, Great Exhibition and World Fair, 1851–1939*. Manchester: Manchester University Press.

Grezner, E. (2000) 'Setting the Stage for a New Germany: Architecture and the Scene of Berlin', *Area*, 4(6): 219–42.

Guardian (1999) 'He Built the Dome. Fortunately He Didn't Choose the Colour', 26 July.

— (2000) 'Diary of a Disaster: From Bragging to Bail-Out', 4 Aug.

— (2002a) 'Rebuilding the Rubble', 29 Feb.

— (2002b) 'Architects Compete to Give Liverpool's Waterfront Extra Grace', 12 Nov.

— (2004a) 'Tower Power', 11 June.

— (2004b) 'First Stone Laid at Freedom Tower', 5 July.

— (2004c) 'Liverpool Scraps Plans for Cloud', 20 July.

— (2004d) 'Liverpool's "Diamond Knuckleduster" axed', 23 July.

— (2004e) 'Fall from Grace Angers Architect with Waterfront Vision', 24 July.

— (2004f) 'The Ali G of Urban Planning', 24 July.

Gutman, R. (1968) 'What Architectural Schools Expect from Sociology',

Journal of Architectural Education, 22(2/3): 13–20.

— (1988) *Architectural Practice: A Critical View*. Princeton, NJ: Architectural Press.

— (1992) 'Architects and Power: The Natural Market for Architecture', *Progressive Architecture*, 73(12): 39–41.

— (2007) *Architecture from the Outside*. Princeton, NJ: Princeton University Press.

Habermas, J. (1989a) 'Modern and Postmodern Architecture', in *The New Conservatism: Cultural Criticism and the Historians' Debate*. Cambridge, Mass.: MIT Press.

— (1989b) *The Structural Transformation of the Public Sphere*. Cambridge: Polity Press.

— (1990) *The Philosophical Discourse of Modernity: Twelve Lectures*. Cambridge: Polity Press.

Hacking, I. (1999) *The Social Construction of What?* Cambridge, Mass. Harvard University Press.

Haladane, J. (1999) 'Form, Meaning and Value: A History of the Philosophy of Architecture', *Journal of Architecture*, 4 (Spring): 9–20.

Halbwachs, M. (1980) *The Collective Memory*. New York: Harper & Row.

— (1992) *On Collective Memory*, trans. Lewis A. Coser. Chicago: University of Chicago Press.

Hall, S. (1996) Introduction: 'Who Needs "Identity"?', in S. Hall and P. du Gay (eds), *Questions of Cultural Identity*. London: Sage.

Hall, T. and P. Hubbard (eds) (1998) *The Entrepreneurial City*. Chichester: John Wiley.

Hansard (1998) 'Architecture and Design in Public Building'. <www.publications.parliament.uk/pa/ld199798/ldhansrd/vo980112/text/80112-07.htm#80112-07_spnew6>. Accessed Jan. 2009.

— (1999) Millennium Dome (religious content). <www.publications.parliament.uk/pa/cm199899/cmhansrd/vo990329/debtext/90329-04.htm>. Accessed Mar. 2010.

Harbison, R. (1993) *The Built, the Unbuilt and the Unbuildable*. London: Thames and Hudson.

Harvey, D. (1979) 'Monument and Myth', *Annals of the Association of American Geographers*, 69(3): 362–81.

— (1985) *The Urbanisation of Capital*. Oxford: Blackwell.

— (1989) 'From Managerialism to Entrepreneurialism: The Transformation of Urban Governance in Late Capitalism', *Geografiska Annaler, Series B: Human Geography*, 71B(1): 3–17.

— (1990) *The Condition of Postmodernity*. Oxford: Blackwell.

— (2000) 'Cosmopolitanism and the Banality of Geographic Evils', *Public Culture*, 12(2): 529–64.

Hay, C. (1999) *The Political Economy of New Labour: Labouring Under False Pretences?* Manchester: Manchester University Press.

Hayden, D. (1996) *The Power of Place: Urban Landscapes as Public History.* London: MIT Press.

— (2003 [1981]) 'What Would a Non-Sexist City Be Like?' in R. T. LeGates and F. Stout (eds), *The City Reader.* London: Routledge.

Hayes, W. H. (2002) 'Architectural Criticism', *Journal of Aesthetics and Art Criticism,* 60(4): 325–29.

Hays, M. K. (1984) 'Critical Architecture: Between Culture and Form', *Perspecta,* 21: 14–29.

— (1995) 'Architecture Theory, Media, and the Question of Architecture', *Assemblage,* 27: 41–46.

Hedetoft, U. (1995) *Signs of Nations: Studies of Political Semiotics of Self and Other in Contemporary European Nationalism.* Aldershot: Dartmouth Publishing.

Herrero, M. (2007) *Irish Intellectuals and Aesthetics: The Making of a Modern Art Collection.* Dublin: Irish Academic Press.

Hersey, G. (2001) *The Monumental Impulse: Architecture's Biological Roots.* Cambridge, Mass.: MIT Press

Hewison, R. (1987) *The Heritage Industry.* London: Methuen.

Heynen, H. (1999a) *Architecture and Modernity: A Critique.* Cambridge, Mass.: MIT Press.

— (1999b) 'Petrifying Memories: Architecture and the Construction of Identity', *Journal of Architecture,* 4 (Winter): 369–90.

Hill, J. (2003) *Actions of Architecture: Architects and Creative Users.* London: Routledge.

Hillier, B. (1996) *Space is the Machine: A Configurational Theory of Architecture.* Cambridge: Cambridge University Press.

Hirst, P. (2005) *Space and Power: Politics, War and Architecture.* Cambridge: Polity Press.

Hitchcock, H. R. (1954) *Early Victorian Architecture in Britain.* New Haven, Conn.: Yale University Press

Hobhouse, C. (1950 [1937]) *1851 and The Crystal Palace.* London: John Murray.

Hobsbawm, E. (1983a) 'Introduction: Inventing Traditions', in E. Hobsbawm and T. Ranger (eds), *The Invention of Tradition.* Cambridge: Cambridge University Press.

— (1983b) 'Mass-Producing Traditions: Europe, 1870–1914', in E. Hobsbawm and T. Ranger (eds), *The Invention of Tradition.* Cambridge: Cambridge University Press.

— (1990) *Nations and Nationalism since 1780: Programme, Myth, Reality.* Cambridge: Cambridge University Press.

Hobsbawm, E. and T. Ranger (eds) (1983) *The Invention of Tradition.* Cambridge: Cambridge University Press.

Holmes, D. (2000) *Integral Europe: Fast-Capitalism, Multiculturalism, Neofascism.* Princeton, NJ: Princeton University Press.

House of Commons Library (1998) 'Millennium Dome Research Paper', 98/32 (12 Mar. 1998).

House of Commons Select Report (2002) Select Committee Report on the on the Millennium Dome.

Hubbard, P. (1996) 'Urban Design and City Regeneration: Social Representations of Entrepreneurial Landscapes', *Urban Studies*, 33(8): 1441–61.

Huyssen, A. (1995) *Twilight Memories: Marking Time in a Culture of Amnesia*. New York: Routledge.

— (1996) 'Monumental Seduction', *New German Critique*, 69: 181–200.

— (1997) 'The Voids of Berlin', *Critical Inquiry*, 24(1): 57–81.

Imig, D. and S. Tarrow (eds) (2001) *Contentious Europeans: Protest and Polity in an Emerging Polity*. New York: Rowman & Littlefield.

Imrie, R. and E. Street (2009) 'Risk, Regulation and the Practices of Architects', *Urban Studies*, 46(12): 2555–76.

Isenstadt, S. (2001) 'Recurring Surfaces: Architecture in the Experience Economy', *Perspecta*, 32: 108–19.

Jacobs, D. (2004) 'Pacifying National Majorities in the Brussels Capital Region: What about the Immigrant Minority Groups?', in E. Lantschner and A. Morawa (eds), *European Yearbook of Minority Issues*, vol. 2. Leiden: Martinus Nijhoff Publishers.

Jacobs, J. (1961) *The Death and Life of Great American Cities*. New York: Random House.

James-Chakraborty, K. (2000) *German Architecture for a Mass Audience*. London: Routledge.

Jameson, F. (1997a) 'The Constraints of Postmodernism', in N. Leach (ed.), *Rethinking Architecture: A Reader in Cultural Theory*. London: Routledge.

— (1997b) 'Is Space Political?', in N. Leach (ed.), *Rethinking Architecture: A Reader in Cultural Theory*. London: Routledge.

Jencks, C. (1980) 'Introduction to Section 1', in G. Broadbent, R. Bunt and C. Jencks (eds), *Signs, Symbols, and Architecture*. Chichester: John Wiley.

— (1995) *The Architecture of the Jumping Universe; A Polemic: How Complexity Science is Changing Architecture and Culture*. London: Academy Editions.

— (2004) *Iconic Buildings: The Power of Enigma*. London: Frances Lincoln.

— (2007) *Critical Modernism: Where is Post-Modernism Going?* London: Wiley-Academy.

Jenkins, R. (1992) *Pierre Bourdieu*. (Key Sociologists). London: Routledge.

Jenkins, S. (2005) 'Give These People an Inch and They Take a City', *Guardian*, 15 Sept.

Jessop, B. (1990) *State Theory: Putting the Capitalist State in its Place*. Routledge: London.

— (2004) 'Critical Semiotic Analysis and Cultural Political Economy',

Critical Discourse Studies, 1(2): 159–74.
— (2007) *State Power*. Cambridge: Polity Press.
Jessop, B. and S. Oosterlynck (2007) 'Cultural Political Economy: On Making the Cultural Turn without Falling into Soft Economic Sociology', *Geoforum*. <http://www.sciencedirect.com/science/journal/00167185>. Accessed Jan. 2010.
Johnson, M. (1996) 'Once Upon a Sign: Relationship of Architecture and Narrative in the United States Holocaust Memorial Museum', *Journal of Architecture*, 1 (Autumn): 207–25.
Jones, Katherine (in preparation) 'EU Cultural Policy, Place-Making and Contested Identities', unpub. PhD thesis, Department of Geography, King's College London.
Jones, P. (2002) 'Architecturing Modern Nations: Architecture and the State', in G. Delanty and E. Isin (eds), *Handbook of Historical Sociology*. London: Sage.
— (2006) 'The Sociology of Architecture and the Politics of Building: The Discursive Construction of Ground Zero', *Sociology*, 40(3): 549–65.
— (2007) 'Cosmopolitanism and Europe: Describing Elites or Challenging Inequalities?', in C. Rumford (ed.), *Cosmopolitanism and Europe*. Liverpool: Liverpool University Press.
— (2009) 'Putting Architecture in its Social Place: A Cultural Political Economy of Architecture', *Urban Studies*, 46(12): 2519–36.
Jones, P. and M. Krzyżanowski (2008) 'Identity, Belonging and Migration: Beyond Constructing "Others"', in G. Delanty, R. Wodak and P. Jones (eds), *Identity, Belonging and Migration*. Liverpool: Liverpool University Press.
Jones, P. and S. Wilks-Heeg (2004) 'Capitalising Culture: Liverpool 2008', *Local Economy*, 19(4): 341–60.
Jones, Peris S. (2003) 'Urban Regeneration's Poisoned Chalice: Is there an *Impasse* in (Community) Participation-based Policy?', *Urban Studies*, 40(3): 581–600.
Jordy, W. H. (1983) 'American Architecture between World's Fairs: Richardson, Sullivan, and McKie', *Archives of American Art Journal*, (23)4: 27–33.
Kaika, M. and K. Thielen (2006) 'Form Follows Power', *City*, 10(1): 59–69.
Kamali, M. (2006) *Multiple Modernities, Civil Society and Islam: The Case of Iran and Turkey*. Liverpool: Liverpool University Press.
Kambuj, D. M. (1980) 'Marxist Position in Aesthetics of Architecture', *Social Scientist*, 9(2/3): 86–95.
Kastoryano, R. (2002) *Negotiating Identities: States and Immigrants in France and Germany*. Princeton, NJ: Princeton University Press.
Kennedy, P. (2004) 'Linking the Local and the Global: Transnational Architects in a Globalizing World', in F. Eckhard and D. Hassenpflug (eds), *Urbanism and Globalization*. Frankfurt: Peter Lang.

Kerr, J. (2002) 'The Uncompleted Monument: London, War, and the Architecture of Remembrance', in I. Borden, J. Rendell, J. Kerr and A. Pivaro (eds), *The Unknown City*. Cambridge, Mass.: MIT Press.

Kidson, P., P. Murray and P. Thompson (1965) *A History of English Architecture*. Harmondsworth: Pelican Books.

King, A. D. (ed.) (1990) *Buildings and Society*. London: Routledge.

— (1995) 'Writing Colonial Space: A Review Article', *Comparative Studies in Society and History*, 37(3): 541–54.

— (2000) 'Thinking with Bourdieu against Bourdieu: A "Practical" Critique of the Habitus', *Sociological Theory*, 18(3): 417–33.

Klein, N. (2000) *No Logo: Taking Aim at the Brand Bullies*. New York: Picador.

Knox, P. (1998) *Design Professionals and the Built Environment*. London: Nichols.

— (2010) *Cities and Design*. London: Routledge.

Koolhaas, R. (2006) 'Evil Can Also Be beautiful', *Der Speigel*, 27 Mar. <http://service.spiegel.de/cache/international/spiegel/0,1518,408748,00.html>.

Kornwolf, J. D. (1975) 'High Victorian Gothic; or, the Dilemma of Style in Modern Architecture', *Journal of the Society of Architectural Historians*, 34(1): 37–47.

Kostof, S. (1999) *The City Shaped: Urban Patterns and Meanings Through History*. London: Thames and Hudson.

Kuhn, T. S. (1962) *The Structure of Scientific Revolutions*. Chicago: University of Chicago Press.

Kultermann, U. (1994) 'The Context of Tradition and Cultural Identity: Regionalism and Contemporary European Architecture', in P. M. Lützeler (ed.), *Europe After Maastricht*. Oxford: Berghahn Books.

Kymlicka, W. and W. Norman (2000) 'Citizenship in Culturally Diverse Societies: Issues, Contexts, Concepts', in W. Kymlicka and W. Norman (eds), *Citizenship in Diverse Societies*. Oxford: Oxford University Press.

Ladd, B. (1998) *The Ghosts of Berlin: Confronting German History in the Urban Landscape*. Chicago: University of Chicago Press.

Lamont, M. and S. Aksartova (2002) 'Ordinary Cosmopolitans: Strategies for Bridging Racial Boundaries among Working-Class Men', *Theory, Culture and Society*, 19(4): 1–25.

Lane, T. (1999) *Liverpool, City of the Sea*. Liverpool: Liverpool University Press.

Langer, C. and U. Steglich (1995) 'Interview with Daniel Libeskind', *Architronic: The Electronic Journal of Architecture*. <http://corbu2.caed.kent.edu/architronic/v5n2/v5n2.05.html>. Accessed Mar. 2001.

Larson, M. S. (1993) *Behind the Postmodern Façade: Architectural Change in Late-Twentieth Century America*. Berkeley: University of California Press.

— (1994) 'Architectural Competitions as Discursive Events', *Theory and Society*, 23: 469–504.

— (1997) 'Reading Architecture in the Holocaust Memorial Museum: A Method and an Empirical Illustration', in E. Long (ed.), *From Sociology to Cultural Studies: New Perspectives*. Oxford: Blackwell.

— (2004) 'Grounding the Postmodern: A Story of Empirical Research on Fuzzy Concepts', in R. Friedland and R. Mohr (eds), *Matters of Culture: Cultural Sociology in Practice*. Cambridge: Cambridge University Press.

Lasswell, H. D. (1979) *The Signature of Power: Buildings, Communication, and Policy*. New Brunswick, NJ: Transaction Books.

Leach, N. (1999) (ed.) *Architecture and Revolution: Contemporary Perspectives on Central and Eastern Europe*. London: Routledge.

— (2002) 'Belonging: Towards a Theory of Identification with Space', in J. Hillier and E. Rooksby (eds), *Habitus 2000: A Sense of Place*. Aldershot: Ashgate.

Lefebvre, H. (1991) *The Production of Space*. Oxford: Blackwell.

Levy, D. and N. Sznaider (2002) 'Memory Unbound: The Holocaust and the Formation of Cosmopolitan Memory', *European Journal of Social Theory*, 5(1): 87–106.

Libeskind, D. (2001) *Daniel Libeskind: The Space of Encounter*. London: Thames and Hudson.

— (2004) *Breaking Ground: Adventures in Life and Architecture*. London: Riverhead.

Life Without Buildings (2000) *Any Other City*. Glasgow: Tugboat Records.

Lipman, A. (1969) 'The Architectural Belief System and Social Behaviour', *British Journal of Sociology*, (20)2: 190–204.

Lipstadt, H. (2000) 'Memoryware', *Assemblage*, 41 (Apr.): 45.

— (2003) 'Can "Art Professions" be Bourdieuean Fields of Cultural Production? The Case of the Architecture Competition', *Cultural Studies*, 30(3–4): 319–40.

Lisle, D. (2004) 'Gazing at Ground Zero: Tourism, Voyeurism and Spectacle', *Journal for Cultural Research*, 8(1): 3–21.

Liverpool City Council (2004a) 'Fourth Grace Scrutiny Panel: 18 August 2004'. <http://councillors.liverpool.gov.uk/Published/C00000709/M00002858/$$$Minutes.doc.pdf>. Accessed Apr. 2009.

— (2004b) 'Summary of Key Evidence – Fourth Grace'. <http://councillors.liverpool.gov.uk/Published/IssueDocs/4/5/6/4/I00014654/$4thgracekeyevidencefinal.doc.pdf>. Accessed Feb. 2011.

— (2004c) 'Report to Joint Regeneration and Environment and Culture Select Committee. 4th Grace Scrutiny', 14 Dec. <http://councillors.liverpool.gov.uk/Published/IssueDocs/4/5/6/4/I00014654/$4thGrace.doc.pdf>. Accessed Jan. 2008.

Liverpool Daily Post (2002) 'Public Chance to Vet Fourth Grace', 5 Nov.

— (2004a) 'Fourth Grace Axed to Save Kings Dock Arena', 29 July.

— (2004b) 'Collapse of Fourth Grace Will Hit Investment and Confidence', 23 July.

— (2004c) 'Prescott Drawn into Fourth Grace Wrangle', 23 July.

Liverpool Echo (2002) 'You Will Grow to Love My Cloud', 9 Dec.

— (2004) 'Why the Cloud Had to be Sacrificed', 19 Aug.

Liverpool Fourth Grace. <www.liverpoolfourthgrace.co.uk>. Accessed July 2005 (no longer current).

Liverpool Vision (2000) *Strategic Regeneration Framework.* <www. liverpoolvision.co.uk>.

— (2003) *Delivering the Vision: Annual Review 2002/3.* <www. liverpoolvision.co.uk>.

— (2004) 'Fourth Grace Announcement', Press Release, 19 July.

— (2005) 'Lighting'. <www.liverpoolvision.co.uk/project3b.html>. Accessed Dec. 2009 (no longer current).

Loftman, P. and B. Nevin (1996) 'Going for Growth: Prestige Projects in Three British Cities', *Local Economy*, 33(6): 991–1019.

Lowenthal, D. (1985) *The Past is a Foreign Country.* Cambridge: Cambridge University Press.

Lower Manhattan Development Corporation (2003) 'Renew NYC'. <www.renewnyc.com>. Accessed Jan. 2010.

MacDonald, S. (1996) *Theorizing Museums: Representing Identity and Diversity in a Changing World.* Oxford: Blackwell.

MacLeod, S. (2011) 'Towards an Ethics of Museum Architecture', in J. Marstine (ed.), *Routledge Companion to Museum Ethics: Redefining Ethics for the Twenty-first Century Museum.* London and New York: Routledge.

Macsai, J. (1985) 'Architecture as Opposition', *Journal of Architectural Education*, 38(4): 8–14.

Malik, K. (1996) *The Meaning of Race.* London: Palgrave.

Margalit, A. (2002) *The Ethics of Memory.* London: Harvard University Press.

Marshall, R. (2001) *Waterfronts in Post-Industrial Cities.* London: Spon Press.

Marshall, T. H. (1987 [1950]) *Citizenship and Social Class.* London: Pluto Press.

Martin, T. and A. Casault (2005) 'Thinking the Other: Towards Cultural Diversity in Architecture', *Journal of Architectural Education* (Autumn): 3–16.

Marx, K. (1957) *Capital.* London: Dent.

Massey, D. (2002) 'Living in Wythenshawe', in I. Borden, J. Rendell, J. Kerr and A. Pivaro (eds), *The Unknown City.* Cambridge, Mass.: MIT Press.

— (2004) 'Geographies of Responsibility', *Geografiska Annaler B (Human Geography)*, 86(1): 5–24.

Mattern, S. (2003) 'Just How Public is the Seattle Public Library? Publicity,

Posturing, and Politics in Public Design', *Journal of Architectural Education*, 57(1): 5–18.

Mayo, J. M. (1985) 'Political Avoidance in Architecture', *Journal of Architectural Education*, 38(2): 18.

— (1996) 'The Manifestation of Politics in Architectural Practice', *Journal of Architectural Education*, 50(2): 76–88.

McGuigan, J. (2003) 'The Social Construction of a Cultural Disaster: New Labour's Millennium Experience', *Cultural Studies*, 17(5): 669–90.

McGuigan, J. and A. Gilmore (2002) 'The Millennium Dome: Sponsoring, Meaning and Visiting', *International Journal of Cultural Policy*, 8(1): 1–20.

McNeill, D. (2000) 'McGuggenisation: Identity and Globalisation in the Basque Country', *Political Geography*, 19: 473–94.

— (2005) 'In Search of the Global Architect: The Case of Norman Foster (and Partners)', International Journal of Urban and Regional Research, 29(3): 501–15.

— (2009) *The Global Architect: Firms, Fame, and Urban Form*. London: Routledge.

McNeill, D. and M. Tewdwr-Jones (2003) 'Architecture, Banal Nationalism and Reterritorialization', *International Journal of Urban and Regional Research*, 27(3): 738–43.

Misztal, B. A. (2003) *Theories of Social Remembering*. Milton Keynes: Open University Press.

Mooney, G. (2004) 'Cultural Policy as Urban Transformation? Critical Reflections on Glasgow, European City of Culture 1990', *Local Economy*, (19)4: 327–40.

Mosse, G. L. (1994) *The Nationalization of the Masses: Political Symbolism and Mass Movements in Germany from the Napoleonic Wars through the Third Reich*. London: Cornell University Press.

Munford, E. (2002) *The CIAM Discourse on Urbanism, 1928–1960*. Cambridge, Mass.: MIT Press.

Nalbantoğlu, G. B. and C. T. Wong (eds) (1997) *Postcolonial Space(s)*. New York: Princeton Architectural Press.

Neuman, D. (ed.) (1994) *Critical Architecture and Contemporary Culture*. Oxford: Oxford University Press.

New York Times (2004) 'The 9/11 Memorial: How Pluribus Became Unum', 19 Jan.

Nobel, P. (2005) *Sixteen Acres: Architecture and The Outrageous Struggle for the Future of Ground Zero*. New York: Metropolitan Books.

Observer (2003a) 'Will He Be the Hero for Ground Zero?', 2 Feb.

— (2003b) 'Ground Hero', 22 June.

— (2003c) 'Landmarks of Hope and Glory', 26 Oct.

Ochsner, J. K. (1995) 'Understanding the Holocaust through the US Holocaust Museum', *Journal of Architectural Education*, (48)4: 240–49.

Olick, J. K. (1998) 'What Does it Mean to Normalize the Past? Official Memory in German Politics since 1989', *Social Science History*, 22(4): 547–71.

Olick, J. K. and J. Robins (1998) 'Social Memory Studies: From "Collective Memory" to the Historical Sociology of Mnemonic Practices', *Annual Review of Sociology*, (24): 105–40.

Ousterhout, R. (1995) 'Ethnic Identity and Cultural Appropriation in Early Ottoman Architecture', *Muqarnas*, (12): 48–62.

Panteli , B. (1997) 'Nationalism and Architecture: The Creation of a National Style of Serbian Architecture and its Political Implications', *Journal of the Society of Architectural Historians*, 56(1): 16–41.

Parsons, T. (1968 [1937]) *The Structure of Social Action*. Toronto: Free Press/Macmillan.

Pawley, M. (2000) 'The Rise and Fall of the Reichstag', in N. Foster (ed.), *Norman Foster: Rebuilding the Reichstag*. London: Weidenfeld & Nicolson.

Pearce, M. and G. Stewart (1992) *British Political History 1867–1990*. London: Routledge.

Peck, J. and J. Tickell (1994) 'Too Many Partners: The Future for Regeneration Partnerships', *Local Economy*, 9(3): 251–65.

Pevsner, N. (1968) *The Sources of Modern Architecture and Design*. Harmondsworth: Pelican Books.

Poggi, G. (2002) 'The Formation of the Modern State and the Institutionalization of Rule', in G. Delanty and E. Isin (eds), *Handbook of Historical Sociology*. London: Sage.

Public Broadcasting Service (PBS) (n.d.) 'Treasures of the World: Guernica'. <www.pbs.org/treasuresoftheworld/guernica/glevel_1/5_meaning.html>. Accessed Dec. 2011.

Rakatansky, M. (1995) 'Identity and the Discourse of Politics in Contemporary Architecture', *Assemblage*, 27: 8–18.

Rapoport, A. (1982) *The Meaning of the Built Environment: A Nonverbal Communication Approach*. London: Sage.

Richard Rogers Partnership (n.d.). <www.richardrogers.co.uk>. Accessed Feb. 2005.

Robbins, B. (2002) 'What's Left of Cosmopolitanism?', *Radical Philosophy*, 116: 30–37.

Roche, M. (2000) *Megaevents and Modernity: Olympics, Expos and the Growth of Global Culture*. London: Routledge.

— (2001) 'Citizenship, Popular Culture and Europe', in N. Stevenson (ed.), *Culture and Citizenship*. London: Sage.

— (2002) 'Social Citizenship: Grounds of Social Change', in E. Isin and B. Turner (eds), *Handbook of Citizenship Studies*. London: Sage.

— (2009) *Exploring the Sociology of Europe: An Analysis of the European Social Complex*. London: Sage.

Rubin, B. (1979) 'Aesthetic Ideology and Urban Design', *Annals of the Association of American Geographers*, 69(3): 339–61.

Rudofsky, B. (1981 [1964]) *Architecture without Architects: A Short Introduction to Non-Pedigreed Architecture*. Albuquerque: University of New Mexico Press.

Ruskin, J. (1992 [1849]) 'The Lamp of Memory', in M. Wheeler and N. Whiteley (eds), *The Lamp of Memory: Ruskin, Tradition and Architecture*. Manchester: Manchester University Press.

— (1920 [1854]) 'Monumental, Memorial and Sepulchral Statuary', *Burlington Magazine for Connoisseurs*, 37(208): 46–47.

Said, E. W. (1985) *Orientalism*. Harmondsworth: Penguin.

Saint, A. (1983) *The Image of the Architect*. London: Yale University Press.

Sassatelli, M. (2002) 'Imagined Europe: The Shaping of a European Cultural Identity through EU Cultural Policy', *European Journal of Social Theory*, 5(4): 435–51.

Saunders, W. S. (2005) 'Preface', in W. S. Saunders (ed.), *Commodification and Spectacle in Architecture*. London: University of Minnesota Press.

Sayer, A. (1999) 'Valuing Culture and Economy', in L. Ray and A. Sayer (eds), *Culture and Economy after the Cultural Turn*. London: Sage.

— (2001) 'For a Critical Cultural Political Economy', *Antipode*, 33(4): 687–708.

Schutz, A. (1972) *The Phenomenology of the Social World*. London: Heinemann Educational Books (First published as *Der sinnhafte Aufbau der sozialen Welt*. Vienna: Springer, 1932).

Schwartz, D. (1997) *Culture and Power: The Sociology of Pierre Bourdieu*. Chicago: University of Chicago Press.

Scruton, R. (1977) *The Aesthetics of Architecture*. London: Methuen.

Shore, C. (2000) *Building Europe: The Cultural Politics of European Integration*. London: Routledge.

Sklair, L. (2005) 'The Transnational Capitalist Class and Contemporary Architecture in Globalizing Cities', *International Journal of Urban and Regional Research*, 29: 485–500.

— (2006) 'Iconic Architecture and Capitalist Globalization', *City*, 10(1): 21–47.

— (2009) 'Commentary: From the Consumerist/Oppressive City to the Functional/Emancipatory City', *Urban Studies*, 46(12): 2703–11.

Speer, A. (1978) 'Responsibility and Response', trans. D. Domer, *Journal of Architectural Education*, (32)2: 18.

Spens, M. (1999) 'Jewish Museum, Berlin, Germany', *Architectural Review* (Apr.): 42–44.

Der Spiegel (2007) 'Evil Can also Be Beautiful: Interview with Rem Koolhaas', 27 Mar. <www.spiegel.de/international/spiegel/0,1518,408748,00.html>. Accessed May 2010.

Spillane, L. (1997) *Nation and Commemoration: Creating National*

Identities in the United States and Australia. Cambridge: Cambridge University Press.

Stern, R. (1994) 'The Postmodern Continuum', in W. Lillyman, M. Moriary and D. Neuman (eds), *Critical Architecture and Contemporary Culture*. Oxford: Oxford University Press.

Stevens, G. (1996) 'The Historical Demography of Architects', *Journal of the Society of Architectural Historians*, 55(4): 435–53.

— (1998) *The Favored Circle: The Social Foundations of Architectural Distinction*. Cambridge, Mass.: MIT Press.

Stråth, B. (2002) 'A European Identity: To the Historical Limits of the Concept', *European Journal of Social Theory*, 5(4): 387–401.

— (2008) 'Belonging and European Identity', in G. Delanty, P. Jones and R. Wodak (eds), *Belonging, Identity and Migration*. Liverpool: Liverpool University Press.

Strydom, P. (2000) *Discourse and Knowledge: The Making of Enlightenment Sociology*. Liverpool: Liverpool University Press.

Sudjic, D. (2004) 'A Quiet War Over Iconic Visions', *Observer*, 8 Aug.

— (2005) *The Edifice Complex: How the Rich and Powerful Shape the World*. London: Allen Lane.

— (2006) 'Building a Bolder Future', *Observer*, 20 Aug.

Süssmuth, R. (2000) Foreword to N. Foster (ed.), *Norman Foster: Rebuilding the Reichstag*. London: Weidenfeld & Nicolson.

Sutton, Ian (1999) *Western Architecture: A Survey from Ancient Greece to the Present*. London: Thames and Hudson.

Tafuri, M. (1999 [1976]) *Architecture and Utopia*. Cambridge Mass.: MIT Press.

Therbon, G. (2002) 'Monumental Europe: The National Years. On the Iconography of European Capital Cities', *Housing, Theory and Society*, 19: 26–47.

Thierse, W. (2000) Foreword to N. Foster (ed.), *Norman Foster: Rebuilding the Reichstag*. London: Weidenfeld & Nicolson.

Thorne, R. (1980) 'Places of Refreshment in the Nineteenth-Century City', in A. D. King (ed.), *Buildings and Society*. London: Routledge.

Thornley, A. (2000) 'Dome Alone: London's Millennium Project and the Strategic Planning Deficit', *International Journal of Urban and Regional Research*, 24(3).

Throsby, D. (2006) 'The Economics of the Creative City: Iconic Architecture and Urban Experience', in R. Freestone, W. Randolph, C. Butler-Bowdon and B. Elton (eds), *Talking about Sydney: Population, Community and Culture in Contemporary Sydney*. Coogee: University of New South Wales Press.

Till, J. (2007) 'Architecture and Contingency', *Field: A Free Journal of Architecture*, 1(1): 120–35.

— (2009) *Architecture Depends*. Cambridge, Mass.: MIT Press.

Tombesi, P. (1999) 'The Carriage in the Needle: Building Design and Flexible Specialization Systems', *Journal Architectural Education*, 52(3): 134–42.
— (2001) 'A True South for Design? The New International Division of Labour in Architecture', *arq: Architectural Research Quarterly*, 5(2): 171.
Tonkiss, F. (2005) *Space, the City and Social Theory: Social Relations and Urban Forms*. Cambridge: Polity Press.
Toulmin, S. E. (1992) *Cosmopolis: The Hidden Agenda of Modernity*. Chicago: University of Chicago Press.
Tschumi, B. (1994) *Architecture and Disjunction*. Cambridge, Mass.: MIT Press.
Tzonis, A., and L. Lefaivre (1992) *Architecture in Europe Since 1968: Memory and Invention*. London: Thames and Hudson.
Unwin, S. (1997) *Analysing Architecture*. London: Routledge.
Urban Regeneration Companies. <www.urcs-online.co.uk>. Accessed Jan. 2008.
Urry, J. (2002) *The Tourist Gaze: Leisure and Travel in Contemporary Societies*, 2nd edn. Beverly Hills, Calif.: Sage.
Vale, L. J. (1992) *Architecture, Power, and National Identity*. New Haven, Conn.: Yale University Press.
Venturi, R., D. S. Brown and S. Izenour (2002 [1997]) *Learning from Las Vegas: The Forgotten Symbolism of Architectural Form*. Cambridge, Mass.: MIT Press.
Vidler, A. (1991) 'Researching Revolutionary Architecture', *Journal of Architectural Education*, 44(4): 206–10.
Wacquant, L. (1989) 'Towards a Reflexive Sociology: A Workshop with Pierre Bourdieu', *Sociological Theory*, 7(1): 26–63.
— (2003) *Body and Soul: Notebooks of an Apprentice Boxer*. New Haven, Conn.: Yale University Press.
Wagner-Pacifici, R. and B. Schwartz (2001) 'The Vietnam Veterans Memorial: Commemorating a Difficult Past', in L. Spillman (ed.), *Cultural Sociology*. Oxford: Blackwell.
Ward, T. (1970) 'Totalitarianism, Architecture and Conscience', *Journal of Architectural Education*, (24)4: 35–49.
Weber, M. (1951) *Theory of Economy and Society*. New York: Free Press.
— (1958) *The Protestant Ethic and the Spirit of Capitalism*, trans. Talcott Parsons. New York: Scribner's.
Weiss, K. (1994) '211th Session of German Parliament, Bonn, 25 February 1994: Wrapping of the Reichstag'. <www.bln.de/k.weiss/te_wrapp.htm>. Accessed Feb. 2000.
Which Future for Ground Zero? (2003) 'Petition to Conduct an Architectural Design Competition for the Rebuilding of Ground Zero'. <www.phoenixproject.info/history/orgpetition.html> (no longer current).
Whyte, W. (2006) 'How Do Buildings Mean? Some Issues of Interpretation in the History of Architecture', *History and Theory*, 45(2): 153–77.

Wigley, M. (2005) *Architecture Australia*. <www.architectureaustralia. com>.

Wilkinson, P. (2000) *The Shock of the Old*. London: Macmillan.

Wilks-Heeg, S. (2003) 'From World City to Pariah City? Liverpool and the Global Economy, 1850–2000', in R. Munck (ed.), *The City in Transition? Liverpool in Comparative Perspective*. Liverpool: Liverpool University Press.

Williams, R. (2004) *The Anxious City: English Urbanism in the Twentieth Century*. London: Routledge.

Wilson, E. (1992) *The Sphinx in the City: Urban Life, The Control of Disorder and Women*. Berkeley: University of California Press.

Winter, J. and E. Sivan (eds) (2000) *War and Remembrance in the Twentieth Century*. New York: Cambridge University Press.

Wise, M. Z. (1998) *Capital Dilemma: Germany's Search for an Architecture of Democracy*. New York: Princeton Architectural Press.

Wodak, R., R. de Cillia et al. (1999) *The Discursive Construction of National Identity*. Edinburgh: Edinburgh University Press.

Wolfe, T. (1999 [1981]) *From Bauhaus to Our House*. London: Bantam.

Wright-Mills, C. (1971 [1959]) *The Sociological Imagination*. Harmondsworth: Penguin.

Young, J. E. (1992) 'The Counter-Monument: Memory against Itself in Germany Today', *Critical Inquiry*, (18)2: 267–96.

— (1993) *The Texture of Memory: Holocaust Memorials and Meaning*. New Haven, Conn.: Yale University Press.

— (2000) *At Memory's Edge: After-Images of the Holocaust in Contemporary Art and Architecture*. New Haven, Conn.: Yale University Press.

— (2010) 'Horst Hoheisel's Counter-memory of the Holocaust: The End of the Monument'. <www.chgs.umn.edu/museum/memorials/hoheisel/>.

Yuval-Davis, N. (1996) *Gender and Nation*. London: Sage.

Zukin, S. (1995) *The Cultures of Cities*. Oxford: Blackwell.

Index

192

Printed and bound by CPI Group (UK) Ltd, Croydon, CR0 4YY

09/06/2025

14685807-0001